Revenge in the Name of Honour

The Royal Navy's Quest for Honour and Vengeance in the Single Ship Actions of the War of 1812

Nicholas James Kaizer

Helion & Company

Helion & Company Limited
Unit 8 Amherst Business Centre
Budbrooke Road
Warwick
CV34 5WE
England
Tel. 01926 499619
Email: info@helion.co.uk
Website: www.helion.co.uk
Twitter: @helionbooks

Published by Helion & Company 2020
Designed and typeset by Mach 3 Solutions Ltd (www.mach3solutions.co.uk)
Cover designed by Paul Hewitt, Battlefield Design (www.battlefield-design.co.uk)

ISBN 978-1-912866-72-4

British Library Cataloguing-in-Publication Data.
A catalogue record for this book is available from the British Library.

To my parents, for their never-ceasing support

Contents

List of Maps

Preface

The genesis of this book was in my MA thesis, on which it is based. I have long been fascinated by the Nelsonic era of the Royal Navy, and like many young naval historians I was drawn to the rare but exciting single-ship actions which captivated the popular imagination of the time. During research at Acadia University I encountered the testimony given by Captain James Dacres during his court martial for losing his ship, HMS *Guerriere*. In his defence he boldly exclaimed to the court that he would be happy to be given another ship of *Guerriere*'s strength to try his luck against USS *Constitution* once again. This defence kindled my interest because of how much it contrasted with historical consensus of the action. From N.A.M. Rodger to Andrew Lambert, all agree that *Guerriere* was hopelessly outgunned by the larger American heavy frigate; and yet Dacres declared the defeat was attributed to nothing more than luck and wished to be given another crack at it. British historiography, it seems, is out of step with the mood of the Napoleonic era Royal Navy itself – and has been since the first major works on the War of 1812 were published, by William James.

To explore this topic required, among other things, exploring the mindset of a host of naval officers where few personal accounts survive. As such, this work – and the thesis which predated it – employs a hybrid biographical and microhistory approach. The few surviving personal accounts and letters (relatively unaffected by any of the biases associated with publication) are used in conjunction with official accounts and reports, such as dispatches and court martial minutes, to examine the opinions and actions of the officers of the North American squadron, set against the context of the contemporary Royal Navy over all. The themes of the personal accounts are compared with those found in the official archival record and with the actions undertaken by the Royal Navy to draw conclusions about the general mood of the Navy regarding its contests with its United States counterpart. This is then compared with the public discourse on the actions in Britain (principally through the *Naval Chronicle*) and in Halifax, which is often neglected in British naval historiography, as highlighted by Nova Scotian historians like Marc Drolet, Julian Gwyn, and Keith Mercer.

As a graduate student in Halifax, I was separated from the documents necessary to undertake this study by the Atlantic Ocean. Fitting, I suppose, as this story saw Britain so separated from the events in North America which so captivated them. I owe an enormous debt to the staff of Dominion Archives (now Library and Archives Canada) who, in the 1910s, copied extensive amounts of North American-related Admiralty records and brought them back to Canada, and without these resources this project may not have been feasible. To those archivists, past and present, and indeed those of each far distant archive I consulted: thank you. And as painful as it is for a Canadian to admit, I am also indebted to the US Naval Historical Center for their excellent War of 1812 naval sourcebook series. Without these records, my original MA project never would have weighed anchor.

I owe extreme gratitude to all of those who have helped and guided me in the completion of this work and the study which preceded it, most notably Jerry Bannister and Paul Doerr, my ever patient and knowledgeable MA and honours supervisors, and the wider community of historians here in Nova Scotia. The members of the Canadian Nautical Research Society, whose feedback and questions helped shape the final form of this work, too deserve my thanks. To the talent behind Blue Nautilus Art, Elizabetha Tsitrin, I am indebted for the prolonged hours of editing and the beautiful cover artwork. I am thankful also to Florian Richter, for his excellent illustrations, and to Jacqueline Reiter for her extensive editing and feedback. And finally, to the series editor, Andrew Bamford, without whose guidance and dedicated efforts this work never would have made sail.

Nicholas James Kaizer, 2019

Introduction

Early in the afternoon of 19 August 1812, while on route back to the British naval base in Halifax, lookouts of HMS *Guerriere* – a 16-year-old French-built frigate of the Royal Navy – spotted another frigate on the horizon. Not long after, one of her lieutenants made her out to be the American frigate USS *Constitution*, which had escaped from the grasp of *Guerriere* and her consorts a month earlier. Without hesitation, Captain James Dacres reduced sail and moved to engage the American frigate in what proved to be the first single-ship frigate action of the War of 1812. When the guns fell silent that evening, *Guerriere* had been smashed to pieces and the American frigate appeared unscathed.

By the end of the year, *Constitution*, under a new captain, claimed another British fifth-rate frigate; a third was captured by her sister, USS *United States*. Two British sloops of war were likewise defeated in single-ship actions against American opponents. The only naval victory for the Royal Navy was the capture of an American sloop, *Nautilus*, in a vastly one-sided affair – hardly anything to celebrate.

American contemporaries rightly celebrated the naval victories in 1812, and continued to do so in the following century. The British Royal Navy was the pre-eminent naval power in the world, and *Guerriere*'s surrender was the first time a British ship had struck its colours to a relatively equal force in over a year. Over the two decades of warfare since the start of the French Revolutionary Wars, in fact, the Royal Navy had won every major fleet action, nearly every minor battle, and the vast majority of single-ship actions. Britons from Scotland to Nova Scotia had been fed on a diet of news of naval victories and were convinced their navy was invincible. The serving officers of the Royal Navy attached great personal and professional pride to the triumphs and reputation of the service. Yet by New Year's Eve of 1812, the British had been humbled five times in single-ship actions with no meaningful victories of their own. The American public, who had not expected much of their tiny navy, was overjoyed at *Constitution*'s success over the seemingly invincible Royal Navy.

Next to the titanic struggles of the French Revolutionary and Napoleonic Wars, which saw a revolution in the scale and intensity of warfare, the War of 1812 has largely been forgotten in the United Kingdom, and even in the United States. What remains of popular memory, and indeed some of the historiography of the conflict, focuses on what each side wanted to remember. The Americans remember the triumphs of *Constitution* and her sister in 1812 and 1815, the successful defence of Fort McHenry, the Battle of New Orleans, and their ability to hold their own against the greatest naval power in the world. The British, on the other hand, tend to remember the successful defence of Canada, the burning of the White House, and the much-celebrated *Shannon–Chesapeake* action, all while focusing on the fact that Britain's true enemy was Napoleon Bonaparte.

British narratives of the single-ship actions of 1812 are quick to remind readers that the *Constitution* and her sisters were unusually powerful frigates carrying well over 50 guns of calibres normally not carried on board such vessels, with broadsides at times double that of the standard British fifth-rate 38-gun frigates that opposed them. However, while they are right to point out that the American frigates – rated at 44 guns – in fact carried far more weapons, they neglect to acknowledge that the standard fifth-rates did as well. Still, the disparity in broadside weight between the opposing frigates in the three single-ship actions in 1812 was immense, amounting to the Americans having a 50 percent advantage in firepower. In the opinions of historians and of contemporaries who followed naval news closely, the British were outmatched, but still the Royal Navy and the public were deeply shocked by these losses. The British, after two decades of warfare, expected their ships to triumph against even vastly superior odds. Perhaps there is no greater example of this sentiment than that expressed by Captain Dacres during his court martial for losing HMS *Guerriere*:

> Notwithstanding the unlucky issue of the affair such confidence have I in the exertions of the officers and men who belonged to the *Guerriere*, and I am so aware that the success of my opponent was owing to fortune, that it is my earnest wish, and would be the happiest period of my life, to be once more opposed to the *Constitution*, with them under my command, in a frigate of similar force to the *Guerriere*.[1]

What led James Dacres to declare this, after witnessing first-hand *Constitution*'s heavier guns utterly destroying his ship, and seeing his own shot bounce off the hull of 'Old Ironsides'? What led to the outrage in the British press over the defeats? What led a rather preoccupied Arthur Wellesley, the future Duke of Wellington, to state in an 1813 letter that 'I think we should have peace with America before the season for opening the campaign in Canada, if we could take one or two of these damned frigates'?[2] And what impact did these single-ship actions have on naval policy and the actions of the officers of the Royal Navy's North American squadron?

1 The National Archives (TNA), ADM 1/5431, Testimony of Captain James Dacres, CM *Guerriere*.

2 Wellington to Beresford, 6 February 1813, quoted in Kevin D. McCranie, *Utmost Gallantry: The US and Royal Navies at Sea in the War of 1812* (Annapolis, MD: Naval Institute Press, 2011), p.90.

It is true that the three single-ship actions in 1812 are often over-emphasised and over-studied, despite their having no impact on the American invasion of Canada or on Britain's ability to blockade the eastern coastline of the United States. Yet these actions – victories and defeats – mattered deeply to the Royal Navy and the British cultural sphere. Even in the twenty-first century, when the War of 1812 has largely been forgotten in the United Kingdom, the occasional British tourist still comes to Halifax looking to learn about the victory of Captain Philip Broke of the *Shannon*.

In 2012, the Government of Canada organised a commemoration of the War of 1812, a subject rarely studied in Canadian schools and largely forgotten by the Canadian public. It was hardly surprising, then, that many Haligonians were surprised that summer to see historical re-enactors prowling the streets of Halifax with mock press gangs, scarlet-coated marines on guard, and sailors manning mock gun batteries on the waterfront. Indeed, due to the prevalence of American media in Canada, many young Canadians would have been surprised to find that their forefathers fought against the Continental Congress during the American Revolutionary War, let alone that they had fought a second war against the United States. However, the mood of nineteenth-century Halifax could not have been more different; they were at the forefront of the naval war and their identities were firmly British, and Haligonians were deeply attached to the British Navy. Several of the notable single-ship victors and losers during the conflict had been based in Halifax, the largest port in British hands in North America. There were tensions between the town and the North American squadron over impressment, tensions which sometimes escalated into riots, but the problem was no different than in any other British colony, and in many ways Haligonians enjoyed a nearly unprecedented 'degree of freedom from impressment' in the British empire.[3]

Halifax's press followed the war in Canada, in Europe, and on the high seas closely. The exploits of Britain's frigate captains and their American foes were followed with a particular dedication. Philip Broke, captain of HMS *Shannon* when she captured USS *Chesapeake*, was a household name for decades following the war, and a Halifax-born officer on board HMS *Shannon* would go on to become the longest serving officer in the Royal Navy's history.

What the actions lacked in strategic importance they made up for in flair and in public and professional interest in Britain and America. The Madison administration, lacking any real gains from the conflict they themselves had declared, turned to the successes of USS *Constitution* to claim victory, and a national myth was subsequently built around them. In Britain naval prowess was a central tenet of its national identity, and these American victories had shaken this self-image to its very core. The losses made some question Britain's naval mastery; others looked for any excuse possible to reconcile the setbacks with their understanding of British greatness. Most called for revenge. The single-ship actions were contests of honour and naval chivalry

3 Keith Mercer, 'Sailors and citizens: press gangs and naval–civilian relations in Nova Scotia, 1756–1815', *Journal of the Royal Nova Scotia Historical Society*, 10 (2007), p.108.

played out from the coastal waters of Nova Scotia to the far side of the world, matching the best, and sometimes the worst, that each navy had to offer. Much has been written about the victories of the Royal Navy during the Napoleonic period, but little has been written about its defeats. The impact of these actions and the way the British world understood them provides an interesting analysis of the culture and fighting spirit of the Royal Navy.

* * *

By 1812, the Royal Navy had established itself as the world's pre-eminent fighting force, largely because of its expansive and meticulous supply and logistical apparatus and its large professionalised officers corps. These officers nearly always joined as apprentice officers (young boys who hoped to learn the art of command and seamanship at sea), holding various titles such as captain's servant or volunteer in the latter years of the Napoleonic Wars.

As they grew older, they became midshipmen and master's mates, teenage officers who learned how to sail, navigate, and – most importantly – how to lead. They were often in command of subdivisions of men, sections of gun batteries, boarding parties, and prize ships. Most of these boys entered the Navy in a decentralised manner, being admitted to a ship by its captain with no input from the Admiralty. A small number, including several officers involved in actions during the War of 1812, began their naval careers by attending the shore-based Royal Naval Academy, a school designed by the Admiralty with the (largely failed) goal of centralising the entry of officers into the Royal Navy. Among its graduates was Captain Philip Broke, who would have been a classmate of Francis and Charles Austen, Jane Austen's naval brothers, as well as of John Carden and Henry Chads, both of whom fought in the 1812 actions. While the school was dismissed by contemporaries and early historians, the actual education provided was pretty good, but during the period few naval officers entered the service through it. Throughout the age of sail, the primary route to an officer's commission remained the quarterdeck.[4]

The men who made up the Royal Navy's officer corps in the 'long eighteenth century' were a diverse group, ranging from title-holding aristocrats to those born into abject poverty. At least two officers were of enslaved African descent and possibly born slaves themselves. Most came from somewhere in between, frequently from professional, political, and military backgrounds. It was a unique institution in Britain and indeed in Europe at the time, as the Royal Navy made genuine social mobility possible. Many of the most famous peers (those holding aristocratic titles) of the Royal Navy during the Napoleonic period – including Nelson, Pellew, and St Vincent – were not of noble birth, and instead earned their social status through service at sea. Because of the demands of sea service, the Royal Navy became a semi-bourgeois profession; social status and connections still mattered a great deal, but the professional realities of the Navy created

4 John Blatchly, 'Broke – his youth and education', in Tim Voelcker (ed.), *Broke of the Shannon and the War of 1812* (Barnsley: Seaforth Publishing, 2013), p.78.

a socially unique institution. Certainly, societal connections were a boon to a naval career in Britain, just as they were to a career in the Army, but social connections and birth were not guarantors of a successful career.[5]

The conceptual roots of naval officers, like those of Army officers, lay in the noble commanders of past eras. During the defence against the Spanish Armada, for instance, the commander-in-chief of the Royal Navy was not the famous Vice Admiral Sir Francis Drake but Charles Howard, a scion of the Dukes of Norfolk and cousin of Queen Elizabeth. In the early navy of the Kings of England, commanders were military men, not sailors. This gradually changed, however, with the development of a permanent and professional navy during the latter half of the seventeenth century. In the eighteenth century, naval officers were professionally trained seamen, and while the upper class of British society continued to make up a considerable portion of the Navy's officers, professional skill and seamanship became more important drivers in officers' advancement. This was in part out of necessity: unlike the army, which continued to be dominated by the gentry and nobility throughout the period, there was a great deal of professional skill required to command ships at sea. Seamanship and navigation skills could only be acquired through experience at sea, and in theory the opening steps to a career as a naval officer were open to all with ability. These requirements strained the historic convention of the social status of military commanders and resulted in a system where the sons of dockyard clerks could, and did, share the wardroom with the son of the King. However, being the King's officers, even those of the lowliest birth were expected to be gentlemen; the class over all struggled on the margins of gentility and with the concept of honour.

Gentility and honour were old concepts, and both were intimately connected with nobility and birth. As officers in the King's service might be elevated to the status of gentleman without the familial ties to back them up, they were very self-aware of their reputation and sense of honour. Since there was no test of birth for entry into the profession, duty and skill came to underpin the honour of naval officers.[6] Admiral Lord St Vincent once remarked that 'the honour of an officer may be compared to the chastity of a woman, and once wounded may never be recovered.'[7] It was the supreme virtue of the Royal Navy, representing one's duty, gentlemanliness, and zeal.

As the Royal Navy developed into a professional fighting force in the 'long eighteenth century', the influence of men of humble origin in the

5 Adam Nicolson, *Men of Honour: Trafalgar and the Making of the English Hero* (London, New York, Toronto, and Sydney: Harper Perennial, 2005), pp.102–114; Tom Wareham, 'The duration of frigate command during the Revolutionary and Napoleonic Wars', *The Mariner's Mirror*, 86:4 (2000), pp.420–421; Tom Wareham, *The Star Captains: Frigate Command in the Napoleonic Wars* (London: Chatham Publishing, 2001), p.35; 'To the Right Honourable the Lords Commissioners of the Admiralty, 1809', in Nicholas Tracy (ed.), *The Naval Chronicle: The Contemporary Record of the Royal Navy at War* (London: Chatham Publishing, 1998), Vol.2, pp.355–356.

6 N.A.M. Rodger, 'Honour and duty at sea', *Historical Research*, 75:190 (2002), pp.427–435.

7 Tim Voelcker, 'Victories or distractions', in Tim Voelcker (ed.) *Broke of the Shannon and the War of 1812* (Barnsley: Seaforth Publishing, 2013), p.71.

officer class slowly grew. It was not uncommon for a man like James Cook (the son of a farm labourer) to be granted a commission; indeed, he was a contemporary of post captain John Perkins, whose mother was a Jamaican slave. As the nineteenth century dawned, however, the pendulum began to swing in the opposite direction, and the upper classes began to assert greater influence over entry into the Royal Navy. As long as there was a demand for quality officers in the wartime Navy, it remained possible for men from obscure origins to rise. Provo Wallis, the son of a Halifax dockyard clerk, entered the Navy in the middle of a series of Admiralty reforms designed to better control entry and advancement into the service, but thanks to his role in the much-celebrated *Shannon–Chesapeake* action, Wallis rose to become Admiral of the Fleet. However, many of his peers suffered in the peacetime Navy as it increasingly became important, not only to pass for lieutenant based upon professional skill, but also to pass 'for a gentleman.'[8] By 1818, four years after the final end of the Napoleonic Wars, nearly 90 percent of commissioned Royal Navy officers were unemployed and on half-pay, which disproportionately impacted those of humble origin.[9]

Those young officers who sought a commission had to pass an examination that tested seamanship and professional skill. While described as onerous and an effective measure of controlling competency of the Navy's lieutenants (by establishing a baseline level of skill required for entry), it is worth mentioning that very few midshipmen actually failed the examination. Nor did passing the examination guarantee one's promotion. It was not uncommon for passed midshipmen never to receive a commission, an occurrence that became more common as the war progressed and particularly during periods of peace. There was intense competition for promotion within the Royal Navy, even when the fleet was fully manned in wartime. Promotion sprees at the beginning of conflicts – as the Navy re-armed – resulted in periods of promotion stagnation, such as late in the Napoleonic Wars, when the lists of lieutenants, commanders, and captains far exceeded the demand for officers. This only worsened during times of peace, when large portions of the fleet were laid up in ordinary.

Once one received one's commission as a lieutenant, the next step was that of commander – previously called master and commander (captains of small unrated vessels called sloops of war). A fundamental problem was that there were always far more commanders than there were unrated ships, and upon promotion many never served again. Many lieutenants were only ever promoted to commander into retirement.[10] Becoming a post captain was the most coveted step; post captains commanded the Navy's rated ships, from tiny frigates to massive ships of the line. It was particularly desirable because of the nature of promotion past that point. Captains were promoted to admirals based on their seniority – the Admiralty could not promote a

8 Voelcker, 'Victories or distractions', pp.439–442.

9 Martin Wilcox, '"These peaceable times are the devil": Royal Navy officers in the post-war slump, 1815–1825', *The International Journal of Maritime History*, 26:3 (2014), p.471.

10 Evan Wilson, 'Social background and promotion prospects in the Royal Navy, 1775–1815', *English Historical Review*, 131:550 (2016), p.538.

captain to admiral without first promoting every captain of higher seniority to him. If a captain lived long enough, he was guaranteed to be promoted to admiral, bringing with it a boost in status and pay. Again, this did not ensure security, and many admirals never served at sea after promotion. Rather than be promoted into the three-tiered red, white, and blue admiralty system, some became what was called 'yellow' admirals (effectively meaning retirement). Still, a half-pay post captain earned far more than a half-pay commander, and he was guaranteed another boost in pay upon reaching flag rank. If an officer was worried about a future on half-pay, the notion of retiring as a half-pay rear admiral was preferable to retiring as a half-pay commander.

Some appointments and commands were more desirable than others, particularly over the issue of prize money and activity. Naval officers frequently complained about low pay, as pay rates had not increased to keep up with inflation throughout the eighteenth century. Officers were expected to adhere to the social conventions of their status as gentlemen, carrying costs of participating in society though hosting dinners, keeping elaborate stores for officers' messes, and maintaining expensive tailored uniforms for long voyages at sea. For officers of poorer backgrounds this was a difficult status to maintain on just their salary. This is where one of the key naval incentives came in – prize money was widely sought after by naval officers and seamen alike. It was a fundamental part of the Navy's system of incentives, alongside honours and titles. Captains could potentially earn small fortunes while performing their duties, but this was a rarity.[11] The captain of a ship of the line on blockade, for instance, was unlikely to make any significant captures, while captains serving far from busy shipping lanes might be hard pressed to find enemy ships at all. Frigate captains were the most likely to prey on enemy shipping or to encounter the enemy's warships, and so frigates were the most desired commands available in the wartime navy.[12]

As a result of the limited number of appointments and crowded promotion field, the culture of the Royal Navy officer corps was heavily influenced by competition. As with any competitive job field, candidates with established reputations and connections had an advantage. Officers who demonstrated ability, determination, aggression, and zeal were the most likely to receive desirable appointments and commands. Social and political connections were certainly an advantage for naval officers, but so too were professional connections, which were becoming increasingly more influential in the Napoleonic period, and those officers with a zealous reputation were most likely to catch the eye of the senior officers. Britain's naval strategy often hinged upon aggressive action and reflected virtues of bravery and professionalism in its naval officers. Driven by competition

11 Douglas W. Allen, 'The British Navy rules: monitoring and incompatible incentives in the age of fighting sail', *Explorations in Economic History*, 39 (2002), pp.204–230; Gabriela A. Frei, 'Prize laws in the War of 1812', in Tim Voelcker (ed.), *Broke of the Shannon and the War of 1812* (Barnsley: Seaforth Publishing, 2013), pp.52–56; D.A.B. Ronald, *Young Nelsons: Boy Sailors During the Napoleonic Wars* (Oxford: Osprey, 2012), pp.207–211.

12 Wareham, *Star Captains*, p.160; Wareham, 'Duration of frigate command', pp.412–423.

and the wider culture, naval officers approached command at sea with an aggressive ethos. Battles were eagerly sought and fought in direct, ferocious close-quarter fashion.[13]

Governed by the Articles of War, the Royal Navy expected aggressive action above all else. Sometimes, this even resulted in officers being punished for seemingly not fighting hard enough, even if their actions made strategic sense. Famously, Vice Admiral John Byng was executed following his decision to abandon what he saw as an impossible mission. Half a century later, Vice Admiral Robert Calder was forced into retirement following the indecisive Battle of Cape Finisterre. Calder had failed to destroy the French fleet, but his actions that day forced the French admiral to abandon his mission and return home; the mission in question was to link up with the French fleet at Brest and escort Napoleon's *Grande Armée* across the Channel in 1805.[14] In both cases, however, the Navy and the nation had expected an annihilating victory, not simply a strategic win.

While Britain and France had long struggled for naval mastery, during the French Revolutionary and Napoleonic Wars the Royal Navy attained a dominant position very quickly. The Royal Navy won every major battle, as well as the majority of minor actions. Most of the major actions were fought in the period before the Peace of Amiens; following the resumption of war, Britain's Navy was able to blockade the major French, Spanish, and Dutch fleets in port. The only notable expedition of Napoleon Bonaparte's battle fleets following 1803 culminated in the decisive Battle of Trafalgar. It is often misleadingly stated that this battle destroyed French naval power. In fact, France continued to build ships of the line and maintained large fleets in Brest and Toulon, fleets-in-being which continued to worry the Royal Navy until the wars concluded in 1815. What Trafalgar did do, however, was strike a crushing blow to France's post-revolution naval morale, from which the navy struggled to recover. Nelson's victory was shattering, and the French navy remained under blockade for the rest of the war, giving the British a free hand to operate worldwide.[15] Led by the well-trained officers of the Royal Navy, British warships were nearly consistently able to outperform their French and Spanish counterparts in crucial aspects of naval warfare: seamanship, manoeuvrability, and the speed and accuracy of gunfire, which together decided many engagements.[16]

While the great fleet actions such as Cape of St Vincent, the Nile, and Trafalgar captivated the British public and continue to dominate the Royal Navy's story today, they were relatively rare events. Only about a dozen such fleet actions were fought during the French Revolutionary and Napoleonic

---

13 Nicholas James Kaizer, 'Professionalism and the fighting spirit of the Royal Navy: rules, regulations, and traditions that made the British Royal Navy an effective fighting force during the French Revolutionary and Napoleonic Wars, 1793–1815' (Honours thesis, Acadia University, 2015).

14 Kaizer, 'Professionalism', pp.61–64, 99–100.

15 Martin Robson, *A History of the Royal Navy: The Napoleonic Wars* (London and New York: I.B. Tauris & Co, 2014), pp.142–143.

16 Allen, 'British Navy rules', p.209; Michael Duffy, 'The gunnery at Trafalgar: training, tactics, or temperament?', *The Journal for Maritime Research*, 7:1 (2005), p.145.

Wars, and most naval officers never participated in one. Instead, most action at sea was smaller in scale. Hundreds of actions, ranging from firing a shot across the bow of an enemy merchant or privateer to actions between small squadrons, occurred throughout the period. Most were not even contests; it was not uncommon for a single ship to be opposed by several, or for a lone frigate to be trapped by a ship of the line. Small cruisers such as sloops were frequently faced by frigates.[17] Occasionally, however, two ships of the same class met and fought in what were known as 'single-ship actions.' What these lacked in frequency they made up for in impact back home, and during the period Britain's record was exemplary. Of the 45 single-ship frigate actions fought between the Royal Navy and France between 1793 and 1814, 35 were outright British victories, seven were inconclusive, and only three were French victories.[18] In a handful of these British victories a smaller British frigate defeated its heavier French counterpart, establishing a precedent that consolidated the Royal Navy's hubristic culture.

Three types of frigates existed during the Napoleonic period, a result of a century of advances in ship-building and the development of larger frigates mounting heavier armaments. The first were designed to carry between 20 and 28 guns and were called sixth-rates by the Royal Navy and *corvettes* by the French. HMS *Surprise*, made famous as the favourite command of Patrick O'Brian's Jack Aubrey, was a ship of this type. They were the oldest type of frigate, and by the Napoleonic Wars they had become obsolete as larger frigates became more commonplace. By the end of the eighteenth century, the most common frigate designs (called fifth-rates by the Royal Navy) were generally rated between 30 and 40 guns and carried main batteries consisting of 12- or 18-pounder long guns, often with secondary batteries of carronades on their quarterdecks and forecastles. Unlike long guns, the typical naval cannon, carronades, were murderously effective short-range weapons. Most ships did not actually carry the exact number of guns they were rated for – 38-gun frigates commonly had closer to 48 cannon on board, as was the case for HMS *Java* and HMS *Guerriere*.[19] Their captor, USS *Constitution* (rated 44 guns), carried 54 guns and carronades of a significantly larger calibre, and two her sisters, also rated 44 guns, carried 56 during the War of 1812. This strange trend came about with the invention and adoption of carronades in the 1770s. Initially, carronades were only considered supplementary guns and not intended to replace a warship's primary guns, which made up its official rate, but over the decades ships began swapping out their weather deck-mounted long guns for carronades, and it was not until 1817 when the Royal Navy began to count every carronade towards a ship's official rate. Further, a ship's armament was fluid and captains frequently shifted and swapped guns. A 38-gun frigate remained a 38-gun frigate even if the captain removed or added a handful of guns. While not normally a good indication

17 Mark Lardas, *British Frigate vs French Frigate: 1973–1814* (London: Osprey, 2013), pp.4–5, 69–70.

18 Lardas, *British Frigate vs French Frigate*, p.69.

19 Rif Winfield, *British Warships in the Age of Sail, 1793–1817: Design, Construction, Careers and Fates* (London: Chatham Publishing, 2005), pp.176–181.

of the exact number of shipboard weapons, the official rate was usually a good indication of strength in relation to other frigates.

During the 1790s, the trend towards building larger and larger frigates continued and French shipyards began experimenting with ships rated at 40 or 44 guns, carrying main batteries of 24-pounders – long guns which had previously only been carried by ships of the line. The appearance of these heavy frigates in the first years of the French Revolutionary Wars caused some concern among the Royal Navy, and following the capture of the French 40-gun *Pomone* in 1794 the British began building their own heavy frigates armed with 24-pounder main batteries. Three British 64-gun ships (*Indefatigable*, *Anson*, and *Magnanime*) were *razéed* into 44-gun frigates that kept their 24-pounder main batteries. Purpose-built ships rated at 38, 40, and 44 guns, such as HMS *Endymion* and HMS *Cambrian*, were constructed and designed to carry 24-pounder main batteries.[20] Later in the war, however, the Royal Navy realised that their ordinary fifth-rate frigates armed with 18-pounder batteries were able to handle the new French heavy frigates. During the 1803 re-armament, Britain no longer perceived France's heavy frigates as a great concern, so much so that Britain's own heavy frigates were placed at a low priority for manning and fitting for service at sea.[21]

However, a separate naval innovation had taken place across the Atlantic. In response to maritime threats posed by Algiers pirates, a reluctant United States Congress authorised the construction of six frigates and the founding of the United States Navy. The construction and fitting of these warships was plagued by delays and mishaps, largely the fault of Congressional opposition, and it was not until 1800 – six years after the Naval Act was passed – that the final of the six frigates was launched. Three of these frigates (*Constitution*, *President*, and *United States*) were of a radical design: they were heavily built, which made them both excellent sailors and structurally very sturdy, able to withstand more punishment than other frigates. Most importantly, they were much more heavily armed than their French or British counterparts; though rated at 44 guns, each carried between 50 and 60 guns in all, including 24-pounder main batteries and heavy carronades. The founders of the American Navy knew it was too small to go toe-to-toe with European battle fleets, so these frigates were designed to be capable of tackling any frigate in existence while being able to run from any force they could not handle.[22]

When the War of 1812 broke out, these heavy American frigates entered a naval arena dominated by the Royal Navy, high from two decades of overwhelming success. In the words of American historian and future President Theodore Roosevelt, 'A continuous course of victory, won mainly

---

20 Robert Gardiner, *Frigates of the Napoleonic Wars* (Annapolis, MD: Naval Institute Press, 2000), pp.9–48; Winfield, *British Warships*, p.132; Mark Lardas, *American Heavy Frigates, 1794–1826* (Oxford: Osprey, 2003), p.11.

21 Gardiner, *Frigates of the Napoleonic Wars*, pp.9–48.

22 Ian W. Toll, *Six Frigates: The Epic History of the Founding of the US Navy* (New York and London: W.W. Norton and Company, 2006), pp.49–58; Lardas, *American Heavy Frigates*, pp.4–22; Gardner, *Frigates of the Napoleonic Wars*, pp.89–97.

The sails of a square-rigged ship

1	*Flying jib*	**12**	*Mainsail (course)*
2	*Jib*	**13**	*Main topsail*
3	*Fore topmast staysail*	**14**	*Main topgallant*
4	*Foresail (course)*	**15**	*Main royal*
5	*Fore topsail*	**16**	*Mizzen staysail*
6	*Fore topgallant*	**17**	*Mizzen topmast staysail*
7	*Fore royal*	**18**	*Mizzen topgallant staysail*
8	*Main staysail*	**19**	*Mizzen topsail*
9	*Main topmast staysail*	**20**	*Mizzen topgallant*
10	*Middle staysail*	**21**	*Mizzen royal*
11	*Main topgallant staysail*	**22**	*Spanker*

Illustration by Elizabetha Tsitrin

by seamanship, had made the English sailor overweeningly self-confident.'[23] What hope did the tiny United States Navy have against the Royal Navy's North American squadron when the War of 1812 broke out? The British entered the conflict with the weight of invincibility behind them, and a massive numerical advantage in ships, guns, and men. By contrast, the United States Navy was under-supplied and neglected. Neither the American political establishment nor the American population much cared for the Navy – many had opposed the creation of a permanent naval force at all – but the successes of these heavy frigates in the War of 1812 would endear them to the American people.

* * *

This volume explores the 'culture of victory' and the fighting spirit of the post-Nelsonic Royal Navy through its experience of loss and subsequent struggles in the War of 1812. The three single-ship actions involving *Constitution* and *United States* in 1812 are frequently discussed in British and American accounts of the conflict, as is the *Shannon–Chesapeake* action in 1813. In many British accounts, the events of 1812 are dismissed as inconsequential, and historians generally consider 'the disparity in force [to be] a sufficient explanation.' for the failure.[24] Would this justification have been well-received at the time? How were the forgotten actions in 1813 and 1814, and the final fights of USS *President* and USS *Constitution* in 1815, perceived by the Royal Navy and its adoring public?

In a system where one's career and personal honour were tied to duty, zeal, and an aggressive ethos in action, where triumphing against vastly superior odds was not unheard of and running from superior forces (to a degree) was severely discouraged, the impact of five single-ship losses in one year was significant. The British world had to grapple with these losses and understand their implications for Britain's naval reputation. The public was outraged and horrified by the losses; newspapers in London and Halifax expressed a sense of shock, and many commentators in the *Naval Chronicle*, the most prominent naval publication, called for revenge – indeed, they often called for annihilation through overwhelming force. In responding to public outrage, the Admiralty shifted to a more conservative strategy in North America, focusing on blockades conducted by powerful squadrons that would protect the Royal Navy from further embarrassing defeats. Civilian and naval administrators alike reasoned that one-on-one fights with America's heavy frigates were too great a risk.

The officers serving in the North American squadron saw these losses in a different light, and annihilation through overwhelming force or neutralisation through blockades did not interest captains like James Dacres, James Yeo, Richard Kerr, Thomas Capel, Philip Broke, Henry Hope, and

23 Theodore Roosevelt, *The Naval War of 1812 or the History of the United States Navy During the Last War with Great Britain* (New York: G.P.Putnam's Sons, 1882), p.24.

24 N.A.M. Rodger, *The Command of the Ocean: A Naval History of Britain, 1649–1815* (New York: W.W. Norton, 2005), p.568.

Hassard Stackpoole, who sought to restore the honour of the Royal Navy through victories in even contests – single-ship actions. In extreme cases, this desire for revenge led to the outright violation of orders that jeopardised blockading missions for the chance of bringing about a single-ship action; such endeavours off Boston led to the escape of USS *President* and USS *Congress*, a blunder only rectified by the victory of HMS *Shannon* over USS *Chesapeake* a month later. A conflict quickly emerged in the Royal Navy's North American squadron between the virtue of naval chivalry and the strategic interests of the fleet and the nation. Just what 'duty' meant came into question, as some officers violated orders to seek out contests of honour in the name of their duty to their naval service and their country.

The War of 1812 was considered a side-show against the wars in Europe by contemporaries; one Canadian newspaper even described the conflict in his own backyard as 'our puny war.' Yet whereas modern British historians have largely forgotten or neglected this conflict, the naval exploits of the American conflict were still important to contemporaries. Side-show or not, the losses of 1812 generated a consuming insecurity and urge for revenge and highlighted contrasting visions of honour and duty within the Royal Navy. In that way the conflict mattered to Britons and to the Royal Navy. Many perceived that British honour was at stake, and that honour could only be restored through revenge against the upstart American Navy.

1

'A Perfect Unmanageable Wreck': Opening Acts in the Naval War of 1812

There is some truth to the historiographical view of the War of 1812 as a war of independence. The Revolutionary War had established the United States of America as an independent nation, but many Britons still regarded the Americans as something not quite at the level of a civilised country. Many British diplomats complained about the perceived lack of integrity of its statesmen, and even at the tendency of those same statesmen to interact with foreign counterparts in 'the filthiest dresses'.[1] British statesmen and intellectuals saw the American people as crass and vulgar and their government as a strange and doomed experiment. The ideological basis of American liberty itself was British, and so was the basis for America's economic and commercial prosperity – so many Britons thought.[2] Certainly, the United States in its first few decades of independence was a strange nation by modern European standards. Its cities were tiny, and customs duties provided its primary source of revenue.[3] Congress had resisted both the development of a standing army and a standing navy – neither force was anything to compare with the continental military forces that had developed during the transformative Napoleonic period. But the United States had a burgeoning maritime economy, a large pool of trained merchant sailors, and growing trade relations around the world. It is no surprise that relations between America and her former colonial master grew strained in this period.

As America's commercial sector grew and its trade reached distant markets, so too did British anxieties. British traders worried about competition from the United States, and British policymakers were insistent that the Americans should be denied access to European markets under blockade by the Royal

1 Stephen Budiansky *Perilous Fight: America's Intrepid War with Britain on the High Seas, 1812–1815* (New York: Alfred A. Knopf, 2010), pp.30–33.

2 Budiansky, *Perilous Fight*, pp.30–33.

3 Budiansky, *Perilous Fight*, p.36.

Navy. This came to a head in 1807, when the British government issued a series of decrees, known as the Orders in Council (1807), which authorized Royal Navy ships to stop neutral ships attempting to trade in French ports. The Royal Navy seized many American ships on this pretext.[4] The British could not understand why the Americans (self-proclaimed champions of liberty) would want to support the economies of Napoleonic France and its autocratic allies. Americans, by contrast, resented Britain's attempts to stifle their rights to free trade.

The frequent seizure of American merchant ships was hard enough for the United States to stomach, but it came with an issue even more inflammatory: impressment. During the long eighteenth century, the wartime Royal Navy was stretched to its limits by a shortage of manpower – there were simply not enough volunteers to supply the fleet. While its extent has sometimes been exaggerated in historical memory, impressment was nonetheless the means by which the Royal Navy kept its ships properly manned. Under British law, any British subject with maritime experience was liable to be pressed, or forcibly recruited, into the Royal Navy during wartime. Legally, of course, this should not have been a problem for Americans; they were not British subjects. However, this highlighted a fundamental conflict between America's concept of citizenship and Britain's idea of subjects of the Crown. While American citizenship could be earned by sailors from another country – and there were many sailors in American ships who were born in Britain – the British did not believe that one could renounce being a subject of the King. As such, anyone who was born in England, Wales, Scotland, Ireland, or any of Britain's colonies was liable to impressment, regardless of their American status, and thousands of sailors with American citizenship were impressed during the Napoleonic period.[5] Over 10,000 sailors with some claim to American citizenship were impressed at this time; 3,000 were later released, but many of those who remained bound to the fleet were still not British subjects.[6] One of the most outrageous incidents occurred in 1807, when an attempt to extract deserters from the American frigate USS *Chesapeake* resulted in several American sailors being killed by fire from the British ship of the line HMS *Leopard*. Four years later, HMS *Guerriere* stopped the USS *Spitfire* and impressed a Massachusetts citizen from Maine (at the time a district in Massachusetts). In response, USS *President* was dispatched to patrol the coast to prevent any further incidents. During her cruise she came across the 20-gun post ship *Little Belt*. The two ships entered a tense stand-off, broken by one nervous sailor from one of the two ships firing a gun. In moments, a much larger broadside smashed *Little Belt* to pieces. John Rodgers, *President*'s captain, later claimed that he mistook her for HMS *Guerriere*, much to the outrage of *Guerriere*'s Captain James Dacres.

4 Budiansky, *Perilous Fight*, pp.38–44.

5 Budiansky, *Perilous Fight*, pp.50–53; Alan Taylor, *The Civil War of 1812: American Citizens, British Subjects, Irish Rebels, and Indian Allies* (New York: Alfred A. Knopf, 2010), pp.4–6, 411–412.

6 Julian Gwyn, *Frigates and Foremasts: The North American squadron in Nova Scotia Waters, 1745–1815* (Toronto and Vancouver: UBC Press, 2003), pp.130–131.

Notions of sovereignty, respect, and of course 'free trade and sailors' rights' were augmented by other points of contention between the American republic and the British monarchy. Great Britain was allied to a variety of indigenous polities, most notably the Confederacy led by Tecumseh in both modern Canada and the United States. British support made attempts at westward expansion more difficult for American settlers, who were frequently warring with their indigenous neighbours over native land. Further, there were many in the United States who felt that the American Revolution was unfinished. Beyond matters of respect and sovereignty, Britain still held territories in North America. The colonies of Upper and Lower Canada, Nova Scotia, Prince Edward Island, and Newfoundland had largely resisted joining the American Revolutionary War, despite their close ties with the other American colonies. Some in the United States thought that the revolution would not be complete until 'the final expulsion of England from the American continent.'[7] These grievances pushed a reluctant American political establishment into declaring war on the United Kingdom. Ironically, just days after war was declared but before news had reached London, the new British Prime Minister Lord Liverpool revoked the contentious Orders in Council, hoping for a more practical and conciliatory relationship with the United States. Instead, land and naval forces in North America were setting out for war.

Both the British and Americans expected that war between the two countries would play to America's advantage on land and to Britain's advantage by sea.[8] The American Navy was vastly outnumbered by the seemingly-invincible Royal Navy's North American squadron. Most of Britain's Army was tied up in Europe, and Upper and Lower Canada were only lightly defended. Former President Thomas Jefferson famously remarked that invading and conquering Canada would be 'a mere matter of marching.' Only Halifax was considered to be a formidable British outpost.[9] However, the subsequent invasions of Canada in 1812 were frustrated by the logistical issues of invading a such a vast and rugged region, the incompetent management of the American forces (even Jefferson admitted the army was in a sorry state), the tenacity of General Isaac Brock's generalship, the unexpected determination of his soldiers and militia, and the important contribution of Britain's indigenous allies. Three separate American invasions failed: two armies were defeated by Brock's British and First Nations forces, and a third army simply refused to cross the border late in 1812 due to terrible morale. Jefferson's boastings could not have been more wrong.[10]

---

7 Thomas Jefferson to William Duane, 4 August 1812, *Founders Online, National Archives* (online), available at https://founders.archives.gov/documents/Jefferson/03-05-02-0231 (accessed 11 April 2019).

8 Gwyn, *Frigates and Foremasts*, p.133.

9 Donald Hickey, *The War of 1812: A Forgotten Conflict* (Urbana, IL, and Chicago: University of Illinois Press, 1990), p.73; Thomas Jefferson to William Duane, 4 August 1812, *Founders Online, National Archives* (online), available at https://founders.archives.gov/documents/Jefferson/03-05-02-0231 (accessed 11 April 2019).

10 Hickey, *War of 1812*, pp.72–99; Pierre Berton, *The Invasion of Canada: 1812–1813* (Toronto: McClelland and Steward, 1980); pp.101–305; Nicole Eustace, *1812: War of the Passions of Patriotism* (Philadelphia, PA: University of Pennsylvania Press, 2012), pp.36–75.

No one expected that America's tiny navy would pose a threat to the North American squadron, but it was only at sea where the Americans saw success in the first year of the War of 1812.

Rodgers and Broke on the Hunt

It was no thanks to the American government that the United States Navy was ready for war when it was declared; their ships and ports had never been well supplied, even in the lead-up to the declaration of war. Of the navy's three heavy frigates, eight smaller frigates, and nine sloops, only about half were seaworthy, let alone provisioned and ready to sail.[11] Still, when news reached New York of the outbreak of war, Commodore John Rodgers was able to put to sea quickly with the few American warships ready for sea. He and his fellow officers were enthusiastic and eager to use their advantage of surprise to cripple the local British forces before reinforcements arrived.[12] He put to sea in command of the 44-gun heavy frigate USS *President*, accompanied by her sister USS *United States*, the 36-gun frigate *Congress*, and the sloops *Hornet* and *Argus*. American naval strategy was disjointed; the President Madison had not put much thought into it himself, and the Secretary of the Navy Paul Hamilton had ordered Rodgers to put to sea to seek out isolated British cruisers in American waters, with the understanding that he would return immediately after having struck at the British. Instead, Rodgers went out intending to do as much harm as he could, seeking to intercept a British West Indies convoy and to take full advantage of Britain's state of unpreparedness. In effect, Hamilton had lost control of half of his naval forces.[13]

Rodgers's powerful squadron never found the convoy, but on 23 June, it did happen upon one of Britain's lone cruisers in American waters: the 36-gun HMS *Belvidera*. Her unusually long-serving captain (since 1800) was Richard Byron, a veteran of several actions over the past two decades of war. When his lookouts spotted several strange sails that proved to be Rodgers's squadron, Byron was unaware that war had broken out, and stood towards them to investigate while preparing his ship for action. When the private signal was not returned and he realised he was facing a very powerful squadron, Byron tacked away, not wanting to risk capture.[14] As the chase

11 Marc Drolet, 'The North American squadron of the Royal Navy, 1807–1815' (PhD dissertation, McGill University, 2008), pp.174–175.

12 Secretary of the Navy Hamilton to Commodore John Rodgers, Navy Department, 21 May 1812, in William S. Dudley, Christine F. Hughes, and Tamara Moser Melia (eds.), *The Naval War of 1812: A Documentary History*, Vol.1: 1812 (Washington DC: Naval Historical Center, Department of the Navy, 1985), p.118; Commodore John Rodgers to Secretary of the Navy Hamilton, US Frigate *President*, Staten Island, 3 June 1812, in *Naval War of 1812*, Vol.1, pp.119–120; Lieutenant Oliver H. Perry to Secretary of the Navy Hamilton, New Port, 6 June 1812, in *Naval War of 1812*, Vol.1, p.127.

13 McCranie, *Utmost Gallantry*, pp.26–27.

14 Roosevelt, *Naval War of 1812*, p.74; Library and Archives Canada (LAC), MG12 ADM1/502, C-12863, Captain Richard Byron to Vice-Admiral Herbert Sawyer, HMS *Belvidera*, Halifax harbour, 27 June 1812.

ensued, *Belvidera* proved to be an excellent sailor, and only Rodgers's *President* was able to keep up with her. She slowly gained on the British frigate through the morning and afternoon as the breeze settled, and it was not until 4:20 p.m. that *President* opened fire. Her shot ripped through *Belvidera*'s stern, killing and wounding several as the British returned fire. Within 10 minutes one of *President*'s guns burst, wreaking havoc on her decks. Sixteen men were killed or wounded, including Rodgers himself, who nonetheless remained on deck, determined to close with the enemy.

The chase continued into the evening, and despite her earlier set-back the *President* gained steadily on *Belvidera*. Throughout the chase, *President* and *Belvidera* kept up a steady exchange between their bow and stern chasers, each inflicting considerable mischief on each other's rigging and decks. By the third hour, *President*'s gunnery had inflicted enough damage on the British frigate to slow her down, and even the rest of the American squadron were starting to catch up. As USS *Congress* opened fire, Byron desperately ordered the ship to be lightened; an anchor and several boats were cut away, while 14 tons of water were dumped overboard. Lightened, *Belvidera* was able to escape, much to Rodgers's disappointment. Unbeknownst to Rodgers, the West Indies fleet that he had set out in search of had been in his vicinity when *Belvidera* was spotted. Had Rodgers not chased the British frigate for nearly a full day, it is very likely he would have intercepted the convoy and its escort.[15]

While limping home to Halifax, Byron informed his commanding officer, Vice Admiral Herbert Sawyer, of his disappointment at having to flee. He told the admiral 'I thought it my duty to make a firm retreat from three Frigates of the largest Class' and added that 'the necessity of retreat was painful to everyone on board.'[16] Assuring his superiors of the strong fighting spirit of his men was an important part of his account of the action. In this action, Byron stated that he had carried out his duty to flee from a superior force but emphasised that being obliged to so had dismayed him and his crew. They were hoping for a fight and fled only because risking an action against such a superior force would have been foolhardy, to say the least. Both Byron and one of his officers, whose letter was anonymously printed in the *Naval Chronicle*, reflected on the *President*'s tactics of bearing up at several points in the action to fire ineffectual broadsides at the British. Both this officer and Byron questioned this tactic, as both reasoned that *President* could have caught up with them if she had stayed on course.[17] The anonymous officer went far enough to accuse Rodgers of cowardice and of not wishing to risk trading broadsides with *Belvidera* alone. He also included a statement comparing the weight of metal between the *Belvidera* and the American squadron to drive home to his correspondents that his frigate was indeed outmatched,

15 Roosevelt, *Naval War of 1812*, pp.74–77; McCranie, *Utmost Gallantry*, pp.27–28.

16 LAC, MG12 ADM1/502, C-12863, Byron to Sawyer, 27 June 1812.

17 LAC, MG12 ADM1/502, C-12863, Byron to Sawyer, 27 June 1812; Extract of a letter from an officer on board HMS *Belvidera*, Halifax, 27 June, *The Naval Chronicle for 1812: Containing a General and Biographical History of The Royal Navy of the United Kingdom; With a Variety of Original Papers on Nautical Subjects*, Vol.28: July to December (London: Joyce Gold, 1812), pp.104–105.

though incorrectly listed *Constitution* and *Essex* among Rodgers's ships.[18] Neither officer was happy that their first action in the new conflict had been so defensive.

Neither, it seems, was Vice Admiral Sawyer. Upon *Belvidera*'s arrival in Halifax and his learning of the outbreak of war, Sawyer had to decide how the squadron based in Halifax would proceed. Because of heightened tensions with the United States over the last few years, the Admiralty had increased the size of the North American squadron to its greatest extent since the beginning of the Napoleonic Wars, including a 64-gun ship of the line, seven frigates, eight sloops, and six smaller vessels. This was bolstered by warships in the smaller West Indies commands, but the Royal Navy presence in North America was still well below what had been available during the American Revolutionary War. Sawyer effectively did not have more ships available than his American counterpart, at least until reinforcements arrived from Britain, and he was responsible for protecting local shipping, watching enemy ports, and cruising against American shipping.[19] He was further hampered by the sordid state of the Halifax dockyard, a lack of supplies and provisions, and a severe shortage of men.[20] Despite Sawyer's concern over the lack of available ships and his concern about the chances his fifth-rate frigates had against the American 44s, Sawyer opted for an offensive strategy.[21] On the 5th he dispatched most of his force under the command of Captain Philip Broke of HMS *Shannon* (38 guns), along with the admiral's own flagship HMS *Africa* (64 guns), Byron's *Belvidera*, and the small frigate *Aeolus* (32 guns), joined on the 9th by HMS *Guerriere* (38 guns) under Captain James Dacres. His remaining frigates were dispatched to guard important regions of trade, including the Bay of Fundy.[22] In doing so, Sawyer left himself without the means of communication with the bulk of his naval forces, putting him in the same helpless position as Secretary Hamilton, and left Halifax, Britain's primary naval base in North America, defenceless.

Broke was ordered to put to sea to 'capture or destroy all ships under the American flag in consequence of the [declaration of war]', and particularly to hunt down the squadron under Rodgers's command.[23] In consequence of his inability to issue orders to the detached squadron, Sawyer left the exact course and plans for the cruise up to Broke. Ironically, it was exactly the strategy that Rodgers wanted; it left America's ports open for returning merchant ships, allowed the warships to prepare for sea unmolested by British observation, and left Britain's convoys vulnerable to American cruisers.[24] Despite Sawyer's

18 Extract of a letter from an officer on board HMS *Belvidera*, Halifax, 27 June, *Naval Chronicle*, Vol.28, pp.104–105.

19 Drolet, 'North American squadron', pp.176–181; McCranie, *Utmost Gallantry*, p.29; Gwyn, *Frigates and Foremasts* pp.134–136.

20 Budiansky *Perilous Fight*, p.159.

21 Gwyn, *Frigates and Foremasts*, pp.134–136.

22 McCranie, *Utmost Gallantry*, p.53.

23 LAC, MG12 ADM1/502, Admiral's Dispatches, North America, C-12863, Vice Admiral Sawyer to Captain Philip Broke, HMS *Africa*, Halifax, 11 July 1812.

24 George C. Daughan, *1812: The Navy's War* (New York: Basic Books, 2011), pp.73–82; Spencer Tucker, *Stephen Decatur: A Life Most Bold and Daring* (Annapolis, MD: Naval Institute Press, 2005), p.112.

own anxieties about leaving Halifax unprotected, he judged it to be the best option available until reinforcements arrived, and Broke himself must have been ecstatic at the opportunity of hunting Rodgers down.

Captain Philip Broke, throughout the whole of his time in command during the Napoleonic Wars, was frustrated by a lack of activity. As captain of the frigates HMS *Druid* and HMS *Shannon* he saw little action, and spent most of his time relegated to convoy duty.[25] In early 1811, while on blockade duty off France, he expressed his annoyance at America's neutrality and the resulting fact that the 'silly American' ships he encountered were not fair game.[26] Later that year, he was transferred to quiet Halifax, where he informed his wife of his hope that 'the Congress may find some brisker work for us next month.'[27] By early 1812 he was hopeful, informing his wife that 'the American government will make war if they dare, and are trying to persuade their people that the Prince Regent is a personal enemy of theirs.'[28]

His longing for a conflict between Britain and America in part stemmed from his general desire to fight and win a single-ship action. More than once, Broke's correspondence with his wife demonstrated his longing for such an action, and in 1811 he even stated that he would offer any French frigate captain his share of prize money if one would 'come out voluntarily to give me an opportunity of going home with honor.'[29] In September, following the outbreak of war, he similarly bemoaned that 'I would give all our prizes for an American frigate.'[30] This longing for action, particularly for single-ship actions, was not uncommon among British naval officers. Most yearned for such an opportunity of winning fame and fortune, made even more enticing because such actions were rare. only about five percent of captains ever fought an evenly matched opponent in a single-ship action. Winning such actions came with extensive glory and prize money, and occasionally honours and titles.[31] Given his great interest in an American conflict, Broke must have rejoiced when *Belvidera* arrived in Halifax with the news, and Broke was dispatched with a squadron to hunt down Rodgers. Many naval officers were excited about renewed prospects of prize taking and actions against very capable opponents. Captains thought winning actions against the Americans would be a greater source of honour and glory than against their French counterparts.[32] Broke was correct that war with the United States would break the monotony of blockade duty and convoy escort that had plagued him in years previous, but it was the possibility of action that really enticed him. Even in the event of a war with the United States, Broke confided to his wife that 'our services will be brilliant for a short while and

25 Wareham, *Star Captains*, p.160.
26 Suffolk Record Office (SRO), HA 93/9/59, Philip Broke to Louisa Broke, 31 January 1811.
27 SRO, HA 93/9/82, Philip Broke to Louisa Broke, 3 November 1811.
28 SRO, HA 93/9/92, Philip Broke to Louisa Broke, 19 January 1812.
29 SRO, HA 93/9/68, Philip Broke to Louisa Broke, 28 April 1811.
30 SRO, HA93/9/112, Philip Broke to Louisa Broke, 14 September 1812.
31 Wareham, *Star Captains*, p.160.
32 Wade Dudley, *Splintering the Wooden Wall: The British Blockade of the United States, 1812–1815* (Annapolis, MD: Naval Institute Press, 2003) pp.44–50.

Captain Philip Bowes Vere Broke, an unassuming but exceptional frigate captain; Artist: William Greatbach (Library and Archives Canada)

then there will be nothing but *blockade* and I may as well go home.'[33]

For now, Broke was content to set out in pursuit of the enemy squadron, as he explained to his wife:

> we shall probably sail in a few days, but with such a force as will *sweep the seas* clear of all enemies and shall then reap our harvest. I grieve at this as a patriot, my Loo, but as a naval officer must rejoice at it... We are all sanguine in our expectations of soon sweeping their Navy into our ports and sending (or rather bringing) home a convoy of good prizes.[34]

Broke was soon frustrated, however, by the realisation that his

> *particular object*, Rodgers and his squadron, are far away from where I was sent to look for them. However, my Admiral has given me liberal scope to do all we can and we yet hope that us much – although we have been in a *fever of anxiety* since we sailed. An American frigate escaped us by her rapid sailing last week. We will have her yet.[35]

The frigate in question was USS *Constitution* under the command of Captain Isaac Hull, who had just departed Annapolis on 5 July in hopes of joining Commodore Rodgers on his hunt. She instead chanced upon Rodgers's pursuers on the night of the 17th. Early the following morning, as *Constitution* approached the nearest of the approaching frigates, lookouts confirmed that it was not Rodgers's squadron at all, but instead their first look at the enemy. Hull was a very confident captain, and though his crew was fresh and 'unacquainted with a ship of war'[36] he was sure that 'we shall have nothing to fear from any single deck Ship; indeed: unacquainted as we now are, we should I hope give a good account of any Frigate the enemy have.'[37] Still, upon realisation that he faced a British squadron, Hull knew that opposing several frigates and a ship of the line was out of the question and turned to flee. HMS *Guerriere* spotted her first and turned in pursuit while signalling to alert Broke and the rest, and a long, gruelling chase began.

33 SRO, HA 93/9/81, Philip Broke to Louisa Broke, 27 October 1811.
34 SRO, HA 93/9/105, Philip Broke to Louisa Broke, 2 July 1812.
35 SRO, HA 93/9/105, Philip Broke to Louisa Broke, 2 July 1812.
36 Roosevelt, *Naval War of 1812*, p.82.
37 Captain Isaac Hull to Secretary of the Navy Hamilton, US Frigate *Constitution*, Annapolis Bay, 2 July 1812, *Naval War of 1812*, Vol.1, p.161.

Unfortunately for Dacres, the British squadron did not initially respond to *Guerriere*'s night signals; the lack of a response caused him to worry that he had sailed so far from Broke and the rest that he had lost them and was instead being approached by Rodgers's squadron, and in consequence he tacked away from the *Constitution*. Dacres did eventually realise his mistake, but this allowed *Constitution* ample time to conceive she was facing an entire British squadron and to make sail away from them. This confusion caused much anxiety in the British force, and subsequently was considered an important factor in *Constitution*'s being able to escape, as Byron stated in a letter to Broke following the action:

> Nothing can exceed my mortification from the extraordinary escape of the *American* frigate, and I am likewise much concerned it should fall so heavily on *Dacres*. ... I am now very sorry I did not answer the *Guerriere*'s signal, but it was so near daylight I thought a day signal might nearly be seen as well. Whatever I did was from the most anxious intention to secure the enemy; and I have to regret that, from a succession of unfortunate circumstances, he should have escaped.[38]

Different historical works have come to different conclusions over the impact of the initial confusion on *Constitution*'s escape from Broke, but Byron and his fellows attributed those 'unfortunate circumstances' as a significant factor in her escape. Broke reported that she was an excellent sailor, and every moment passed and mile gained counted in the chase.

As the morning wore on, the fortune of the British did not improve as the wind died, forcing the combatants to man their boats to haul their large men of war along. *Shannon*, whose boats were joined by others from the squadron, slowly gained on the Americans, who began warping – rowing one of the ship's kedge anchors and dropping her some distance from the ship, then setting men to the gruelling task of hauling on the capstan to drag the ship forwards using the weight of the anchor on the sea bottom. Both crews suffered extreme exhaustion over the long day of hauling and trading ineffectual shots. *Constitution* resorted to dumping 2,000 gallons of water overboard, while *Shannon* was joined by *Guerriere* and *Belvidera*, both struggling to get into range. In the light winds the British frigates were hesitant to come into range. Hull had placed two of his heavy 24-pounders on deck as stern chasers, and those long guns could easily sink the boats providing the British frigates their only means of propulsion. Late that evening they finally found a breeze, and *Constitution*'s lead was now cemented thanks to her sailing qualities and to Hull's excellent seamanship. The chase continued for another full day, but by the morning of the 20th Broke's squadron abandoned the chase, as their quarry was nearly out of sight.[39]

Broke's squadron later did capture an American warship, as Sawyer reported to the Admiralty in early August:

38 SRO, HA 93/6/2/41, Captain Byron to Captain Broke, 20 July 1812.

39 McCranie, *Utmost Gallantry*, pp.34–37; Roosevelt, *Naval War of 1812*, pp.80–89.

> The United States Brig *Nautilus* of 14 guns and 100 men had been sent in here, by His Majesty's Squadron, under the Command of Captain Broke, but I have received no official account of this Capture, the Squadron being then in Chase of an Enemy's Frigate, which I am concerned to say, effected her escape.[40]

The capture of a sloop of war by an entire squadron understandably elicited little excitement in the admiral – of far more concern for everyone involved was the escape of *Constitution*. In the same letter, Sawyer's report of *Nautilus*' capture is contrasted with his report of the capture of privateers by HM Sloop *Colibri*, where he praises her captain and officers for a victory between vastly more equal forces.

As disappointing as this was for Broke, his hope was to seek out and bring Rodgers's squadron to action, as he informed the Admiralty upon meeting with the West Indies convoy Rodgers was searching for: 'we shall at first ensure their safety, and I hope our escorting them may lead to a meeting of the Squadrons.'[41] It was not long, however, before Broke had to admit he had failed:

> We are much disappointed to hear that Rodgers is gone beyond our reach. … We shall now return to his coast & revenge ourselves for the dance he has led us … We are all now bent on punishing the Americans for their malicious war by destroying their trade, as we cannot find their marauders.[42]

In pursuing the enemy's trade, Broke decided to break up his squadron and to cruise separately. On 5 August, he appeared to find luck upon encountering the 36-gun frigate USS *Essex*, under Captain David Porter, while chasing an American merchant ship called *Minerva*. Unfortunately for Broke, Porter mistook a recently captured merchant prize accompanying *Shannon* for another warship and made a quick escape from what appeared to be a hopelessly outmatched fight.[43] Broke, unaware that Porter thought he was facing two frigates, was mortified. He complained that 'she sailed too well for us … he did not like to *fight*, it was well for him he *could run*, and had the night to shade him.'[44] In comparison, Broke's official correspondence following *Constitution*'s escape was relatively tame, doing little more than expressing his disappointment and praising her sailing qualities.[45] Even considering the difference in tone between an official letter and personal correspondence, the contrast is palpable. *Essex*'s escape appeared cowardly to Broke and came after a month of continued frustration over American forces eluding him. It is not surprising that Broke informed his wife that, after catching the *Minerva*, 'we burn'd the ship *in spite*.'[46]

---

40 Vice Admiral Sawyer to Secretary of the Admiralty Croker, HMS *Centurion*, Halifax, 2 August 1812, *Naval War of 1812*, Vol.1, pp.215–216.

41 LAC, MG12 ADM 1/1553, B-2608, Captain's Letters B, Captain Broke to Secretary Croker, 30 July 1812; Daughan, *1812*, pp.60–71.

42 SRO, HA93/9/109, Philip Broke to Louisa Broke, 9 August 1812.

43 McCranie, *Utmost Gallantry*, p.45.

44 SRO, HA 93/9/111, Philip Broke to Louisa Broke, 30 August 1812.

45 LAC, MG12 ADM 1/1553, B-2608, Captain's Letters B, Broke to Croker, 30 July 1812.

46 SOR, HA 93/9/111, Philip Broke to Louisa Broke, 30 August 1812.

The actions of Vice Admiral Sawyer and the Halifax squadron during the opening months of 1812 highlight the eagerness for action among him and his officers. Sawyer dispatched most of his ships in search of a single American squadron, leaving Halifax and local trade exposed. Both he and Broke, in command of the squadron, were eager to bring about an action with the enemy. Byron's correspondence reveals a similar sentiment. All three officers were frustrated, of course, as no notable evenly matched actions occurred at sea during the war's opening months. In fact, the only single-ship action that had thus far occurred pitted a British sloop against the aforementioned frigate USS *Essex*, and the result could hardly have lifted the spirits of Broke and Sawyer.

Essex–Alert action, 13 August 1812

On the 13 August, the British sloop *Alert* was patrolling off Newfoundland for American cruisers and chanced upon the frigate USS *Essex*, commanded by the young and ambitious Captain David Porter. *Essex* was posing as a sloppy merchant ship – as *Alert* was doing herself – and lured the British sloop closer, hoping to bring her to action. Despite the sloop's slow speed, she closed over the morning, and by 11:30 a.m. was approaching *Essex*'s starboard quarter with the intention of raking when Porter ordered his ship to come about and raise the stars and stripes, taking *Alert* and her commander by surprise. Commander Thomas Laugharne was in a terrible position; his sloop, an ex-collier, was horribly slow and hopelessly outgunned, carrying sixteen 18-pounder carronades and two 6-pounders to Essex's forty 32-pound carronades and six 12-pounders. She was not built for combat, and her bulwarks were 'exceedingly slight … and were incapable of resisting an ordinary Musket Ball.'[47] As *Essex* came into the wind, Laugharne decided to make a desperate attack on her to inflict enough damage to effect an escape. However, Porter, in the faster and more manoeuvrable frigate, was able to counter the slower British sloop. *Alert* only managed to fire off three glancing and ineffective broadsides before *Essex* unleashed her broadside of 32-pound carronades; at short range these guns ripped *Alert*'s rigging to shreds and sent her crew into a panic. The frightened crew, including the second-in-command Lieutenant Andrew Duncan, rushed aft to implore Laugharne to surrender.[48] Laugharne's account points out that he was reluctant to strike and only did so upon the assurances of his officers and crew that he had done all he could, portraying his surrender as that of a commander reluctant to quit but swayed by his concern for the safety of his crew. *Alert*, now effectively a floating wreck, struck her colours eight minutes after the start of the action.[49]

47 TNA, ADM 1/5431: CM *Alert*: Comments of Commander Thomas Laugharne, Commander Thomas Laugharne to Admiral John Duckworth, 30 August 1812.

48 George C. Daughan, *The Shining Sea: David Porter and the Epic Voyage of the USS* Essex *during the War of 1812* (New York: Basic Books, 2013) pp.2–3.

49 TNA, ADM 1/5431, CM *Alert*, ADM 1/5431: Laugharne to Duckworth, 30 August 1812, comments of Laugharne, testimonies of William Haggerty (Purser) and Lieutenant Philip Nind.

Surrendering in such a situation was the only reasonable course to take – *Essex* was four times her force, and *Alert* did all she could to fight the action before suffering crippling damage from her opponent's heavy carronades.[50]

The British press, both in Britain and in her colonies, largely ignored the loss of a sloop of war attached to the Newfoundland station; it was overshadowed by news to come of the victories of America's frigates in the War of 1812. While the public had little interest in the action, the officers of *Alert* certainly did, as their future careers were at stake. Commander Laugharne and his officers faced a court martial for the loss of the ship, as every captain did when a ship was lost, whether to enemy action, inclement weather, or accident. Most officers were honourably acquitted for such losses so long as the court determined they had done everything possible to save the ship. Laugharne's conduct was judged to be satisfactory – the court had no quarrel with his decision to strike when he did, as *Alert* was not at all capable of continuing the action. Their view of the action was reflected in that of Sir John Duckworth, the commander-in-chief of the Newfoundland Station: 'It is a consolation to reflect that the Enemy have not gained either credit in conquering so poor an adversary or profit in the acquisition of a vessel so little suited to the purposes of war.'[51] Even so, Laugharne had cause to be concerned; acquittal did not guarantee that he would be welcomed back into active service in such a competitive Navy. At this time there were twice as many commanders as there were sloops to be commanded, and (unlike post captains) inactive commanders often had no prospects of promotion except in retirement. Whereas a post captain in Laugharne's position faced a worst-case scenario of remaining on half-pay indefinitely – although with the likelihood of living long enough to be advanced to admiral by seniority (with the pay and status increase that came with it) – Laugharne remained a commander until his effective retirement in 1832, when he was promoted in recognition of his shore-based coastguard service following the end of the war. He only served at sea briefly from 1814 to 1815 and remained ashore for the rest of his life. His Second Lieutenant, Philip Nind, was himself never promoted past lieutenant.[52]

Alert's senior lieutenant, Andrew Duncan, received an even worse fate. The court martial testimonies revealed that Duncan had joined the shattered crew in urging Laugharne to surrender, and according to commentary in the *Naval Chronicle*, he was 'found guilty of disobedience of orders, and not rendering that assistance to Captain Laugharne that he ought to have done.'[53] To the Royal Navy, the image of a British captain leading his sloop into battle

50 Roosevelt, *Naval War of* 1812, p.80.

51 TNA, ADM 1/477/60, Duckworth to Croker, 31 August 1812.

52 David Syrett and R.L. DiNardo, *The Commissioned Sea Officers of the Royal Navy, 1660–1815* (Aldershot: Scholar Press for the Navy Records Society, 1994) pp.267, 332; TNA, ADM 956/5/65, Thomas Laugharne, Officer Service Record; John Marshall, 'Thomas Lamb Polden Laugharne, Esq.', in John Marshall, *Royal Naval Biography: Or, Memoirs of the Services of all the Flag-Officers, Superannuated Rear-Admirals, Retired-Captains, Post-Captains, and Commanders* (London: Longman, Hurst, Rees, Orme, Brown, and Green, 1835), Vol.4, Part II, pp.479–480.

53 *Naval Chronicle*, Vol.28, p.506.

against a much more powerful frigate was likely very appealing, and would have reminded them of Thomas Cochrane's capture of *El Gamo* in HM Sloop *Speedy* 12 years before.[54] Conversely, the image of a lieutenant appealing to the captain to strike instead invoked notions of cowardice and disgust among the court, even considering how badly outmatched *Alert* was. He may have been correct in urging his commander to strike as the situation was hopeless, but the court could not countenance Duncan's conduct in the action. He was summarily stripped of his rank and dismissed from the service.[55]

If the court was reminded of *Speedy*'s victory under Thomas Cochrane years before, when Cochrane attacked and defeated a 32-gun Spanish frigate that had him vastly outgunned and outmanned, then Captain Porter of USS *Essex* seemed to think Laugharne had actually meant to mimic Cochrane and attack his vastly superior frigate. In a letter following the action, Porter described his admiration for Laugharne's conduct and bravery, stating that:

> We are now well convinced ... that an English Sloop of War, calculating on the Magic of the British name and Terror of British Thunder, has had the assurance to 'commence attack within pistol shot on an American Frigate' for such (they informed us) they knew us to be, and have repeatedly reported, that had we been Frenchmen they would either have taken us, or made their escape.[56]

Even though *Alert* was vastly outgunned and quickly destroyed by *Essex*'s gunnery, Porter was under the mistaken impression that his enemy seriously meant to offer a fight. The Royal Navy had an entrenched reputation for determination and invincibility, and clearly that had made an impression on Porter. His views still influence some American historians today, such as George Daughan:

> In the finest British tradition – going back to Sir France Drake – he was defying the odds and continuing his mad dash toward the much larger frigate, bent on evening the odds by surprising her and hitting her hard before she knew what was up.[57]

Laugharne's plan was not to try and capture *Essex* – his account makes that clear – but still, Porter's initial impression resonates with the analysis of contemporary historians.

Porter lamented in his subsequent correspondence with the Secretary of the Navy that, with any justice, *Alert* would have encountered the sloop USS *Hornet* rather than *Essex*, as 'the forces would then have been more equal.'[58] Capturing a British sloop carried no glory with it, and thus far Porter had been deprived of any meaningful action in the conflict. In July, he encountered

---

54 Arthur Herman, *To Rule the Wales: How the British Navy Shaped the Modern World* (New York: Harper Collins, 2004), pp.400–401.

55 Syrett and DiNardo, *Commissioned Sea Officers*, p.135.

56 Captain David Porter to Secretary of the Navy Hamilton, US Frigate *Essex*, at sea, 3 September 1812, *Naval War of 1812*, Vol.1, p.444.

57 Daughan, *1812*, p.69.

58 Daughan, *1812*, p.69.

the frigate HMS *Minerva*, which was guarding a convoy. He hoped *Minerva* would offer combat and was surprised when she did not. As *Minerva* was defending a convoy, one carrying the 1st Regiment of Foot to the Gulf of St Lawrence, her captain had no choice but to remain with his charges. As much as breaking off to offer combat with an enemy of equal strength would have tempted her captain, risking the convoy in such a manner would likely have earned him a court martial and severe punishment.[59] Still, Porter was disappointed by this, just as Broke had been disappointed that Porter had avoided action with *Shannon*. His esteem for Britain's naval spirit was nevertheless confirmed by the tiny *Alert*, which had seemingly made an ill-fated gamble to take on a fifth-rate frigate on her own.

Constitution–Guerriere action, 19 August 1812

During *Constitution*'s escape from Broke's squadron, Captain Byron worried that Dacres might be wrought with guilt over failing to catch her. If he was, then perhaps Dacres saw a chance to settle the score when his old acquaintance was spotted on the afternoon of the 19th, some 400 miles southeast of Nova Scotia; one of *Guerriere's* lieutenants, Bartholomew Kent, later suggested that this was the case. Dacres was spoiling for a fight with the Americans. He had reportedly issued a challenge in an American paper to John Rodgers of the *President* 'or any other of the large frigates' in response to the *Little Belt* affair. Evidently, Dacres had taken this personally, as he had ordered 'NOT THE LITTLE BELT' to be painted in large letters along his foretopsail.[60] Dacres may have been *en route* to Halifax for much needed repairs, but the chance to win the first victory for the Royal Navy against the American Navy was more than enough. The possibility of running from the fight and towards the certain shame and court martial that would follow, never occurred to Dacres.[61] Hull was also eager for action, as his cruise had thus far been uneventful.[62]

Under these conditions, both ships entered action carrying only their topsails and some topgallants – the typical 'battle sail' rig in action. Dacres was also concerned about the conditions of his masts: they were old and somewhat decayed, and there was a worry that too much strain on them in action might rip them apart. This meant he had to be careful in his manoeuvring to minimise the strain on his masts. Just after 5:00 p.m. *Guerriere* opened with the first shots from her starboard guns, all falling short, and proceeded to wear ship and fire her larboard broadside, inflicting minor damage on *Constitution*'s rigging. Wearing ship, the process of passing a vessel's stern through the wind so to come out on the opposite tack, put much less strain on a square rigged vessel than tacking, which involved passing one's bow

59 Daughan, *1812*, p.60.

60 Toll, *Six Frigates*, p.348.

61 Toll, *Six Frigates*, p.348; Andrew Lambert, *The Challenge: Britain Against America in the Naval War of 1812* (eBook edition) (London: Faber and Faber, 2013), Chapter 2.

62 Roosevelt, *Naval War of 1812*, p.89.

through the wind – considerably faster to execute but more strenuous.[63] He continued to wear, presenting and firing each broadside in succession, over the next 40 minutes as Dacres tried to gain an advantageous position with the weather gauge. Hull was able to frustrate his opponent, however, and continued to manoeuvre to counter him. Both sides exchanged long range shots without inflicting any serious damage on the other.[64]

The two frigates slowly drifted closer over the next hour, and at 6:00 p.m. both captains moved to close the gap, opening fire at close range. A brutal cannonade followed yardarm to yardarm. *Guerriere* got the worse of it; enemy fire ripped through her hull planking and rigging, wreaking havoc on her decks and toppling her mizzenmast. *Constitution*'s rigging suffered, one of her flags was cut away by enemy fire, and her several longboats still secured on her spar deck were smashed to pieces, but she suffered almost no damage to her hull. Much of *Guerriere*'s shot could not penetrate *Constitution*'s strongly-built live oak hull, even at this close range, and one American sailor observed shot simply bouncing off her sides. It was here that her now famous nickname was born.[65] Yet what mattered more in the moment was the increasingly deplorable state of *Guerriere*, the decks of which were strewn in wreckage, and which was now losing her ability to steer because of the heavy drag of the fallen mizzenmast in the water. This allowed *Constitution* to sail out and around her enemy and fire a raking broadside into *Guerriere*'s shattered bows. Still drifting, *Guerriere* now swung round in the water so that her bowsprit passed over *Constitution*'s quarterdeck and became entangled in her rigging. Both sides contemplated boarding the other, but small arms fire prevented either from making the attempt.[66]

Before long the wind shifted, and the two ships separated. As *Constitution* veered away to make repairs, *Guerriere*'s bowsprit was ripped from the hull, and the fore and mainmasts quickly followed. The frigate was left as 'a perfect unmanageable wreck'[67] – defenceless, and without any ability to manoeuvre in the heavy ocean swell. Sailing ships rely on the force of the wind in the sails and on the current against the keel for balance, so without any remaining rigging *Guerriere* was left at the mercy of the waves and rolled heavily. This only exacerbated the chaotic state on her decks, as wreckage tumbled back and forth and several guns on the quarterdeck and forecastle fell overboard. Dacres and his two surviving lieutenants, all badly wounded, were forced to concede that further action was hopeless, as *Constitution* repaired her damaged rigging and moved to cross their bows, guns run out. Rather than risk another raking broadside, Dacres ordered the colours to be struck from the remaining stump of the mizzenmast.[68]

---

63 Lambert, *The Challenge*, Chapter 2.

64 Roosevelt, *Naval War of 1812*, pp.89–90; McCranie, *Utmost Gallantry*, p.48; Lambert, *The Challenge*, Chapter 2.

65 Toll, *Six Frigates*, p.350.

66 Roosevelt, *Naval War of 1812*, pp.90–92; McCranie, *Utmost Gallantry*, p.49; Lambert, *The Challenge*, Chapter 2.

67 Captain James Dacres to Admiral Herbert Sawyer, Boston, 7 September 1812, *Naval War of 1812*, Vol.1, pp.243–245.

68 Roosevelt, *Naval War of 1812*, p.91; McCranie, *Utmost Gallantry*, p.49; Lambert, *The Challenge*, Chapter 2.

Such a loss was shocking for the confident Royal Navy – the sheer number of victories over defeats over the last two decades of war ensured that. The fighting spirit of the Navy was so entrenched that her officers were even expected to triumph against superior force, and their captains were certainly expected to avoid shying away from such fights; the memory of Calder's court martial was still fresh in 1812, and the echo of Byng over a half century earlier still haunted the Navy. Many admirals and captains had led their forces against superior enemies and triumphed; had Dacres not attempted to do so, he would have faced certain public ignominy and professional ruin.[69] Single-ship actions were particularity impactful. Frigate captains yearned for such an opportunity, and for Dacres it was even more important. He was born into a naval dynasty: his father, uncle, brother, and cousin were all serving naval officers, and Dacres had been immersed in naval culture from an early age. By engaging the *Constitution*, he became one of the four or five percent of naval captains to fight in single-ship action.[70] Understandably, he would not have wished to begin his report to the commander-in-chief with the melancholic phrase 'I am sorry to inform you of the capture of H.M. late ship *Guerriere*, by the American frigate *Constitution*.'[71]

The following day, Captain Hull decided to abandon the sinking *Guerriere* and set her on fire. An hour later, she blew up and disappeared below the waves. Dacres and his crew were carried back to Boston as prisoners of war, giving the captain ample time to set out his report on the loss. In reporting the loss of his frigate to Vice Admiral Sawyer, Dacres knew he was drafting a letter which would serve as his professional and public defence; reports from notable actions were nearly always reviewed by the Admiralty and subsequently printed in various newspapers and journals in Britain. His career and reputation were on the line. In addition to describing the particulars of the action, the letter emphasised the havoc that enemy gunnery had inflicted on his officers, crew, and rigging. The wounding of many of his officers (including himself, two lieutenants, and the master) was described as a significant blow to his ship's performance late in the action, although he was careful to defend the honour of said officers, reporting that 'none of the wounded Officers quitted the Deck till the firing ceas'd' and praising them for remaining on duty despite their wounds.[72] Further, he emphasised the extensive damage that *Guerriere* suffered to her hull and rigging, which had left her a floating wreck.[73] The extent of the damage was laid out in full, these points rammed home by the fact that *Guerriere* was so thoroughly wrecked that Hull had abandoned her rather than take her as a prize. Dacres also highlighted the deliberations he had engaged in and his reasoning before ultimately surrendering, the officers concluding that, with the ship about to be raked and 'all attempts to get her before the wind being fruitless,' resisting

69 Lardas, *British Frigate vs French Frigate*, p.71; Toll, *Six Frigates*, p.348; Lambert, *The Challenge*, Chapter 2.

70 Wareham, *Star Captains*, p.160.

71 Captain James Dacres to Admiral Herbert Sawyer, Boston, 7 September 1812, *Naval War of 1812*, Vol.1, pp.243–245.

72 Dacres to Sawyer, 7 September 1812, *Naval War of 1812*, Vol.1, p.244.

73 Dacres to Sawyer, 7 September 1812, *Naval War of 1812*, Vol.1, p.243.

'would only be a needless waste of lives.'[74] Only then, with *Guerriere* in such a dismal and helpless state, had Dacres ordered 'though reluctantly, the Colours to be struck.'[75]

Nearly every historical work on this action – from William James and Theodore Roosevelt to the more modern works of Kevin McCranie, N.A.M. Roger, and Andrew Lambert – discusses the much superior broadside of the *Constitution* compared to that of *Guerriere* and its impact. For British writers, this disparity in addition to the defective state of the British frigate sufficiently explains the loss, and American accounts tend to emphasise additional factors without discounting the disparity in force.[76] Certainly, the British frigate was widely outmatched. *Constitution*, in addition to her much stronger hull, carried six more guns than her opponent, which were of a much larger calibre. Her main battery consisted of 24-pounders; *Guerriere*'s main battery consisted only of 18-pounders, the standard armament for fifth-rates, and so *Constitution*'s broadside shot weighed around 700 pounds to *Guerriere*'s approximately 500 – a nearly 50 percent advantage.[77] Strangely, this fact was omitted by Dacres in his report:

> I hope, in considering the circumstances, you will think the ship entrusted to my charge was properly defended; the unfortunate loss of our masts. the absence of the third lieutenant, second lieutenant of marines, three midshipmen, and twenty-four men considerably weakened our crew, and We only mustered at quarters two hundred and forty-four men, and nineteen boys, on coming into action; the enemy had such an advantage from his marines and riflemen, when Close, and his superior sailing enabled him to choose his distance.[78]

He emphasised the enemy's superiority in crew size and small arms fire, their fewer mounting casualties compared to *Guerriere*, and their superior sailing qualities, but did not ascribe the loss to a superiority in gunnery or broadside weight. Much of the action was fought at close range, so the greater range of the enemy's guns did not play much of a role, but the larger calibre of *Constitution*'s guns, as well as her much stronger hull, were significant factors. However, aside from describing the armament of the enemy, Dacres did not comment on the disparity in force at all.

Upon arriving in Boston, Dacres and his officers were paroled and their men put into a prison hulk on the Charles River. While the port town celebrated the victory and heaped praise upon Hull and his crew, the British prisoners were exchanged and returned to Halifax; neither side early in the conflict had the capacity to house large numbers of prisoners, and so

74 Dacres to Sawyer, 7 September 1812, *Naval War of 1812*, Vol.1, p.243.

75 Dacres to Sawyer, 7 September 1812, *Naval War of 1812*, Vol.1, p.243.

76 Roosevelt, *Naval War of 1812*, pp.90–92; McCranie, *Utmost Gallantry*, p.49; Lambert, *The Challenge*, Chapter 2; William James, *A Full and Correct Account of the Chief Naval Occurrences of the Late War Between Great Britain and the United States of America* (London: Joyce Gold, 1817), pp.96–113; Rodger, *Command of the Ocean*, p.567.

77 Roosevelt, *Naval War of 1812*, pp.90–92; McCranie, *Utmost Gallantry*, p.49; Lambert, *The Challenge*, Chapter 2; James, *Naval Occurrences*, pp.96–113.

78 Dacres to Sawyer, Boston, 7 September 1812, *Naval War of 1812*, Vol.1, p.245.

exchanges were initially common – a situation that would eventually break down over a number of tensions, including the British refusal to return slaves freed from the American south.[79] Upon arriving in Halifax, Dacres and his crew faced a court martial for the loss of the ship, chaired by a committee of senior naval officers, including Captain Broke.

During the trial, Dacres reiterated several points he had made in his initial letter to Sawyer, one being an attempt to board the *Constitution* while his ship was locked against her. Dacres explained that every preparation had been made to carry out such a plan, but that it was called off because 'finding his deck filled with men, and every preparation made to receive us, it would have been almost impossible to succeed.'[80] He also expanded upon his decision to surrender, saying that 'nothing but the unmanageable state of the ship (she being a perfect wreck) could ever have induced me to [strike], conceiving it was my duty not to sacrifice uselessly the lives of the men, without any prospect of success, or of benefit to their country.'[81] To summarise the themes of his letter and court martial defence, Dacres saw his duty as a naval officer to continue fighting, taking whatever risk to his ship and crew so long as there was a chance of victory. Once that prospect disappeared, it was his duty to consider his sense of humanity and responsibility for the safety of his crew.

Dacres concluded his testimony with a bold statement, in which he praised the quality of his crew and attributed the loss solely to misfortune:

> Notwithstanding the unlucky issue of the affair such confidence have I in the exertions of the officers and men who belonged to the *Guerriere*, and I am so aware that the success of my opponent was owing to fortune, that it is my earnest wish, and would be the happiest period of my life, to be once more opposed to the *Constitution*, with them under my command, in a frigate of similar force to the *Guerriere*.[82]

In his statement, which demonstrated his fighting spirit to the court, he makes no mention of the disparity in the number or guns nor broadside weight between *Constitution* and *Guerriere,* and even asserted that he had full confidence of victory in a rematch between the American frigate and 'a frigate of similar force' to his former command. Taken in consideration with his earlier letter, in which he highlighted the enemy's superior small arms fire and the misfortune of *Guerriere*'s extensive rigging damage, this suggests Dacres' genuinely believed that *Constitution*'s victory was owing to fortune, and not to her heavier armament. His interest in facing the enemy again, in a similar ship and with the same praise-worthy crew, too may have been genuine. Alternatively, this bold statement may have been intended to add weight to the case for his acquittal and to protect his professional reputation. Either way, this suggests that this confidence and fighting ethos was common

79 Anthony G. Dietz, *For Their Safekeeping and Accommodation: British Prisoners of War in the United States During the War of 1812* (Harriett G. Dietz [Standard Copyright License], 2011), pp.2–17, 371–386.

80 TNA, ADM 1/5431, Testimony of Dacres, CM *Guerriere*.

81 TNA, ADM 1/5431, Testimony of Dacres, CM *Guerriere*.

82 TNA, ADM 1/5431, Testimony of Dacres, CM *Guerriere*.

and expected of officers of the Royal Navy, and that the bold assertions made would have appealed to the members of the court. Given Broke's own desires to fight and win a single-ship action, it would not be surprising if this speech had moved him. Either out of genuine sentiments, deliberate manipulation, or a combination of both, Dacres's speech defending a disheartening loss enshrines the Royal Navy's fighting spirit, bred over two decades of unparalleled success at sea. Maintaining his professional reputation was important; there was always the risk of being removed from the service, and even an honourable acquittal did not guarantee that Dacres would receive another active command in the Navy. This would be shameful enough for most naval officers, but for someone from the Dacres's naval family it would have been even worse.

However, other officers' accounts differ from Dacres in their analysis of the enemy's superiority. A letter from an anonymous lieutenant during the action was printed in the *Naval Chronicle*, and in it he reflects on the astonishing size of the enemy ship and its armament:

> No one that has not seen the *Constitution* would believe there could be such a ship for a frigate, the nearest ship in the British navy, as to her dimensions and tonnage, is the *Orion*, of 74 guns. She was laid down for a 74-gun ship, is 180 feet long on her upper deck, and 45 feet 10 inches breadth of beam. She had no gangways, but two complete decks, the same as a line-of-battle ship, and is 1630 tons burden.[83]

While he does not comment on the exact number of guns carried by *Constitution*, he does suggest that she had two full rows of guns. Vice Admiral Sawyer's letter also reflects on the importance of *Constitution*'s gunnery and broadside, describing her as 'of very superior force, both in guns and men (of the latter almost double).'[84] Both Dacres's commanding officer and one of his subordinate lieutenants were willing to emphasise *Constitution*'s superior tonnage and broadside to help justify the British defeat, but Captain Dacres did not. This is because Dacres was on trial, but his admiral was not, and the stakes for his officers were not nearly as extreme. It was therefore more important for Dacres to play to the biases of the post-Nelsonic navy.

Sawyer defended Dacres's surrender on the theme of humanity. He assured Croker that, because *Guerriere* had been dismasted and had begun rolling hard enough to render efforts to work the guns ineffective, 'it became a duty to spare the lives of the remaining part of her valuable crew, by hauling down her colours.'[85] Due to the fact that *Guerriere* fought until she had been heavily damaged and placed in a position where she was likely to be raked, Sawyer states that this should 'satisfy their Lordships she was defended to the last.'[86] The last does not refer to the literal last man standing or even to the moment

83 Extract of a letter from an officer, late belonging to HMS *Guerriere*, dated Halifax, 15 October, *Naval Chronicle*, Vol.28, p.426.

84 Copy of a letter from Vice Admiral Sawyer to John Wilson Croker, dated on board HMS *Africa*, at Halifax, 15 September 1812, *Naval Chronicle*, Vol.28, p.316.

85 Sawyer to Croker, 15 September 1812, *Naval Chronicle*, Vol.28, p.316.

86 Sawyer to Croker, 15 September 1812, *Naval Chronicle*, Vol.28, p.316.

ship had sunk, but rather to the last point at which the British could hope for a victory. Subsequent resistance was not only fruitless, but also a waste of lives. The Royal Navy would risk the lives of their sailors so long as victory was possible, but that drive for victory and honour was always tempered by a need to recognise the moment at which all possibility of success had disappeared.

The court agreed with this sentiment, and with Dacres's assertion that misfortune was to blame for the ship's loss and not any shortcomings in her captain, officers, or crew. Their verdict stated that *Guerriere* found herself in such a perilous state due to the 'accident' of losing her masts, adding that this 'was occasioned more by their defective state than from the fire of the enemy, though so greatly superior in guns and men.'[87] Fortune and the ship's defective state were blamed rather than the superior firepower of the enemy frigate. Surrender was justified, then, to save the lives of the 'valuable remaining crew.'[88] Following a trial steeped in the aggressive traditions of the Royal Navy, Dacres and his crew were acquitted.

Dacres was lucky and appointed to HMS *Tiber* before the end of the war. He enjoyed an active career until his promotion to vice admiral in 1848, when he effectively retired. His lieutenants did not fare as well. First Lieutenant Bartholomew Kent served briefly as captain of HM Brig *Nova Scotia*, which was initially considered a minor vessel and therefore a lieutenant's command, but later in the war she was officially rated a sloop of war and handed over to a commander. He was promoted to commander in 1815, but appears not to have enjoyed an active career during the peace.[89] The Third Lieutenant, John Pullman, was never promoted to commander, and his subsequent career was largely forgotten.[90] Ironically, the Second Lieutenant, Henry Ready, had been promoted to commander on 13 August, but was killed in action weeks before news of the promotion would have arrived in Halifax.[91]

Two months into the conflict, the events at sea had done little to satisfy the Royal Navy. News was slow to travel home, and slow even for details of the actions to reach Newfoundland and Nova Scotia. As news of *Guerriere*'s loss spread, though, it sent shockwaves through the Navy and the public. The extent and character of public outrage varied widely. British papers expressed their shock at the loss, while Nova Scotia's papers quietly sat on their distress and awaited further details of the action. When news of *Guerriere*'s loss reached Britain's papers the conflict was still in its early stages. The court martial had assured the captains in Halifax that the ship's loss was primarily due to her defective state and not to enemy gunnery, and news reporting spread that message throughout the empire. Against the French the British had won the vast majority of single-ship actions, many against superior opponents. Therefore, it was expected that the British would win against the Americans. It was simply a matter of time.

87 TNA, ADM 1/5431, Verdict, CM *Guerriere*.

88 TNA, ADM 1/5431, Verdict, CM *Guerriere*.

89 Syrett and DiNardo, *Commissioned Sea Officers*, p.254; 'James Richard Dacres, Esq.', in *Royal Naval Biography*, Vol.2, Part II, pp.972–977; 'Bartholomew Kent, Esq.', in *Royal Naval Biography*, Vol.4, Part I, pp.354–357.

90 Syrett and DiNardo, *Commissioned Sea Officers*, p.369.

91 Syrett and DiNardo, *Commissioned Sea Officers*, p.374.

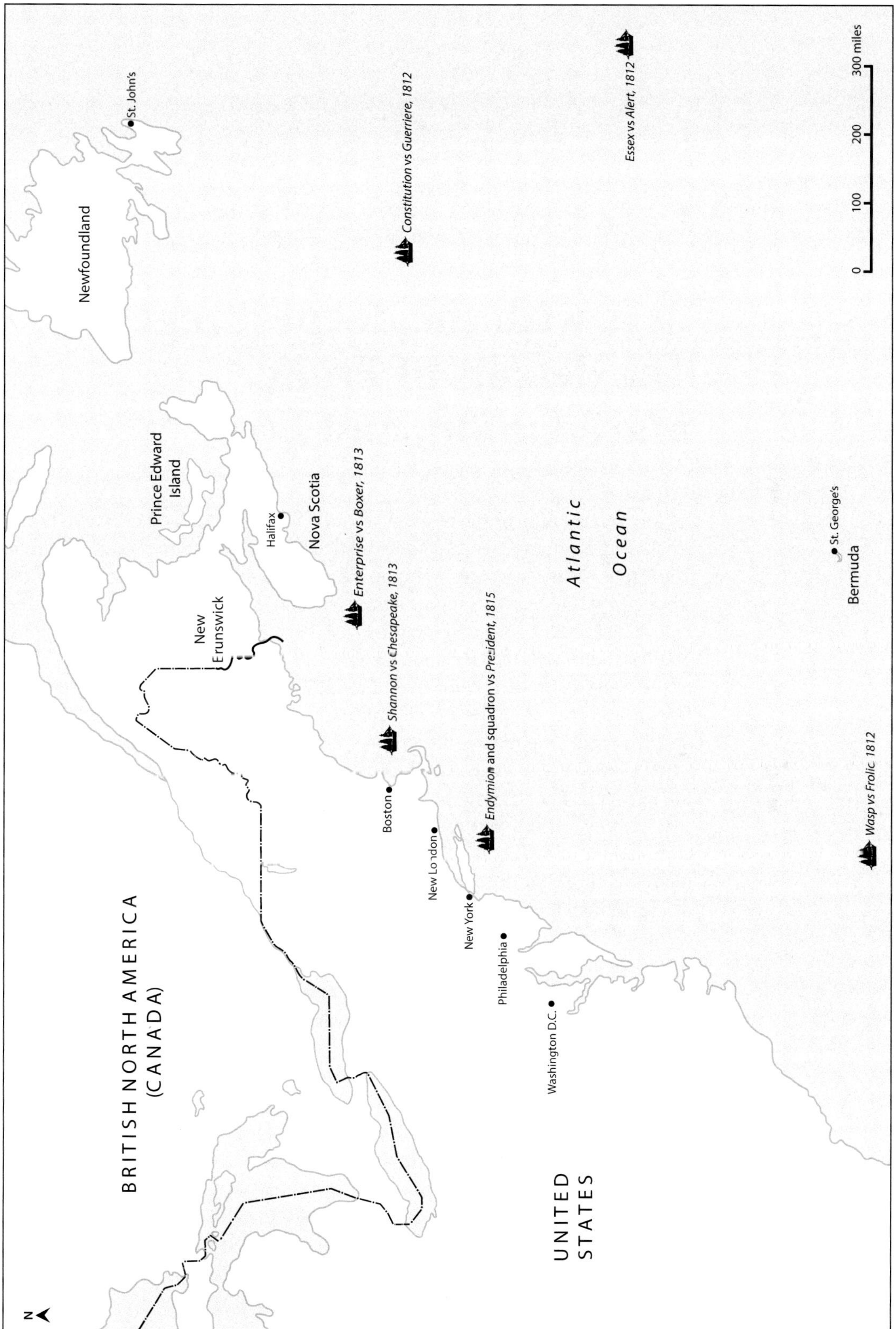

Map 1 Actions along the Eastern coastline of British North America and the United States, 1812–1815.

2

'It is with the deepest regret': The defeats of *Frolic*, *Macedonian*, and *Java*

As the first months of the conflict went on, both navies began to take better stock of the situation and of their available naval assets in North America. The United States was able to equip more of its ships for sea and adopt new strategies, while reinforcements slowly trickled into Halifax from Britain. The British Admiralty, still adjusting to new leadership under Robert Dundas, 2nd Viscount Melville, serving as First Lord of the Admiralty, did not learn of the declaration of war for over a month. Unofficial accounts arrived first from American ships that had departed as the debate raged in Congress, and they did not receive official confirmation announcing the war until Sawyer's dispatches arrived at the end of July. However, these did not include the particulars of what had occurred, nor did they include copies of reports that Sawyer himself had received. Even worse, Sawyer had not ordered the commander carrying the dispatches, Valentine Gardner, to hold mail on board his ship, and in consequence private correspondence containing much of the information Sawyer had omitted found its way into the press. The Admiralty was not pleased to learn of important news and reports from the American conflict from the local press rather than from the commander-in-chief. Sawyer's handling of the opening of the conflict had been very capable, but his poor communication with the Admiralty caused them quickly to lose confidence in him.[1]

Sawyer was replaced as commander-in-chief of the North American squadron by Admiral Sir John Borlase Warren – a senior commander with extensive experience in North America and in dealing with small roving French squadrons. He was chosen also because of his diplomatic abilities; he had helped defuse tensions while commanding in Halifax during the *Leopard–Chesapeake* affair. It was hoped that Warren could negotiate an end to hostilities now that the Orders in Council had been revoked by the new

1 McCranie, *Utmost Gallantry*, pp.56–57.

Prime Minister.[2] Sawyer, having been stripped of his status as commander-in-chief, continued in command of the forces based in Halifax, and was placed under Warren's command, along with his fellow admirals of the Leeward Islands and Jamaica commands. Upon his arrival in Halifax and taking command of his newly unified North American force, Warren found a very desperate situation. Sawyer, insulted at effectively being demoted, requested to be sent home. Warren's commanders in the West Indies were equally annoyed at being relegated to his command, losing their prestigious status as commanders-in-chief. Warren's force, though reinforced, was still inadequate to protect the whole of Britain's sea lanes and blockade America's ports.[3] Worse still, upon his arrival he learned that a large portion of the American Navy, including the three heavy frigates, had got to sea without being intercepted. In consequence, for the rest of 1812, the United States Navy was free to operate throughout the Atlantic.

Wasp–Frolic action, 18 October 1812

In early October, the bulk of America's naval forces proceeded to sea under three separate commands. Commodores Rodgers, Bainbridge, and Decatur departed Boston as thousands of well-wishers lined the docks to send them off, each in command of one of the heavy frigates, a small frigate, and a sloop. This strategy was decided on to minimise the risk of losing the entire force in one action, and to maximise their ability to harass and destroy British commerce.[4] In response, Broke was dispatched in search of the American forces with another squadron, this time with three 38-gun frigates. Warren estimated, based on reports, that Rodgers and Decatur were cruising with *President*, *United States*, and *Congress* – far more than a fair match for *Shannon* and two other fifth-rates. The naval community in Halifax were still convinced that *Guerriere*'s defeat was an anomaly, and they were eager to prove it.[5] Like before, however, Broke never found the enemy in force. The three commodores, after leaving Boston, split up, each cruising separately. It was not long before one of the American cruisers, acting alone, chanced upon one of the many lone warships protecting convoys or undertaking other missions.

One of those cruisers was USS *Wasp*, an 18-gun sloop of war. Under the command of Master Commandment (the equivalent of the modern United States Navy rank commander) Jacob Jones, *Wasp* had set sail from the Delaware on 13 October with orders to join Commodore Rodgers's squadron. On the first night, however, *Wasp* was caught in a gale that carried away her jib boom and six men, of whom only four were saved. This grim start to the cruise was soon overshadowed by the sight of a small convoy of merchant ships escorted by a single 18-gun brig-sloop two days later.

2 McCranie, *Utmost Gallantry*, p.56; Lambert, *The Challenge*, Chapter 3.
3 McCranie, *Utmost Gallantry*, pp.56–57.
4 McCranie, *Utmost Gallantry*, pp.58–59; Tucker, *Stephen Decatur*, pp.112–114.
5 McCranie, *Utmost Gallantry*, p.62.

She was one of the hundred existing *Cruizer*-class brig-sloops, HMS *Frolic*, under Captain Thomas Whinyates, whose crew was busy repairing extensive damage suffered in the same gale and reassembling a convoy of homeward bound merchants scattered in the storm. Whinyates could not have been any less fortunate: his ship was in a bad state of repair, he was short on crewmen, and he had to protect his already battered convoy. To give time for the merchants to escape, *Frolic* steered for the approaching Americana and hoisted Spanish colours.[6]

Whinyates had been promoted to post captain, though he was as yet still unaware of this and still in command of his unrated brig-sloop.[7] Whinyates therefore had more financial security than his counterpart in *Alert*, but the stakes were still high. Victory could earn him laurels, while defeat could cast him ashore on half-pay for the rest of his career. *Wasp* carried an equivalent armament to his sloop; both were armed with sixteen 32-pound carronades along their sides and two lighter chase guns. This meant that any action between the two would need to be at close range, where the full destructive force of the carronades would be most effective.[8] It would, therefore, be deadly. Victory in such an action could easily be forgotten in the public sphere, as victories against equal foes were becoming more and more expected in the Royal Navy, but defeat would amplify the dishonour.

Around noon, the two ships opened fire at close range, running parallel in very heavy seas. Crewmen on both ships opened with enthusiastic cheers, stifled over time by waves which caused the vessels to pitch and roll heavily, disrupting their ability to aim and fire and even submerging the muzzles of the carronades. It was heavy, hard work, but both crews kept up a steady and effective fire. Initially, *Frolic*'s gunnery proved very quick and deceptively effective. They fired three broadsides to the *Wasp*'s two, but due to the rolling of the ship much of that shot went high and cut up the American rigging.[9] Initially, Whinyates later reported, he was confident of victory based on the rate and efficiency of his fire in such conditions, but his ship was already in a worse state than the *Wasp* and damage to her rigging quickly reduced his ability to manoeuvre.[10] *Wasp* also succeeded in throwing more of her shot into the enemy's hull, inflicting considerable damage to her lower masts and crew.

Causalities mounted on both sides, as did rigging damage, but *Frolic* suffered more. Her captain reported that this was largely because of her already extensive damage; indeed, this formed the basis for his defence following the action. In a state of unmanageability, the less wounded *Wasp* was able to slip

6 McCranie, *Utmost Gallantry*, p.73; Roosevelt, *Naval War of 1812*, pp.100–101; James, *Naval Occurrences*, pp.139–141.

7 Syrett and DiNardo, *Commissioned Sea Officers*, p.466; 'Thomas Whinyates, Esq.', in *Royal Naval Biography*, Supplement, Part III, pp.107–108.

8 Lambert, *The Challenge*, Chapter 3.

9 McCranie, *Utmost Gallantry*, p.75; Roosevelt, *Naval War of 1812*, pp.100–101; Jon Latimer, *1812: War With America* (Cambridge, MA: Harvard University Press, 2007), p.104; James, *Naval Occurrences*, pp.140–141.

10 Captain Thomas Whinyates, R.N., to Admiral Sir John B. Warren, R.N., His Majesty's Ship *Poictiers* at Sea, 23 October 1812. *Naval War of 1812*, Vol.1, p.539.

ahead and fire into *Frolic*'s bows. Unable to manoeuvre, the warship drifted into the wind, placing her firmly at a right angle to the Americans' broadside. For 20 minutes she was subjected to the heavy shot of the enemy carronades – devasting weapons at close range. According to Roosevelt, Jones intended to continue raking his opponent, but his crew's excitement led them to rush onto the enemy's deck and carry her by boarding. Unknown to Jones, at this time Whinyates had been trying to organise his own boarding party, seeing it as his only hope, but this proved impossible: by the time that the Americans boarded, Whinyates and each of his officers were wounded and only about 20 men were still standing to repel boarders. Whinyates, still alive but unable to stand on his own, had no choice but to allow the Americans to strike *Frolic*'s colours. As the guns fell silent her masts both collapsed, leaving the prize a dismasted hulk in the heavy swell.[11]

Casualties on both sides were heavy, but *Frolic* suffered the most as so much of her shot had gone high rather than striking the enemy's hull. Whinyates and his Second Lieutenant, Fred Wintle, recovered from their wounds, but the First Lieutenant and the master both succumbed. All had remained on deck despite not even being able to stand on their own, and for that each was praised by the captain in his report.[12] He made it clear that despite his own efficient gunnery, the ship's defective state and the weather conditions were primarily to blame for the loss. Whinyates stated that he was 'convinced if the *Frolick* had not been crippled in the gale I should have to make a very different report to your Excellency.'[13] His men kept fighting, he reported, until nearly everyone had been wounded and every gun had been knocked out of action.[14]

About an hour after *Frolic* was captured, American lookouts spotted a large ship on the horizon, which proved to be the British ship of the line *Poictiers*. Jones realised that he had to flee – even in perfect condition, a sloop of war would be blown to pieces within minutes under fire from a 74-gun ship. This meant abandoning the prize, but Jones's priorities were rightfully with his ship and his men. He ordered the men to set sail, but as the sails filled with wind they disintegrated. The damage *Frolic*'s guns had inflicted on *Wasp* had not been enough to impact her chances in action, but it was enough to doom *Wasp* to capture. She tried to run for another couple of hours but was overtaken by the massive ship of the line. Whinyates had lost the action, but his desperate defence ensured that both sloops would end up in British hands.[15] However, Whinyates did not praise or emphasise the recapture; it was not his victory to report. *Poictiers*' captain did not celebrate the two captures in his report either; rather than proclaiming *Poictiers*' capture of two badly damaged and impossibly outmatched sloops,

11 Whinyates to Warren, 23 October 1812. *Naval War of 1812*, Vol.1, p.539; Roosevelt, *Naval War of 1812*, pp.102–103; McCranie, *Utmost Gallantry*, pp.73–74; Latimer, *1812*, p.104; James, *Naval Occurrences*, pp.139–141.

12 Whinyates to Warren, 23 October 1812, *Naval War of 1812*, Vol.1, p.541.

13 Whinyates to Warren, 23 October 1812, *Naval War of 1812*, Vol.1, p.541.

14 Whinyates to Warren, 23 October 1812, *Naval War of 1812*, Vol.1, p.541.

15 Whinyates to Warren, 23 October 1812, *Naval War of 1812*, Vol.1, p.541; McCranie, *Utmost Gallantry*, p.74; Roosevelt, *Naval War of 1812*, pp.105–106.

Beresford's letter reads like a dutiful statement of his recapture of a prize and his effort to collect the convoy *Frolic* had been captured defending. Like the typical letter informing a superior of the capture of a much smaller warship or privateer, Beresford did not discuss the action or praise the conduct of his officers and men. Capturing a pair of sloops was a trivial matter for a ship of the line. However, he did assure Admiral Warren that 'The conduct of Captain Whinyates, who I regret to say is wounded, and of his crew appears to have been so decidedly gallant, that I have been induced to continue him in command of the *Frolic*, until your pleasure is known.'[16]

Whinyates continued in command of his sloop until his return to port, where he faced a court martial. While the court acquitted Whinyates, he did not remain in command of *Frolic*. She had a new acting captain later that month – a lieutenant who received an official promotion a year later.[17] It is difficult to say if this was the result of Whinyates's loss to *Wasp* (a simple logistical decision considering his wound and the need to keep his ship at sea) or if it was because the command was considered appropriate for a more junior officer at Halifax, given that Whinyates was now a post captain. Regardless, his active career was nearly over following his loss to an equivalent foe. Whinyates did not receive another command until 1815 and then only served another nine months at sea, after which he saw no further active service and was promoted into retirement when his name reached the top of the post captains list in 1846.[18] Ironically, the commander whose ship was ultimately lost fared far better than the one whose ship remained in Royal Navy service due to the relative importance placed by each navy on single-ship actions. Jones and his senior lieutenant Biddle of *Wasp* were both awarded prize money by Congress and promoted. *Wasp* was commissioned as HMS *Loup Cervier*, the French common name for the Canada lynx native to Nova Scotia;[19] later in the war she encountered Captain Jones once again, now in command of the newly-captured and refitted USS *Macedonian*.

United States–Macedonian action, 25 October 1812

In early 1812, months before the outbreak of war, two captains of frigates from rival navies met in Norfolk. One was Stephen Decatur, who held the unofficial rank of commodore in the United States Navy and who was in command of USS *United States*. With him was the British John Surman Carden, in command of the crack new 38-gun frigate HMS *Macedonian*. The two socialised frequently during Carden's stay in Norfolk, and Carden often

16 *The London Gazette*, 22 December, 1812, 16684:2568, Beresford, 'Copy of a Letter from Admiral the Right Honourable Sir John Borlase Warren, Bart., KB, Commander in Chief of His Majesty's Ships: Beresford to Warren, at sea, Oct 23 1812' (online), available at https://www.thegazette.co.uk/London/issue/16684/page/2568.

17 Winfield, *British Warships*, p.297.

18 Syrett and DiNardo, *Commissioned Sea Officers*, p.466; TNA, ADM 196/6/559, Whinyates, Officer Service Record.

19 LAC, MG12 ADM 1 1/503 Admiral's Dispatches, 1812–1813, North America, C 12854, Admiral Sir John Warren to Secretary John Croker, 26 February 1813.

dined with Decatur and his wife. The two officers took a liking to each other, bonding primarily through discussions of their beloved frigates. While *United States* was by far the slowest of the three heavy frigates with the nickname 'Old Wagon', she was still a prestigious command as one of the most powerful frigates in the world and currently carrying a slightly heavier armament than her sisters.[20] *Macedonian* herself was considered an exceptionally fast frigate, and her First Lieutenant, David Hope, considered her to be one of the best-trained frigates in gunnery in the world.[21] It was reported that during one of Carden and Decatur's discussions they had joked about making a wager over a beaver hat on the outcome of a prospective contest between their two frigates. This may be apocryphal, but it is better known that Carden did lecture Decatur on the dangers of over-arming frigates. Carden informed his friend that the British had come to learn that frigates were most effective with 18-pounder armaments, better even than those with 24-pounders. Being lighter, they were easier to handle and could be fired faster and more accurately without sacrificing much in the way of destructive power. This certainly was a conclusion the Royal Navy had reached during their warfare with France, and Carden told Decatur that with experience the United States Navy would come to learn this as well.[22]

When Carden and Decatur met again it was 500 miles south of the Azores. *United States*, after separating from the other American ships, was prowling Britain's trade routes in the eastern Atlantic. *Macedonian* was on her way home after having escorted an East Indiaman south. Both captains were eager for action, and in the early morning began approaching the other.[23] As reported by one of her crewmen, the Macedonians were in their best clothes for Sunday and keen to engage the enemy, save for a handful of Americans on board. One approached the captain and requested to be excused from fighting their countrymen; several Americans had been granted such a request by Dacres when *Guerriere* met *Constitution*. However, Carden angrily dismissed them and sent them back to their station.[24]

At 8:30 a.m., both ships hoisted their colours and ensigns and the *United States* wore and turned away from the wind, intentionally keeping back so that Decatur could make full use of his longer main battery (perhaps hoping to disprove the British experience that lighter armaments were better). On the *Macedonian*'s quarterdeck, First Lieutenant David Hope suggested that they try and close the distance as quickly as possible, hoping either to rake the enemy or force a close action, but Carden was more cautious, instead opting to sail up to windward and gain the weather gauge before moving to

20 Toll, *Six Frigates*, pp.360–361.

21 Colonel David Fitz-Enz, *Old Ironsides: Eagle of the Sea – The Story of the USS* Constitution (Lanham, MD: Taylor Tree Publishing, 2004), p.154; Roosevelt, *Naval War of 1812*, p.108.

22 Toll, *Six Frigates*, pp.360–361; Tucker, *Stephen Decatur*, pp.114–115.

23 LAC, MG12 ADM 1/1663, Captains Letters C, B-2612, John Carden to Secretary John Croker, USS *United States* at Sea, 28 October 1812; McCranie, *Utmost Gallantry*, p.97; Daughan, *1812*, p.131.

24 Toll, *Six Frigates*, p.361; Roosevelt, *Naval War of 1812*, p.110; McCranie, *Utmost Gallantry*, p.63.

close the gap.[25] The weather gauge, simply put, means being to windward of the enemy. Generally, being closer to the wind gives one more ability to manoeuvre than being further to leeward (further from the wind). Modern rules around nautical right of way reflect this, as a sailing vessel to leeward always has right of way over one to windward, as it is assumed that of the two the one to windward will have an easier time manoeuvring. In Carden's case, however, holding the weather gauge did him little good. He had difficultly closing the gap over the next hour, with 'the Enemy keeping two points off the Wind I was not enabled to get as close to her as I could have wished.'[26] This appears quite the feat according to modern nautical terminology – standing two points off the wind would place a square rigger in the 'no sail zone,' often referred to today as 'irons,' as they could not generate the power necessary to move the ship. As Sam Willis points out, however, nautical terminology has changed over the centuries. Historically, sailors measured their point of sail not from the direction of the wind, but from the angle at which their vessel would have been close hauled, just outside of the 'no sail zone.'[27] *United States* was likely sailing between six or eight points from the wind, depending on her own sailing qualities. Still, this was remarkably close hauled. Though she was moving slowly, this made it difficult for the windward *Macedonian* to close the distance.

The gap nevertheless slowly closed, and at around 9:00 a.m. the first broadsides were fired. *Macedonian* clearly proved the faster of the two, but with such a distance between them it was some time before she was close enough for her gunnery to inflict any real damage on the enemy. In the meantime, *United States*' longer 24-pounders began to wreak havoc on the British frigate's rigging, hull, and crew. Spars were knocked away, slowing the British frigate down. Men on deck and below were cut down by enemy shot and ragged splinters were sent flying through the crowded decks as shot pieced and shattered the oak hull. Several guns on the forecastle were dismounted from their carriages and put out of action. The Americans' larger 24-pound shot proved decisive, inflicting much more damage per impact than *Macedonian*'s 18-pound shot. When the gap closed within range of the carronades carried by both vessels, the odds tipped even further in the *United States*' favour. The American carried twenty-four 42-pound carronades to the British's fourteen 32-pounders. They were loaded with cannister and grape and were devastatingly destructive weapons at close range.[28]

The fire of the *United States* inflicted absolute carnage on and below *Macedonian*'s decks as scores of men were killed or wounded, covering the decks with blood. Sounds of gunnery was punctuated by the screams of the dying. The maintopmast, carrying the only sail currently set on the mainmast, was shot away by enemy fire and fell forwards, pushing the foretopmast with

---

25 Toll, *Six Frigates*, pp.361–362; Roosevelt, *Naval War of 1812*, p.108; McCranie, *Utmost Gallantry*, pp.63–64.

26 LAC, MG12 ADM 1/1663, Carden to Croker, 28 October 1812.

27 Sam Willis, 'Capabilities of sailing warships', *The Northern Mariner*, 13:4 (2003), pp.31–32.

28 LAC, MG12 ADM 1/1663, Carden to Croker, 28 October 1812; Toll, *Six Frigates*, p.361; Roosevelt, *Naval War of 1812*, p.110; McCranie, *Utmost Gallantry*, p.63.

it. The mess of canvas, wood, and rope collapsed onto the forecastle, covering the gun platform with wreckage and slowing the ship nearly to a halt. Decatur took advantage of the situation and tacked into the wind, coming up on *Macedonian*'s quarter and sending several devastating raking broadsides clean through her hull. Samuel Leech, one of her sailors, described scenes of absolute horror below: men were ripped apart by the enemy's round shot and grape and the great splinters they threw into the air.[29]

Above deck the situation was no less chaotic. Carden and his officers were struggling to clear the wreckage and regain control of the ship, hoping to use the few sails remaining to approach the enemy and carry her by boarding. Only the mizzenmast and a third of the fore-course remained standing; but, even as men assembled along the gangways with small arms, swords, and pikes, the weakened mizzenmast collapsed over the stern, strewing more wreckage onto the quarterdeck and its weight dragging in the water, rendering the ship completely unmanageable.

At this point Decatur wore round and moved out of range to repair the damage inflicted on his ship's running rigging, while Carden tried to take hold of the situation on board his ship. *Macedonian* now carried only a tattered fore-course, and was otherwise dismasted and at the mercy of the waves. There were over 100 men either dead, dying, or wounded, and carnage was strewn across the deck, adorned by piles of wrecked rigging and canvas. With the guns now silent, there was a steady cry from the wounded throughout the ship. Two of Carden's lieutenants, as well as other officers, were wounded but remained on deck, and Carden summoned them aft for a council. Lieutenant Hope proposed they continue fighting, but as *United States* approached on a course to resume a raking position, Carden opted against it.[30]

Carden's account makes it clear that it was his intention to fight as long as possible, and that his crew did indeed do this. He explained to Croker in his report that 'I soon found the Enemys force too superior to expect success, unless some fortunate chance occur'd in our favor, and with this hope I continued the Battle for two hours and ten minutes.' Over those two hours his ship's rigging was destroyed, leaving *Macedonian* an unmanoeuvrable hulk and in a position to be raked by the *United States*.[31] Carden's defence, as with those of Laugharne, Dacres, and Whinyates, rested on the fact that he and his crew fought and held out as long as he anticipated that they had a chance of victory, and that the *Macedonian* would not have been surrendered 'whilst a man lived on board, had she been manageable.'[32] However, without the ability to manoeuvre and return fire there was no chance of defeating the enemy so continued resistance was pointless.

The aftermath of the action was equally chaotic. With dozens of men being tended to below decks amid the wreckage and carnage, several

29 LAC, MG12 ADM 1/1663, Carden to Croker, 28 October 1812; Toll, *Six Frigates*, p.361; Roosevelt, *Naval War of 1812*, p.110; McCranie, *Utmost Gallantry*, p.63.

30 Toll, *Six Frigates*, pp.361–363; Roosevelt, *Naval War of 1812*, pp.109–110; McCranie, *Utmost Gallantry*, p.64.

31 LAC, MG12 ADM 1/1663, Carden to Croker, 28 October 1812.

32 LAC, MG12 ADM 1/1663, Carden to Croker, 28 October 1812.

sailors broke into the spirit stores and quickly became intoxicated. Leech described some of his compatriots reduced to tears as they saw their messmates cut down; others were angrily prepared to fight the American prize crews as they came on board to take possession of the frigate. Decatur did his best to preserve the property of the defeated officers, and even offered to purchase those stores such as food and wine that they could not carry home with them.[33]

Decatur and Carden greeted each other as friends. The American refused to accept Carden's sword and praised his gallantry, but he could tell that Carden was in a deplorably melancholic state. Carden admitted that he was devastated at losing his ship, believing that he was the first British captain to do so. Decatur's attempts to console him by informing him that Dacres had that unfortunate distinction only partially mollified Carden.[34] He had still lost his ship in one-on-one combat, and *Macedonian* became the first and only British frigate to be brought into an American port as a prize.[35] This and the 'deepest regret' he expressed in his letter to the Secretary of the Admiralty, John Croker, is evident in examining his post-action letters. Carden's letter on the 28th is barely legible, and subsequent letters written in January, while he was still a prisoner in America, were far more legible.[36]

The sense of regret expressed in his letter was of course nothing unique – such sentiments were expressed in the accounts of all the commanders who had thus far lost ships in action to the enemy, particularly Dacres. Also, like Dacres, Carden extensively described the destruction on board his ship and the casualties, and argued that these factors had removed any chance of victory by the end of the action, prompting him to surrender. Carden reported that 'all the Guns on the Quarter Deck and Forecastle disabled but two, and filled with wreckage, two also on the Main Deck disabled, and several shot between wind and water. A very great proportion of the Crew Killed and wounded.'[37] His ship had suffered very heavy damage, was rendered incapable of manoeuvring, and most of his ship's company had been killed or knocked out of action. He then added that he was faced, while in this desperate situation, with an 'Enemy comparatively in good order, who had now shot ahead, and was about to place himself in a raking position without our being enabled to return the fire, being a perfect wreck, an unmanageable Log.'[38] In fact, the *United States* was relatively untouched. It was another testament to the ingenious design of her and her sisters that she had withstood much of *Macedonian*'s fire with very little damage.

In the end, Carden reflected that 'Every effort has been made against the Enemy by myself, my brave Officers, and men, nor should she have been

33 Tucker, *Stephen Decatur*, p.119.

34 Tucker, *Stephen Decatur*, p.119; Toll, *Six Frigates*, pp.365–366; Latimer, *1812*, pp.105–106.

35 Daughan, *1812*, p.131.

36 LAC, MG12 ADM 1/1663, Carden to Croker, 28 October 1812; LAC, MG12 ADM 1/1663, Captains Letters C, B-2612, John Carden to Secretary Croker, New London, America, 6 January 1813; LAC, MG12 ADM 1 1/503 Admiral's Dispatches, 1812–1813, North America, C-12854, John Carden to Admiral John Warren, New London, America, 23 January 1813.

37 LAC, MG12 ADM 1/1663, Carden to Croker, 28 October 1812.

38 LAC, MG12 ADM 1/1663, Carden to Croker, 28 October 1812.

surrendered whilst a man lived on board, had she been manageable.' He praised the conduct of his First Lieutenant, David Hope, who had suffered a head wound near the close of the action but promptly returned to the deck, 'displaying that greatness of mind and exertion, which who it may be equalled, can never be excelled.' The Third Lieutenant was also wounded, but remained at his post. Carden spoke very highly of his officers' conduct and bravery during the action. His narrative was that of a gallant crew fighting an unmanageable ship against impossible odds.[39]

Carden's account differed from Dacres's in one key aspect, however. Following the action, he reflected that he

> ceased to wonder at the result of the Battle; the *United States* is built with the scantline of a seventy four gun Ship, mounting thirty long twenty four pounders on her Main Deck, and twenty two forty two pounders, Carronades, with two long twenty four pounders on her Quarter Deck and Forecastle. Howitzer Guns in her Tops, and a travelling Carronade on her upper Deck, with a Complement of four hundred and seventy-eight pick'd Men.[40]

Whereas Dacres had ignored the superior broadside and size of his opponent entirely, Carden emphasised the fact, linking it with the size and skill of the enemy's 'pick'd Men.' He does not argue that the superior broadside was the sole justification for defeat, but presents it as a nonetheless important factor in the action. By contrast, Dacres's defence hinged more on the advantage the enemy had in marines and riflemen rather than in gunnery.

Unlike Dacres, who came from a naval dynasty, Carden's entry into the Navy was peculiar. His father was an army officer, and he only joined the Navy at 17 after being privately educated ashore at the Royal Naval Academy. He had no familial ties to the Royal Navy and had spent half of his life ashore, whereas Dacres and most other naval officers had served at sea from a young age; they had been immersed in the Navy and its culture for the whole of their adult lives, and for a good portion of their childhoods as well. As such, the traditions of odds-defying confidence that Dacres demonstrated may not have been as hard-set in Carden's psyche, which may suggest why he was more willing to emphasise the enemy's superiority in firepower in his report. Still, Carden did not use the superiority of the enemy as his sole defence – it is one factor of several that he uses to explain the odds he was facing and the circumstances that resulted in the complete disabling of his ship. It was the damage inflicted, not the weight of the enemy broadside on its own, that sealed his fate.

Carden and his crew remained in New London for several months. Carden only returned to Bermuda, one of the two principal naval bases in the western North Atlantic, in March. Dacres's stay in Boston was much shorter, and this was perhaps a sign that the amicable relationship between the two combatants regarding prisoners was beginning to break down. In May, Carden and his crew were tried by court martial on board Warren's

39 LAC, MG12 ADM 1/1663, Carden to Croker, 28 October 1812.
40 LAC, MG12 ADM 1/1663, Carden to Croker, 28 October 1812.

flagship HMS *St Domingo*, with Captain Henry Hotham presiding. Carden told the court that

> *Macedonian* became more crippled every broadside… The swell was great and the *Macedonian* roll'd heavy as her canvas and spars was reduced by the enemy's shot. The enemy shot ahead and left the *Macedonian* a perfect wreck we having only about one third of the foresail left to the yard, every other sail having shot away, we now endeavored to clear the wreck which had all fallen on deck, the mizzen foremast forward and the fore and main ones after, and to get the ship before the wind, which had considerable abated in consequence of the heavy cannonading. But while this effort was making the mizzen mast, being very much wounded by shot, fell over the stern, the wreck of which in the water rendered the ship totally unmanageable, and the enemy … now placing himself under our stern, the congruent circumstances occurred as stated in my Public Letter.[41]

He further emphasised the superior dimensions and broadside of the enemy ship and the superior size of her crew, adding that there were a good number of British sailors or Royal Navy veterans aboard. It was not, in Carden's mind, a defeat that robbed Britain of prestige or reputation, as 'My county has lost a ship but I consequentially feel that is all she has lost; Victory over such a superiority of force could not be obtained.'[42]

During the course of the court martial, much of the questioning focused on the first hour of the action, when *Macedonian* was slowly closing the gap but under fire from *United States*' longer-range guns, in the process suffering damage to her rigging and hull. That this was caused by his intention to secure and hold the weather gauge was much criticised by the court, and even more so by later historians. Indeed, some such as Lambert blame the loss entirely on Carden's endeavour to hold the weather gauge, which prevented him from closing until it was too late. As Willis argues, the weather gauge is not as simple in terms of naval warfare as it is often presented. While holding the weather gauge is often presented as a guarantee of success, in reality it was but one factor in naval warfare, one that is wildly misunderstood by most historians.[43]

Here, the naval officers presiding over the court martial seemed to agree that holding the weather gauge gave Carden little advantage and pressed this in their questioning. Lieutenant Hope, when questioned, agreed. Hope stated that at the opening of the action

> it appeared to me that we could have borne up and crossed her bow. Captain Carden asked the masters opinion, and … the master said he thought it was better to engage her to leeward and I gave it as my opinion it was no consequence whether she was engaged to windward or to leeward, on account of the sea as long as we went close alongside of the enemy.[44]

41 TNA, ADM 1/5436, Captain John Carden's Narrative, CM *Macedonian.*

42 TNA, ADM 1/5436, Captain John Carden's Narrative, CM *Macedonian.*

43 Sam Willis, *Fighting at Sea in the Eighteenth Century: The Art of Sailing Warfare* (Woodbridge: The Boydell Press, 2008), p.113.

44 TNA, ADM 1/5436, Lieutenant David Hope's Testimony, CM *Macedonian.*

Hope described more than one opportunity where he believed that alternative tactics may have enabled the *Macedonian* either to rake the enemy or bring her to close action.[45] Raking broadsides, especially at close range, could be devasting, and a close-range action earlier on, while *Macedonian* still had her rigging and gun battery intact, may have reduced the advantage the *United States* enjoyed because of her longer guns. In his rebuttal, Carden maintained that bringing the enemy to close action sooner was impossible, and argued that

> It ever was my intention (impossible to accomplish) from the first moment I made the stranger out to be an enemy to engage him as close alongside on The same tack to windward, as the yards of the ship would allow, at the same time to advantage by a way more preferable circumstances that might offer, but that more preferable one I never did perceive, and as I hear every circumstance fully in my mind, I feel conscious it never existed, or was apparent to me.[46]

Carden's strategy was to hold the weather gauge and then to bring the enemy to close action, whereas Hope argued that the priority should be to force a close action first. This alludes to a common theme in British tactics in the age of sail, as Royal Navy officers preferred fighting at close range. While Carden maintained that close-range action proved impossible, he was careful in every account to state that it was indeed his intention to force such an action.

Macedonian did have a marked advantage in sailing ability and speed, and this was poorly utilised. Decatur, by sailing so close to the wind, robbed the advantage of the weather gauge from the British, meaning that the approach would be long, and during that time the longer guns Carden had once derided as ineffective proved their worth by knocking away spars, guns, and men. But bringing the ship to close action early on would not necessarily have put the ship in a better situation, as the *United States* carried very powerful 42-pound carronades, making her short-range broadside even more deadly than her long-range one. Hope believed that bringing a close action early with their rigging and broadside intact would have given them a chance to outmanoeuvre their opponent to compensate for the heavier broadside; the other officers questioned did not agree with this, but did think that bringing about a close action earlier would have made the American victory far more costly.[47] The court agreed with the First Lieutenant in their verdict:

> previous to the commencement of the action, from an over anxiety to keep the weather gage an opportunity was lost at closing with the enemy, and that owing to this circumstance the *Macedonian* was unable to bring the *United States* to close action until she had received material damage.[48]

45 TNA, ADM 1/5436, Lieutenant David Hope's Testimony, CM *Macedonian*.

46 TNA, ADM 1/5436, John Carden's Rebuttal, CM *Macedonian*.

47 TNA, ADM 1/5436, Lieutenant David Hope's Testimony, CM *Macedonian*; Tucker, *Stephen Decatur*, pp.115–118.

48 TNA, ADM 1/5436, Verdict, CM *Macedonian*.

They believed that, under the right conditions and with the right tactics, an 18-pounder frigate had the ability to tackle and defeat a 24-pounder adversary at close action. Even with two American victories suggesting otherwise, they remained confident in the abilities of British frigates. As such, Carden's defeat was not blamed on the enemy's superiority in guns and men, but on failing to bring about a close action.

Tactical failure, however unfortunate, was not enough to convict Carden of wrongdoing. While he was criticised by Hope, neither Hope nor any of his officers questioned Carden's gallantry or courage, and the members of the court admired his determination to tackle such a superior foe. They described his conduct as courageous and praised him for inspiring his men in action, and concluded that his failure to close with the enemy did not originate 'in the most distant wish to keep back from the engagement.'[49] It was not cowardice or hesitation that caused the loss, but bad judgement. Carden's conduct satisfied the court, and he was honourably acquitted.

The wider naval community, however, was not satisfied with Carden's conduct. Many were surprised and shocked by his failure to bring about a close action.[50] He was eventually promoted to flag rank but only as a retiree, and was never again offered another active appointment following his loss to *United States*.[51] His lieutenants fared better, but Mottley and Bulford both struggled for active employment in the peacetime navy and were promoted to commander in retirement. Hope, the only officer to share the court's opinion that at close range there had been a real chance of victory, enjoyed a more active career, eventually reaching the rank of post captain.[52]

Criticised by peers and civilian alike, Carden's reputation remained linked to his defeat in 1812. This motivated him to draft a memoir of his naval career in which he defended his conduct during the action and attempted to pin his failed career following the battle onto a feud with the Secretary of the Admiralty.[53] His memoir depicted a brave British crew being overwhelmed by the enemy's force and by ill fortune, and asserted that *Macedonian* could have out-sailed and run from the enemy, adding that the Admiralty would soon prohibit British frigate captains from fighting 44-gun frigates such as *United States*. This implied that running was justified, given the superior armament he was facing, but Carden reminded the reader that had he done so he 'should have Suffer'd an Ignominious Death for Cowardice.'[54] Lambert echoes that sentiment in his discussion of Dacres's loss to *Constitution*. He argues that, despite the decayed state of HMS *Guerriere*, had Dacres run from

49 TNA, ADM 1/5436, Verdict, CM *Macedonian*.

50 Tracy, *Naval Chronicle*, Vol.5, pp.71–72; McCranie, *Utmost Gallantry*, p.66.

51 TNA, ADM 196/3/363, John Carden, Officer Service Record; Syrett and DiNardo, *Commissioned Sea Officers*, p.72.

52 Syrett and DiNardo, *Commissioned Sea Officers*, pp.61, 227, 323; TNA, ADM 196/5/347, Samuel Mottley, Officer Service Record; TNA, ADM 196/4/583, David Hope, Officer Service Record; 'David Hope, Esq.', in *Royal Naval Biography*, Vol.3, Part II, pp.111–124.

53 Wareham, *Star Captains*, p.157; John Surman Carden, *A Curtail'd Memoir of Incidents and Occurrences in the Life of John Surman Carden, Vice Admiral in the British Navy* (Oxford: Clarendon Press, 1850), pp.280–284.

54 Ibid, 270.

the action, he would have been chastised and dishonourably discharged.[55] Carden attacked and failed, and while he was honourably acquitted, his career in the Navy came to an end. Instead, it was Decatur who returned home to America in triumph and began fitting out both *United States* and the newly captured *Macedonian* for further action against the Royal Navy. As disheartening as the war had been so far, it was not over yet.

Constitution–Java action, 29 December 1812

News of *Guerriere's* loss reached Britain in early October, which precipitated a shockwave of disbelief and horror, though as far as the British public were aware *Guerriere's* defeat was an isolated disaster. News of *Macedonian's* loss still had not reached Britain by early November, when Captain Henry Lambert was fitting out HMS *Java* for a voyage to the East Indies. Lambert, *Java's* captain since August, likely did not expect his next cruise would have much at all to do with the new war with the United States. On 12 November *Java*, crowded and heavily laden, set sail for the East Indies. On board was senior lieutenant Henry D. Chads (a loyal follower of Lambert), a crew containing a fair number of landsmen, and the newly appointed Governor of Bombay Lieutenant General Sir Thomas Hislop. With him was a staff of about 100 and another dozen men appointed to military and civilian posts in the East.[56]

The cruise out was long and uneventful in such a crowded ship. Lambert, though an experienced naval officer, exercised the men at gunnery only once, focusing instead on turning the large number of relatively useless crewmen into proper seamen. Over all the crew was ill-disciplined and inexperienced, so Lambert, Chads, and the other officers had their work cut out for them. On 29 December, well into the journey, lookouts from *Java* spotted an unknown warship not far from the coast of Brazil, and Lambert stood in to investigate.

She had encountered USS *Constitution*, refitted following her action with *Guerriere* and under the new command of Commodore William Bainbridge. One of the navy's most senior captains whose career had survived several mishaps, losses, and long periods away commanding merchant ships during peacetime, Bainbridge had initially been pegged for command of *Constitution*, but the rush of the outbreak of war had interrupted that. Upon Hull's return home, however, he had been ordered to relinquish command to his senior. If Hull was disappointed in having to give up the ship, he may have welcomed the opportunity of a shore appointment: his brother had just died, and he needed time to grieve and put his family affairs in order. The crew, however, did not welcome the change in command.[57]

55 Lambert, *The Challenge*, Chapter 3.

56 McCranie, *Utmost Gallantry*, pp.77–78; Toll, *Six Frigates*, pp.375–376; James, *Naval Occurrences*, pp.168–169; Lambert, *The Challenge*, Chapter 3.

57 McCranie, *Utmost Gallantry*, p.58; Toll, *Six Frigates*, pp.373–374; Fitz-Enz, *Old Ironsides*, p.148.

Commodore William Bainbridge, although he was disappointed at being given *Constitution*, would go down in history from her quarterdeck. (Naval History and Heritage Command)

They responded to Bainbridge hoisting his commodore's pennant with a near mutiny. Hull had been popular, and Bainbridge's reputation was stained by his surrender of a frigate during the conflict with Barbary Corsairs; some of his current crew had been made prisoners of war because of the incident. Worse for Bainbridge was his overall disappointment with his ship. *Constitution* today is remembered as the pride of the early United States Navy and the only remaining ship in the fleet to have sunk an enemy warship in action. There is great prestige associated with the ship, but in 1812 she was one of three sisters and firmly considered the second of the three. *United States* was painfully slow, but equalled *Constitution* in battle honours so far. *President*, the youngest of the three, was by far the best sailor and the preferred command for America's senior naval officers. Bainbridge even offered $5,000 (over $100,000 in value today, around the annual salary of a senior United States Navy captain or junior rear admiral) to Rodgers – currently in command of *President* – to exchange ships; Rodgers, placing more value on the chance to cruise in *President*, refused.[58]

Upon realising that the enemy was an American frigate, probably one of the class that had shocked the nation by capturing *Guerriere*, Lambert did not hesitate and cleared for action.[59] This was not Lambert's first action, nor even his first single-ship action. As the young captain of the 20-gun HMS *Wilhelmina*, he had successfully fought off the 36-gun privateer frigate *Psyché* in 1804. Upon his return to the East Indies in command of the heavy frigate *San Fiorenzo* he had encountered the same ship, now a frigate in the French navy, and, with a significant advantage in armament, had captured her. However, he also had the unfortunate distinction (along with Chads) of losing his frigate HMS *Iphigenia* at the Battle of Grand Port, considered to be Britain's greatest naval disaster of the Napoleonic Wars and the only naval action commemorated on the *Arc de Triomphe*. While Lambert had been fully acquitted of the loss (and much of the responsibility for it lay at the feet of the squadron commander anyway), the defeat nonetheless had a profound impact on the character of the Royal Navy.[60] Reputation and duty were everything to naval officers, and though Lambert had complained about the quality of his crew even before setting sail, he had no hesitation about bringing this American frigate to action.[61]

58 Toll, *Six Frigates*, pp.373–374; Fitz-Enz, *Old Ironsides*, pp.148–150.

59 James, *Naval Occurrences*, p.169; Lambert, *The Challenge*, Chapter 3.

60 Stephen Taylor, *Storm and Conquest: The Battle for the Indian Ocean, 1808–1810* (London: Faber and Faber, 2007), 299.

61 Lambert, *The Challenge*, Chapter 3.

The two ships slowly approached over the morning and into the afternoon, each ship manoeuvring 'to obtain advantageous positions'.[62] *Java* proved to be the superior sailor and kept the weather gauge throughout the early portion of the action, but Bainbridge's seamanship enabled him to at least keep *Java* from obtaining any raking positions while failing to reach any such position himself. The two ships, continuing to manoeuvre and slowly close the distance between them, began firing around 2:00 p.m., with *Constitution* opening with round shot, grape, and cannister.[63] Both parties claimed they were avoiding close action in the opening broadsides, but the action was still fought at relatively close range.[64] If they were each frustrated at not being able to close faster with the enemy, they must both have been focusing more on gaining a better position than on bringing about a close action.

Java appeared to have the better of her opponent early on. The opening broadsides inflicted little damage on either ship, but *Java* successfully maintained the weather gauge and her fire cut away some of the enemy's running rigging. Worse for Bainbridge, *Java*'s shot smashed the ship's wheel to pieces, momentarily depriving her of steerage. *Java* continued to manoeuvre to try and cross the enemy's stern at very close range; with damage to the wheel and rigging, *Constitution* was helpless to respond, and *Java* fired a crushing broadside into the frigate's stern.[65] Several men were wounded by British gunnery and musketry, including Bainbridge himself, who was struck by a musket ball in his left hip. Moments later, British round shot smashed through the copper railing of the aft hatchway, causing a fragment of ragged metal to ricochet off and cut into the wounded commodore's right thigh.[66]

Being to the leeward of the enemy, most of the accumulating gun smoke was being blown away from *Java* and smothering the *Constitution*'s decks. In that state her crew continued to keep up a heavy fire from the 24-pounders and heavy carronades, while men rushed below to secure control of the tiller in the wardroom. *Constitution* continued to suffer, but so too did *Java*, whose headsails were cut up and the end of her bowsprit and jibboom was shot away. Bainbridge, his trousers now drenched in his own blood but refusing to go below, ordered further sails to be set to compensate for the enemy's superior speed and then ordered the ship to come about, hoping to find a more advantageous position. As had happened a dozen times since the action began, Lambert ordered *Java* to counter the manoeuvre, swinging her bow around into the wind to place her on the opposite tack and avoid being raked. This was when the impact of *Constitution*'s gunnery paid off: with her

62 Lieutenant Henry D. Chads to Secretary of the Admiralty John W. Croker, United States Frigate *Constitution*, off St Salvador 31 December 1812, *Naval War of 1812*, Vol.1, p.646.

63 Chads to Croker, 31 December 1812, *Naval War of 1812*, Vol.1, p.646; Journal of Commodore William Bainbridge: Tuesday 29 December 1812, *Naval War of 1812*, pp.640–641; Roosevelt, *Naval War of 1812*, pp.119–121; Toll, *Six Frigates*, p.376; McCranie, *Utmost Gallantry*, pp.78–79.

64 Chads to Croker, 31 December 1812, *Naval War of 1812*, Vol.1, p.646; Journal of Commodore William Bainbridge: Tuesday 29 December 1812, *Naval War of 1812*, Vol.1, pp.640–641.

65 Roosevelt, *Naval War of 1812*, p.121; Toll, *Six Frigates*, pp.376–377; McCranie, *Utmost Gallantry*, pp.78–79.

66 Toll, *Six Frigates*, p.377.

headsails and bowsprit so cut up, *Java* could not tack quickly enough, and she was caught still passing through the wind by *Constitution*, which had successfully worn and now firing a devastating raking broadside into her stern.[67]

Around 3:00 p.m., Captain Lambert realised that he had lost his advantageous position and that the enemy's fire was beginning to take its toll on his ship and crew. Rather than continue the cannonade and manoeuvring, which had initially worked in his favour but was proving increasingly difficult and costly, Lambert steered *Java* for the enemy, assembling boarders with cutlasses and pikes. *Java* made to crash against *Constitution*'s quarter, but heated fire from the Americans continued to batter her and at the last moment smashed through the base of the foremast, which quickly collapsed into the sea, slowing the ship nearly to a halt just before the enemy. *Java* had sailed close enough so that her wounded bowsprit drifted over the enemy's stern, getting caught in her rigging, but not close enough for her boarders to get across. Instead, *Constitution*'s stern chasers opened with grape and cannister into the tightly packed boarders in the forecastle. For a few moments the British frigate was stuck, subject to the fire of the stern chasers, manned by a pair of quick-working gun crews.[68]

As the ships disentangled, Bainbridge wore his ship round, taking a position astern of the enemy and firing away. *Java*'s mainmast was struck and the maintopmast and topgallant masts collapsed over the side, covering the guns and gun crews with wreckage. At 3:30 p.m. Lambert was shot through the chest by a musket ball, collapsing unconscious, and was carried below. His wound was mortal – the ball had just missed his heart and shattered the captain's sternum. Lieutenant Henry Chads, himself lightly wounded, was left in command without any ability to get the ship underway. She was left at the mercy of *Constitution*'s gunnery. Over the next hour Bainbridge slowly circled the enemy, sailing along her larboard side before bringing his frigate across *Java*'s shattered bows, guns firing as they bore. Having raked the enemy, *Constitution* came back around and sailed along her starboard broadside, guns firing as they bore, knocking more guns out of action. Chads lamented that his gunners (many of whom wounded by enemy fire, musketry, or simply by falling blocks and tackles) could only respond with a handful of guns due to the spread of canvas and wreckage over the side. Many men were diverted from their stations to put out fires, as the canvas repeatedly caught fire as cannon belched smoke from either ship.[69]

For another half-hour *Constitution* continued to pour broadsides into her enemy, and her fire caused the mizzenmast to fall by the board, covering the British's engaged side with still more wreckage. *Java*'s fire had so slackened by 4:00 p.m. that Bainbridge suspected she had struck. In response

67 Roosevelt, *Naval War of 1812*, pp.121–122; Toll, *Six Frigates*, pp.376–377; McCranie, *Utmost Gallantry*, pp.78–79.

68 Roosevelt, *Naval War of 1812*, pp.121–122; Toll, *Six Frigates*, pp.376–377; McCranie, *Utmost Gallantry*, pp.78–79.

69 Roosevelt, *Naval War of 1812*, pp.121–123; Toll, *Six Frigates*, pp.376–379; McCranie, *Utmost Gallantry*, pp.78–79.

he disengaged, sailing out of range to conduct badly needed repairs to his cut-up rigging. *Java* was left a complete wreck, nearly dismasted and rolling in the waves. For the next hour 'every exertion was made' to put *Java* back into some semblance of fighting shape. A new ensign was hoisted to replace the one lost with the mizzen, signifying to the distant Americans that the fight was not over. Much of the wreckage was cleared so the gun crews could resume their place, and a jury-rigged sail was set from the stumps of the foremast and bowsprit. However, as Chads tried to get the ship before the wind the mainmast finally fell, again covering the starboard side with wreckage. Their efforts undone, Chads assembled the remaining officers to take stock of the situation.

Aside from a tattered jury-rigged sail forward, the ship was completely dismasted and rolling heavily in the waves. Her intact wheel and tiller mattered little without any propulsion and the ship was completely unmanageable. Over 100 men were absent from their stations, either dead or badly wounded below, and about a dozen guns throughout the ship were completely out of action. Several of those still intact were covered by wreckage that needed to be cleared away. At this time the enemy was slowly making her approach and the officers, including Lieutenant General Hislop, concluded that their only hope was for the *Constitution* to make an error and approach close enough for the Javas to make a second boarding attempt. Understandably, Bainbridge did not make such an error – he prepared to take up a raking position, and all of the remaining officers on board *Java* concluded that further resistance was fruitless. The ensign was struck before *Constitution* could resume the action.[70]

Thus far, the action with *Java* had been the bloodiest victory for the Americans. Accounts vary as to the number of American casualties but appear to amount to around 30.[71] *Java*'s shot had inflicted considerable damage, including imbedding round shot in her masts, but it was not enough to put the ship in any real material danger. Bainbridge himself remained on deck until well into the night, only having his wounds dressed hours after the guns fell silent. Meanwhile, Chads reported 22 dead and over 100 wounded, and the ship itself was a complete ruin and slowly sinking. Bainbridge ordered her set alight on New Year's Eve, carrying the prisoners to San Salvador and releasing them on parole before heading back to America. On route she was spotted by two British squadrons, one commanded by none other than Philip Broke once again, but *Constitution* escaped from both in a storm and returned triumphant to Boston early in 1813.[72]

With Lambert in critical condition, Chads was now responsible for the over 300 men remaining and worked to secure passage home, as well as informing the Admiralty of the loss as the acting captain who had surrendered the ship.

70 Roosevelt, *Naval War of 1812*, pp.121–123; Toll, *Six Frigates*, pp.376–379; McCranie, *Utmost Gallantry*, pp.78–79.

71 Roosevelt, *Naval War of 1812*, p.123; Gardner W. Harris, *The Life and Services of Commodore William Bainbridge, United States Navy* (Philadelphia: Carey Lea & Blanchard, 1837), p.146; Budiansky, *Perilous Fight*, p.183.

72 McCranie, *Utmost Gallantry*, pp.81–82.

It was not his first experience with defeat – he had served with Lambert during the Battle of Grand Port, when HMS *Iphigenia* was surrendered to the French. Like Carden, Chads had entered the Navy through the Royal Naval Academy, but he also had naval connections: his father, who had died in 1799, had been a post captain. While on board *Constitution*, anchored in Salvador, he began his letter to the Admiralty:

> It is with deep regret that I write you for the information of the Lords Commissioners of the Admiralty that His Majesty's Ship *Java* is no more, after sustaining an action on the 29 Inst for several hours with the American Frigate *Constitution* which resulted in the Capture and ultimate destruction of His Majesty's Ship. Captain Lambert being dangerously wounded in the height of the Action, the melancholy task of writing the detail devolves on me.[73]

Chads's melancholy task was not only to detail the loss of his ship and provide justification for his actions and decisions (and that of his crew); he also had to defend the honour of his captain, who succumbed to his wounds early in January. Bainbridge, suffering from considerable pain due to his two leg wounds, expressed his regret at the death of 'a distinguished and gallant officer, and a most worthy man.'[74] He also did what he could to treat the captured officers generously, using the same gentlemanly courtesy that Hull and Decatur had shown their prisoners. Chads and Hislop later expressed their admiration for the generous treatment they received, although they lamented that the American crew had not treated their counterparts with the same respect.[75]

Chads's account is sparse on details of the action before he took command; as the senior lieutenant, Chads would have held his own specific position in action, likely supervising gun batteries or the quarterdeck. He would not have focused on the battle as a whole until assuming command. He did relate the most important moments of the action, and explained that *Java*'s dire situation arose due to the fact that USS *Constitution* was 'avoiding close action and firing high to disable our masts, in which he succeeded too well.'[76] It was because of damage to *Java*'s rigging that she lost the weather gauge and found herself at the mercy of the *Constitution*'s raking fire. Casualties increasingly mounted, and wreckage put most of the starboard battery out of action. By 4:15 p.m., when the American frigate stood off to make repairs, *Java* was left as 'an unmanageable wreck.'[77] He assured Croker that, during this lull in the action,

> Every exertion was made by us during this interval to place this Ship in a state to renew the action. We succeeded in clearing the wreck of our Masts from our Guns. a Sail was set on the stumps of the Foremast & Bowsprit the weather half of the

73 'Chads to Croker, 31 December 1812', *Naval War of 1812*, Vol.1, p.646.
74 William Bainbridge, quoted in Roosevelt, *Naval War of 1812*, p.124.
75 Budiansky, *Perilous Fight*, p.184.
76 Chads to Croker, 31 December 1812, *Naval War of 1812*, Vol.1, p.646.
77 Chads to Croker, 31 December 1812, *Naval War of 1812*, Vol.1, p.647.

> Main Yard remaining aloft, the main tack was got forward in the hope of getting the Ship before the Wind, our helm being still perfect. the effort unfortunately proved ineffectual from the Main mast falling over the side from the heavy rolling of the Ship, which nearly covered the whole of our Starboard Guns.[78]

The account maintains that even with the captain, the master, and a good portion of the crew wounded or killed, Chads was still trying to keep *Java* in the fight. However, when attempts to repair and get back some control over the frigate failed, *Constitution* again sailed towards *Java*, preparing to rake her 'without a possibility of our returning a shot.'[79]

As the frigate's acting commanding officer, Chads's report highlights that the decision to strike was made collectively, with the frigate's officers and with Lieutenant General Hislop:

> I then consulted the Officers who agreed with myself that on having a great part of our Crew killed & wounded, our Bowsprit and three masts gone, several guns useless, we should not be justified in wasting the lives of more of those remaining whom I hope their Lordships & Country will think they have bravely defended His Majesty's Ship. Under these circumstances, however reluctantly at 5:50 our Colors were lowered from the Stump of the Mizzen Mast and we were taken possession a little after 6.[80]

It was a 'reluctant' decision, one made in the interest of preserving the lives of the crew once it became clear they had done all they could to defend the frigate. As always, the Royal Navy officers were willing to risk a great deal so long as victory remained a remote possibility; once it was judged to be impossible, however, their sense of humanity took over.

Like Carden, Chads did not dismiss the disparity in force between the two frigates in his report. He included a description of the broadsides and dimensions of both, in hopes that they would satisfy the Admiralty that the defeat was an honourable one, given the odds they faced. One officer later placed the blame on his opponent's strength, in addition to the fact that the *Constitution*'s crew was made up of 'our prime sailors,' some from *Iphigenia* and *Guerriere*: 'From the manner in which this action was fought, and the unequalled injury the *Java* sustained beyond the *Constitution*, it appears evident that the American had advantages which do not belong to our frigates.'[81]

Upon their return to England, Chads and the crew of the ship were court-martialled on board HMS *Gladiator*, a small two-decker ship of the line that had never served outside of port in its career, instead serving as a frequent venue for trials. The trail was extensively covered in the *Naval Chronicle*,

78 Chads to Croker, 31 December 1812, *Naval War of 1812*, Vol.1, p.647.

79 Chads to Croker, 31 December 1812, *Naval War of 1812*, Vol.1, p.647.

80 Chads to Croker, 31 December 1812, *Naval War of 1812*, Vol.1, p.647.

81 Unnamed *Java* Lieutenant to 'My Dear Friend', Mercury Cartel, St Salvador, 26 January 1813, *The Naval Chronicle for 1813: Containing a General and Biographical History of The Royal Navy of the United Kingdom; With a Variety of Original Papers on Nautical Subjects*, Vol.29: January to June (London: Joyce Gold, 1813), p.452.

thanks to the submission of several accounts and minutes. The submitter stated that 'the determination shewn by the gallant Chads to commence the second action, whilst the least gleam of hope of ultimate success remained' was worthy of praise and consideration by officers in the service.[82] Chads particularly focused not on his own 'gallant' determination but that of the late Captain Lambert. Despite being the acting captain once Lambert had been taken below, Chads's testimony was modest and focused on the collective nature of his decision-making in the following action,[83] and particularly on the council held during the lull in the action:

> consulted now with the lieutenants Herringham and Buchannan, when it was determined to engage him again, should he give us an opportunity of doing so, with a probability of disabling him, which was now our sole object, but that it would be wasting lives resisting longer, should he resume a raking position, which unfortunately was the case.[84]

His argument was that if they could have continued fighting they would do so, even in their crippled state, but the officers would not risk the lives of their men if *Constitution* assumed a raking position, as they must have assumed she would do. In the opinion of the officers, continuing to fight under raking fire (as they had already done for 40 minutes) would have needlessly risked the lives of the *Java*'s crew with the ship unable to return fire or get before the wind.[85] Consequently, when *Constitution* moved to reassume a position off *Java*'s stern, Chads struck.

While Chads's testimony had been modest, Lieutenant General Hislop enthusiastically defended Chads in his testimony: 'It would be presumption in me to suppose that any testimony of mine can be requisite to give weight to the more substantial proofs which must appear before this honourable court, in manifestation of the exemplary conduct of Lieutenant Chads.' He echoed the sentiment of fighting to the last chance of victory, informing the court of the 'cool, firm, and determined resolution' of Chads to continue the action 'should the possibility of hurting or disabling the enemy's ship present itself.'[86]

Chads was in a very different position from Laugharne, Dacres, Whinyates, or Carden – he assumed command of *Java* late in the action and was not as responsible for the loss as Lambert would have been. However, he was also a relatively junior officer in the Navy and his career was less secure. Thankfully for Chads, the court and the wider Navy were sympathetic. Chads was not only honourably acquitted but promoted to commander later that year, and was a post captain by 1815.[87] He continued active service for some time and finished his career as an admiral, renowned in the Navy as

82 'I.T.L.' to the Editor, Walsworth, *Naval Chronicle*, Vol.29, p.402.
83 TNA, ADM 1/5435, Testimony of Lieutenant Henry Chads, CM *Java*.
84 TNA, ADM 1/5435, Testimony of Lieutenant Henry Chads, CM *Java*.
85 TNA, ADM 1/5435, Testimony of Lieutenant Henry Chads, CM *Java*.
86 TNA, ADM 1/5435, Testimony of Major General Hislop, CM *Java*.
87 Syrett and DiNardo, *Commissioned Sea Officers*, p.77.

a gunnery specialist.[88] The Second Lieutenant, William Herringham, also continued in active service until 1837 upon promotion to post rank.[89] George Buchanan, still a very junior lieutenant as he was only commissioned early in 1812, unfortunately remained a lieutenant for the rest of his career.[90]

As historian Andrew Lambert argues, 'because [Captain] Lambert died heroically, and the ship had been stoutly defended against a more powerful foe, their Lordships were correct to consider the action a matter of some pride.'[91] Overall, the officers of *Java* fared better than their counterparts in previous actions. Of the lieutenants serving in *Alert*, *Guerriere*, *Frolic*, and *Macedonian*, few enjoyed active careers at senior rank following the end of the war. Hope, First Lieutenant of *Macedonian*, was the only one to reach post rank; the rest ended their careers as lieutenants or commanders, and in the case of two were only promoted to that rank in retirement. Lambert asserts this is because of the death of Captain Lambert, which placed further responsibility upon the lieutenants, and because of the acknowledgement that they had fought against such a superior foe. However, the disparity between *Java* and *Constitution* was not noticeably different from the disparity present in the previous two frigate actions. What mattered more was the acknowledgement that the lieutenants had inherited an impossible position upon the death of their commander and had defended the ship as best they could.

* * *

Java was set on fire, quickly exploding as the fire ignited what remained of her powder magazine, on New Year's Eve. It was a fitting end to 1812, which had seen five successive British losses in single-ship actions and no meaningful victories. The British had struggled to locate the enemy, and those that managed to find American cruisers were either frustrated by their ability to escape or were taken in action. It was a thoroughly disappointing year for the Royal Navy, but in defeat these actions, the accounts detailing them, and the subsequent courts martial demonstrate several recurring themes of importance within the post-Nelsonic Royal Navy. The same qualities that led to the victories of the Napoleonic Wars, such as an aggressive ethos and a preference for close action, were exhibited in each account. The contrasting British notions of gallantry and humanity were demonstrated in each: all five commanders defended themselves by stating that they continued fighting, putting themselves and their men at risk, so long as they had a chance of victory and doing their duty, but once they judged that victory was no longer possible their aggressive ethos and fighting spirited gave way to their sense of humanity. Together, zeal and humanity underpinned the honour of these men as officers of the Royal Navy.

88 Lambert, *The Challenge*, Chapter 4; 'Henry Ducie Chads, Esq.', in *Royal Naval Biography*, Vol.3, Part I, pp.237–255.

89 Syrett and DiNardo, *Commissioned Sea Officers*, p.216; TNA, ADM 196/4/517, William Herringham, Officer Service Record.

90 Syrett and DiNardo, *Commissioned Sea Officers*, p.60.

91 Lambert, *The Challenge*, Chapter 4.

In the three frigate actions, each commander's defence rested on the fact that enemy gunnery had reduced their ships to an unmanageable state. This left them unable to manoeuvre or respond effectively to the enemy's fire; they and their men were left at the mercy of the Americans, who retained their ability to manoeuvre and rake the British at will. Yet no one argued that the superiority of the enemy's broadsides was itself to blame for the losses, or even to the situation in which the British found themselves. Dacres completely ignored it; although Carden and Chads acknowledged it and argued that it had played an important role, they maintained that the state of their vessels was a more important factor. Instead of arguing that their ships had suffered so much because of the superiority of the enemy's broadside, they argued that other factors were more or equally important: superior enemy sailing qualities, picked well-trained crews, and fortune. The commanders and their judges believed that, notwithstanding the superior broadsides of *Constitution* and *United States*, if important masts and spars had not been knocked away during key moments of the actions (such as *Java* attempting to hold the weather gauge when tacking across her enemy's stern), the British might have prevailed. Misfortune was the key difference between the defeats inflicted by the Americans and the victories the British had won over the heavy frigates of France.

The courts martial agreed in each case that the loss was not fault of the captains, officers, or ships' companies involved. Only one officer, Lieutenant Andrew Duncan, was dishonourably dismissed. The rest were honourably acquitted, although the nature of their careers following the acquittal were drastically different. Above all, the most successful career post-defeat was enjoyed by Dacres. Perhaps it was his bold defence in his court martial, or his strong naval connections – or perhaps both. Chads was unique in that he was promoted following the defeat; his career was not as active as Dacres's was, but he remained employed for a period after the Napoleonic Wars ended. Laugharne, Whinyates, and Carden were not as fortunate. Their career prospects collapsed once Britain was at peace, and they were among the many naval officers who remained on half-pay in the peace-time navy. There were only so many commands available, and those went to officers with better reputations or connections. Dacres had connections and Chads had distinguished himself. The other three's reputations reflected their losses. Though honourably acquitted, the stain of defeat all but ended their naval careers.

Regardless of their post-battle careers and reputations, none of the officers was criticised for fighting actions against superior forces. Neither Dacres, Carden, nor Chads was told they should have run from a battle in which they would be significantly outgunned. They fought as long as they had a chance of victory, and this was accepted by the courts. In the case of Carden, it was decided that if he had fought the action at close range, he would have had a chance of defeating the enemy. Dacres boldly dismissed the enemy's superiority in his defence entirely. This was the style of the Royal Navy – it harked back to memories of Thomas Cochrane's capture of *El Gamo*, or to the *Sybille–La Forte* action. Running from an enemy, even one that was 50 percent more powerful in men and guns, was not an option for officers of

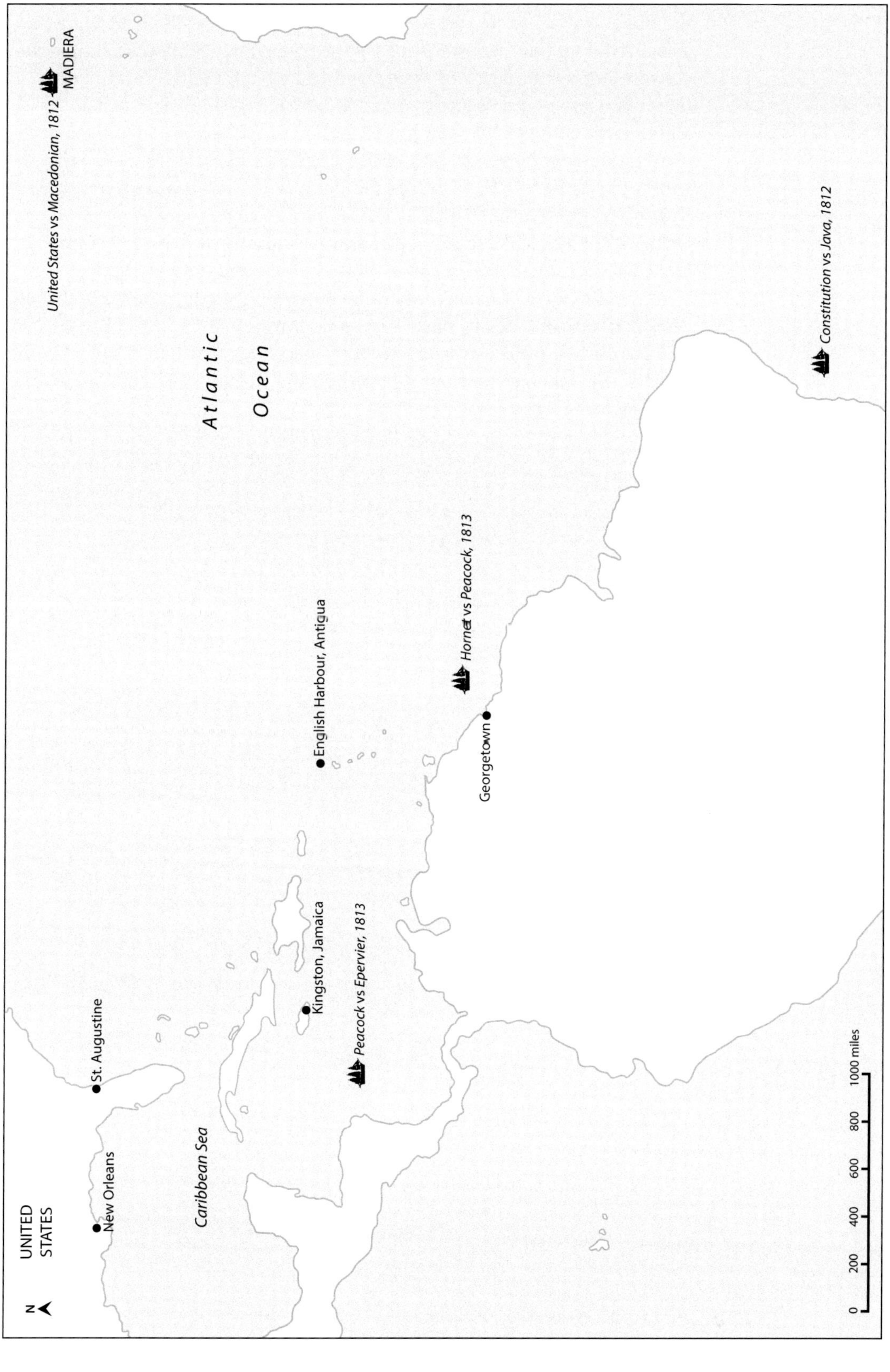

Map 2 Actions in the West Indies and along the Eastern coastline of South America, 1813–1814.

the Royal Navy.[92] Accusations of cowardice, or even of simply keeping back and not doing their utmost to engage the enemy, struck more captains from active service than death or wounds in enemy action.[93] It was a reputation that had made a stark impression on American naval officers such as Porter, and one which impaired their interpretation of the events of 1812. However, just as this aggressiveness was encouraged and expected, so too were the courts perfectly willing to accept the defence that each officer struck once they no longer had a chance at victory. Surrender in and of itself was no crime in the Royal Navy so long as it was determined that the commander and each officer had done everything they could and not held back.

A public outcry followed when the news of the actions broke in Britain. This sparked contentious naval discourse through 1813 in the Royal Navy and the British public over the strategic decisions that had resulted in the defeats, the damage they had inflicted on the Royal Navy's reputation, and the urge for revenge.

92 Lambert, *The Challenge*, Chapter 2.

93 Allen, 'British Navy rules', pp.210–211.

3

'The unlooked for reverse of the medal': Impact of the 1812 losses in Britain and Nova Scotia

News of the American declaration of war was greeted by the British government and press with little enthusiasm. Friends and foes to the United States alike had expected that the tensions between the two governments would be peacefully resolved, particularly after Lord Liverpool assumed the premiership and adopted a more conciliatory policy. Indeed, many voices in Britain's press expressed a sense of anger and frustration at the outbreak of war. *The Times*, an opposition newspaper, stated that conflict with America was not wanted and was regrettable, but there was no need to worry about the outcome.[1] *The Examiner*, a radical paper, hoped both sides would come to realise that such a war could only be ruinous and purposeless, and that peace would quickly be obtained.[2] The disdainful attitude many Britons still had towards the new American republic led many to dismiss the threat posed by the United States, particularly when weighted against the titanic threat that was Napoleon Bonaparte. However, months of conflict and several naval disasters began to turn that public frustration into outright anger and hatred towards the Americans.[3]

News from the war with the United States, on land and on sea, took a long time to break in the United Kingdom. It took time for rumours of events to cross the channel and circulate in British papers; even longer for official reports to arrive. News of HMS *Alert* arrived first. Despite the contest between *Alert* and the frigate *Essex* being wildly uneven, the news of the defeat was still shocking to the British public. It was the first time a British ship had surrendered to another in a single-ship action since 1803. The

1 Andrew Lambert, 'Sideshow? British grand strategy and the War of 1812', in Tim Voelcker (ed.), *Broke of the Shannon and the War of 1812* (Barnsley: Seaforth Publishing, 2013), p.17.

2 Latimer, *1812*, p.102.

3 Latimer, *1812*, p.102.

British public were too used to hearing news of naval successes at sea, and this eclipsed the reality that the contest was virtually impossible for *Alert* to win.[4] It took until October for reports of *Guerriere*'s loss to reach Britain, and that event in particular kicked off a wave of public outcry and melancholy that only got worse as news of the following actions slowly trickled in over the next five months.[5]

Even in Halifax, situated right at the heart of the naval conflict in North America and hosting a large portion of the North American squadron, newspapers had to wait for news and official reports of the actions for some time. Most of the coverage of these actions in fact came from papers printed in London, Boston, or New York, and much of what Halifax learned of the naval losses came from rumour and less than reliable sources. This was difficult for residents, as they were enthralled with the Royal Navy and its exploits. Nelson's career in particular had been closely followed by Nova Scotians, who did not let the lack of official reports and significant time delay in receiving reports prevent them from speculating on rumours of his movements and celebrating his victories. However, just as there were public celebrations of Nelson's victories at the Nile, Copenhagen, and Trafalgar, so too was there public shock and sorrow following the losses of the *Guerriere*, *Alert*, *Macedonian*, *Frolic*, and *Java*, particularly those vessels which had been stationed in Halifax and whose officers and crew were well known in Halifax society.[6]

When the *Acadian Recorder*'s first edition was distributed in mid-January 1813, it was devoted to the loss of HMS *Guerriere*, which had taken place nearly half a year previously. The reason for this was, in the opinion of the *Recorder*:

> every circumstance relating to our Navy, or naval character, most naturally excite our warmest feelings, and as our readers residing in the interior of this and the neighboring Provinces cannot have opportunities of obtaining information from English papers, we consider it our duty to afford them all the intelligence in our power on a subject so interesting: though such communications may sometimes appear stale to those living at the fountain head of news.[7]

As such, a piece of 'stale' news led the *Recorder*'s first edition. Reporting of the previous year's successes in Canada followed in the next edition. Of all of the military and political news from Europe and Canada, it was the naval losses from half a year earlier that the *Recorder* felt would be of most interest to Nova Scotians.

A particularly important voice was the *Naval Chronicle*. It was 'the most important original published documentation of the Royal Navy' during its

4 Latimer, *1812*, p.99.

5 Latimer, *1812*, pp.102–103; Toll, *Six Frigates*, pp.369–371.

6 Keith Mercer, 'Lord Nelson on the mind: naval victories and cultural memory in Nova Scotia', *Trafalgar Chronicle*, 22 (2012), pp.173–178; Keith Mercer, 'Colonial patriotism to "Mystical Chords of Memory": the Halifax celebrations and commemorations of the *Shannon–Chesapeake* battle', *Acadiensis*, 44:1 (2015), p.42.

7 Mercer, 'Lord Nelson', pp.173–178; Mercer, 'Colonial patriotism', p.42.

run of publication, from 1799 to 1819.[8] It was a periodical dedicated to the Royal Navy, written by and for naval officers, though its readership extended into the educated and naval enthusiastic public and even found its way into the offices of foreign governments. Its issues printed news of the Navy's exploits, letters from officers and official dispatches, and hosted discussions on everything from naval expenditure to the welfare of the Navy's warrant officers. Individuals who wrote in to the *Chronicle* did so under pseudonyms that reflected naval or patriotic themes – 'Iron Gun,' 'Albion,' and 'Muzzle to Muzzle' were all common. According to Nicholas Tracy, these letters were 'apparently from Naval Officers.'[9] However, not all were military experts – 'Muzzle to Muzzle' argued that British naval tactics, comprising of bold, close-range action, should be applied by Lord Wellington's armies in Spain, and clearly demonstrated a lack of understanding of the nature of Napoleonic warfare. Other letters were written in a way that suggested the average reader may not be fully aware of naval matters, such as the inner workings of a naval crew. William James, who later would become a prominent naval historian, was one of the commentators during the war, writing under the name 'Boxer.' While the commentators all displayed a strong sense of patriotism and devotion to the British Navy and occasionally an above-average knowledge of naval affairs, their opinions on matters of naval honour, reputation, and strategy suggested many were not well versed in the naval community, and their values, while distinct from those expressed in the wider popular press in Britain, did not reflect those of the serving members of the Royal Navy.

The impact of a handful of single-ship victories in strategic terms mattered little to the Royal Navy. They still enjoyed a considerable advantage in numbers, and the losses did not actually impact their ability to protect British commerce or conduct blockades, both of vital importance to Britain's overall strategy. In fact, as each American victor had either returned home for refit or been captured, America's commerce raiding mission was compromised by their single-ship victories. Rodgers's several cruises in 1812 were far more effective because he did not engage any British warships.[10] Rodgers's achievement had little impact on the British press, although rumours of his movements did appear in the papers in Halifax. In fact, the losses in 1812 were contrasted with various victories and successes – victories in Spain under Wellington, the successful defence of Canada, and various other minor triumphs. These did little, however, to mitigate the sense of sorrow throughout Britain and her colonies. As historian Jon Latimer argues: 'it caused as much consternation as it had joy in America; the news soured that of Salamanca, the burning of Moscow, and Brock's triumph at Detroit. This was the Royal Navy, after all.'[11] Britons, whether in Britain itself or in far flung places like Halifax, were deeply devoted to the Royal Navy and its naval heroes. After two decades of unparalleled success and a steady diet of

8 Tracy, *Naval Chronicle*, Vol.1, p.vii.
9 Tracy, *Naval Chronicle*, Vol.1, p.viii.
10 Lambert, 'British Grand Strategy', p.17.
11 Latimer, *1812*, p.102.

news of victories, this 'unlooked for reverse of the medal'[12] was difficult for Britons to accept. Different segments of the press and different populations understood the losses and their impact on Britain's reputation and naval heroisms in different ways. Everyone had to find a way to come to terms with their beloved naval heroes being defeated by a foe who had so far been largely ignored as a credible threat.

'Sacred spell of invincibility': impact on perceptions of Britain's naval might

In February 1813, George Canning (former Foreign Secretary and future Prime Minister) took to the floor of the House of Commons to speak on the losses of 1812, and declared that 'the sacred spell of invincibility of the British navy was broken by those unfortunate captures.' Canning continued and told the house of his wish that:

> however speedily we must all wish the war to terminate, I hope I shall not be considered as sanguinary and unfeeling when I express my devout wish that it may not be concluded before we have re-established the character of our naval superiority, and smothered in victories the disasters which we have now to lament, and to which we are so little habituated.[13]

Canning's views may have been tempered by his feud with the current Foreign Secretary, Lord Castlereagh, but they nonetheless reflected the mood of the national press and were reflected in a host of popular songs, ballads, caricatures, and cartoons.

Britain's major papers were particularly scornful of the losses. *The Times* first announced news of *Guerriere*'s loss with shock, noting that 'never before in the history of the world did an English frigate strike to an American.'[14] Another issue reported that *The Times* 'declared that far more than a single ship was lost. The invaluable reputation of the Royal Navy was undermined with incalculable consequences.'[15] The *Naval Chronicle* too, following *Java*'s loss, took a grim tone, declaring that 'The subject is too painful for us to dwell upon.'[16] The editors added that the United States 'be made to *feel* the real weight of the British trident, when properly wielded … til not only our losses have been indemnified, our defeats avenged, but the spell be restored.'[17]

The view that the seas were Britain's domains had been built by the successes of the Royal Navy to date, and their steady domination of naval

12 *Naval Chronicle*, Vol.28, p.313.

13 Historic Commons Hansard, HC Debate 18 February 1813, col.643, Hon. George Canning, MP.*Historic Hansard Index, UK Parliament. https://api.parliament.uk/historic-hansard/index.html* (accessed 6 November 2019)

14 James Davey, 'Representing nations: caricature and the naval War of 1812', in Tim Voelcker (ed.), *Broke of the Shannon and the War of 1812* (Barnsley: Seaworth Publishing, 2013), p.160.

15 Quoted in Daughan, *1812*, p.82.

16 *Naval Chronicle*, Vol.29, p.242.

17 'Naval History 1812–1813 (February–March)', *Naval Chronicle*, Vol.29, p.242.

news throughout the Napoleonic Wars. As *The Times* pointed out, 'anyone who predicted such a result of an American war this time last year would have been treated as a madman or a traitor.'[18] Now, it was feared that the loss of the 'spell' of British naval supremacy, in the minds of the *Chronicle* and other papers, had real-world strategic implications. *The Times* expressed their consternation that, while three British frigates had been lost, not one American had been captured in turn, and worried this had granted the Americans a dangerous level of insolence and a freedom of movement on the seas seemingly unopposed by the sea's rightful sovereign, the Royal Navy.[19] In the *Chronicle*, the editors linked the Navy's tarnished reputation with a recent fight between HMS *Amelia* and the French frigate *Aréthuse*: after a long and bloody action, the affair ended in a stalemate, the news of which astounded the editors of the *Naval Chronicle*. 'It is long since any thing like this persevering effort has been witnessed on the part of the French. Is it not obvious that they are stimulated by American triumphs?'[20]

'Albion,' an anonymous contributor who sent in a letter to the *Chronicle*, also felt that the loss of the *Guerriere* to a ship 'rated equal force' was an important and devastating blow to Britain's naval reputation and 'almost unprecedented in the naval annals of Britain.'[21] Its importance was primarily due to the fact that it 'occasioned a loss of reputation to our navy, [and] an increase of character to that of the Americans.'[22] Another, or perhaps the same, 'Albion' argued that these defeats were mortifying, and also concluded that the news had emboldened the French in their action with HMS *Amelia*.[23] He was very concerned that the French were 'now desirous of following the example of the Americans,' both in their pursuit of snapping up British frigates in single-ship actions and in the design of their heavy frigates.[24]

Such events were unthinkable because the Royal Navy was not supposed to lose. The way that Britons understood the character of the British sailor was no longer compatible with defeat, and commentators had to find a way to reconcile their perception of Britain's naval reputation with the news. Some voices pinned the blame on the naval officers themselves. Carden was thoroughly lambasted in the press and in popular culture,[25] and Dacres too received a share of consternation, *The Times* declaring that he should have gone down with the ship rather than strike.[26] According to segments of popular opinion, these officers had personally failed. A myriad of additional explanations erupted to explain the losses. As the Americans were of British heritage, to some it made sense that they had inherited those same cultural traits that made the Royal Navy so impressive.[27] The Earl of Harrowby

18 *The Times*, 20 March 1813, quoted in Latimer, *1812*, p.106.
19 Davey, 'Representing nations', p.160; Toll, *Six Frigates*, p.369.
20 Davey, 'Representing nations', p.160; Toll, *Six Frigates*, p.369.
21 'Albion' to the Editor, Aberdeen, 10 November 1812, *Naval Chronicle*, Vol.29, p.386.
22 'Albion' to the Editor, 10 November 1812, *Naval Chronicle*, Vol.29, p.386.
23 'Albion' to the Editor, 4 April 1813, *Naval Chronicle*, Vol.29, p.291.
24 'Albion' to the Editor, 4 April 1813, *Naval Chronicle*, Vol.29, p.291.
25 Toll, *Six Frigates*, p.371.
26 Toll, *Six Frigates*, p.369.
27 Toll, *Six Frigates*, p.370.

agreed, but still bemoaned that 'It is a cruel mortification… to be beat by these second-hand Englishmen upon our own element.'[28] Others wondered if the Americans had concocted a secret new way of handling their guns, or of producing improved powder and shot.[29] Or perhaps the Royal Navy was simply being ruined by too many aristocrats in its ranks. Perhaps discipline on board ship was either too brutal or too slack, degrading the performance of the English sailors.[30]

British papers were quick to pass judgement on the defeated naval officers, the Navy as a whole, or on the Admiralty's decision-making. In Halifax, however, the press was far more cautious regarding these defeats. There the residents often first learned about events taking place in the American naval theatre from copies of papers from American ports such as Boston or Philadelphia – and regarding American naval victories, the editors of the *Royal Gazette* and *Acadian Recorder* preferred to wait for the British accounts than to go off American ones. As such, in the 16 September 1812 edition of the *Royal Gazette*, editors commented on the recently arrived news of the capture of Halifax-based HMS *Guerriere*:

> We have extracted from late Boston papers the American account of the capture and destruction of His Majesty's Ship *Guerriere* – As we have not had any other particulars of this distressing event, we think it our duty to abstain from any comment whatever.[31]

Similarly, in the first edition of the *Acadian Recorder*, published 16 January 1813, the loss of *Macedonian* was discussed only briefly: 'Of the *Macedonian*'s action we have hitherto had only the American account, and it is but common justice to suspend our judgement 'till we are acquainted with both sides of the question.'[32] Halifax received official British accounts of actions occurring off the North American coastline from the *London Gazette*. It is telling that the Halifax newsmen refrained from printing the readily available American accounts, and felt duty-bound to wait for British reports before reporting on the 'distressing events.' Beamish Murdoch, a Nova Scotian historian and politician who was a young boy during the war, mentioned the 'sad series of disasters' of 1812 in his *History of Nova Scotia* and reflected that, while 'they are only connected with the history of our province indirectly,' their impact 'on the minds of our people was great, stimulating their patriotism and loyalty instead of depressing them.'[33]

News of the *Macedonian*'s loss reached Halifax as late as December, when it was reported briefly in the *Royal Gazette*. Both papers had said very

---

28 James Davey, *In Nelson's Wake: How the Royal Navy Ruled the Waves after Trafalgar* (New Haven, CT and London: Yale University Press, 2015), p.261.

29 Latimer, *1812*, p.106.

30 Latimer, *1812*, p.106.

31 Nova Scotia Archives (NSA), Microfilm Reel 8172, *Royal Gazette*, Wednesday 16 September 1812, 12:611.

32 NSA, *Acadian Recorder*, Saturday 16 January 1813, 1:1 (online), available at https://novascotia.ca/archives/newspapers/archives.asp?ID=752.

33 Beamish Murdoch, *A History of Nova Scotia, or Acadie* (Halifax: J. Barnes, 1867), Vol.3, p.334.

little about her loss by early March, when rumours of *Java*'s loss reached Halifax. The *Acadian Recorder*'s reporting was restrained, as the reporting on *Guerriere* and *Macedonian* had been in the *Gazette* and *Recorder*. In the 6 March 1813 edition the newspaper simply reported that, unreliable as intelligence from American sources was, 'we cannot flatter ourselves that [*Java*] is not destroyed, but from all we can learn, and the tried and established character of Capt. Lambert, we have no doubt the defence of her has been such as to reflect additional lustre on the British name.'[34] On the 20th, however, the *Recorder* printed an American paper's account of the *Constitution*'s triumphant return after defeating HMS *Java*.[35] It seemed that the restraint showed by the *Recorder* when it declined to print American accounts of *Macedonian* and *Frolic* had wavered after three months without news of either action, and the shock of another loss. *The Gazette*'s caution also gave way as news arrived of *Java*'s loss; the same rumours that the *Recorder* had alluded to in the 6 March edition were discussed in detail in the *Gazette*'s 3 March edition. While mostly accurate, this account did erroneously claim that *Java* was set on fire by some of her own crewmembers.[36] The date is reported incorrectly as well, indicating that this account was not the most well informed.

Halifax's papers worked to defend the honour and reputation of their local naval heroes, the officers and crew of ships stationed in Nova Scotian waters. One of the threats to that reputation were the rumours coming from Boston and other American ports, the source of much of their news. One such rumour reached Halifax early in 1813, targeting the crew of HMS *Orpheus*. According to a letter by her captain, the Boston report claimed that the crew of HMS *Orpheus* 'and other ships on this station, would not fight against the American frigates.'[37] The crew of *Orpheus* responded to the rumour with a letter they presented to First Lieutenant Frayrer that included an assertion of their dedication to duty and willingness to fight. That letter, along with an accompanying one penned by the ship's captain, was later printed in one of Halifax's newspapers on Friday 29 January. At the captain's request, they were reprinted in the *Acadian Recorder* the following morning.[38] On 3 February, the following Wednesday, the *Orpheus* letters were again reprinted in the *Royal Gazette*, along with a similar set of letters from the crew and captain of HMS *Atalante*.[39] In Halifax's public discourse there was little room for blaming the Royal Navy's officers for the losses or for insulting their honour.

34 NSA, *Acadian Recorder*, Saturday 6 March 1813, 1:8 (online), available at https://novascotia.ca/archives/newspapers/archives.asp?ID=752.

35 NSA, *Acadian Recorder*, Saturday 20 March 1813, 1:10 (online), available at https://novascotia.ca/archives/newspapers/archives.asp?ID=752.

36 NSA, *Acadian Recorder*, Saturday 20 March 1813, 1:10 (online), available at https://novascotia.ca/archives/newspapers/archives.asp?ID=752.

37 Captain H. Pigot to the Editor, *Naval Chronicle*, Vol.29, p.195; NSA, Microfilm Reel 8172, *Royal Gazette*, Wednesday 3 February 1813, 12:631; NSA, *Acadian Recorder*, Saturday 23 January 1813, 1:2 (online), available at https://novascotia.ca/archives/newspapers/archives.asp?ID=753.

38 NSA, *Acadian Recorder*, Saturday 23 January 1813, 1:2 (online), available at https://novascotia.ca/archives/newspapers/archives.asp?ID=753.

39 NSA, Microfilm Reel 8172, *Royal Gazette*, Wednesday 3 February 1813, 12:631.

The *Naval Chronicle*, too, was invested in defending and championing the honour and gallantry of the members of the Royal Navy. Since its founding, the *Chronicle* had printed material highlighting moments of gallantry for individual officers and for the Navy as a whole, both current events and those from the recent and distant past. The editions following the 1812 losses, however, now had to engage with the distasteful topic of defeat, through which the editors and commentators had to contend with the perceived stain on Britain's reputation and the threat to her 'spell of invincibility.'

In one of the first discussions on the loss of *Guerriere*, the editors of the *Chronicle* stated that British fifth-rate frigates

> should undoubtedly (barring extraordinary accidents) cope successfully with a 44-gun ship of any nation; but if that 44, by advantage of wind and superior sailing, should be able to choose her position, and vary her distance as may suit her convenience, it becomes problematical whether an English 38 could conquer her adversary under such circumstances; which seem to have been those attending this action.[40]

In their view, British frigates were expected to triumph over heavier frigates, except when the enemy was fortunate in having a superior position and excellent handling. This understanding meant that, in their eyes, there was no stain on the honour or abilities of the defeated British crews. With better luck and a less able foe, they certainly would have succeeded, but facing such a superiority meant that there was no shame in defeat.[41] This view was reiterated following the loss of *Macedonian*, when the *Chronicle* concluded that that USS *United States*' superior size and broadside (described as 'a frigate in name only') and 'the circumstances [of *Macedonian*'s capture] were such as are universally deemed honourable to Captain Carden and his brave crew.'[42]

A commentator in 1813 agreed, telling the editor that while the losses of 1812 were a massive blow to Britain's naval reputation and to its ability to protect trade in the West Indies, he did not extend the blame to the officers and crew who fought the action; '*inglorious*, I say, because unsuccessful; but I am ready to bear testimony to the gallant and noble exertions of the officers and ships' companies who have been obliged to yield (after *seeking the* combat) to the enemies' superiority; which we have *now only* been taught to acknowledge.'[43]

'Frigates in name only': reconciliation through the disparity of force

A few papers, such as *The Morning Chronicle*, a paper violently opposed to the Liverpool ministry, argued that the disparity in force between Britain's fifth-rates and America's heavy frigates vindicated the defeated officers and

40 *Naval Chronicle*, Vol.28, pp.313–314.

41 *Naval Chronicle*, Vol.28, p.314.

42 *Naval Chronicle*, Vol.29, p.74.

43 'Albion' to the Editor, *Naval Chronicle*, Vol.29, p.115.

sailors of guilt.[44] The *Naval Chronicle* latched onto this understanding as well, but for the most part Britain's press and public did not consider the disparity in force, and in some cases did not understand the actual difference between a frigate armed with 24-pounders and one armed with 18 pounders. The fact that the frigates had been beaten by superior enemies provided little comfort;[45] the Royal Navy was supposed to be invincible, after all. The Royal Navy had perpetually been victorious, even against superior odds, and to many there seemed little difference between an American 44-gun frigate and a British 38-gun frigate. Naval battles were not supposed to be matters of arithmetic.[46] William James, who went on to write several important, if biased, early histories of the war and on the Royal Navy, believed this when he first heard of the actions as a Jamaica Vice Admiralty Court lawyer detained in America:

> The account that an American 44, had captured a British 49, gun frigate, reached the author, when a prisoner in the United States. An Englishman, early accustomed to regard the navy as the bulwark of his country, and not aware of any difference between the nominal or *rated*, and the real force of a ship, might well feel a degree of humiliation in the *Guerriere*'s loss.[47]

James's sense of shock and determination to learn the truth – and his desire to reconcile his understanding of the Royal Navy's supremacy with the losses – led him into a literary career, though it took time for James to reach the conclusion that *Constitution* really had outclassed *Guerriere*. Early in the war there were few voices that made that argument, and it took some time before papers such as *The Times* also came to that realisation.[48]

The *Naval Chronicle*, however, was quick to come to that conclusion. From the start, the editors had argued that the disparity in force was sufficient to explain the losses and to defend the honour of the Royal Navy, even if they still thought that British fifth-rates were capable of defeating superior opponents under certain circumstances. Many of the journal's commentators also latched onto this explanation, some going even further. In a letter submitted in March 1813, 'J.C.' stated that 'there is no cause for regretting the late disasters at sea, *viz.* the capture of the *Guerrier*, *Macedonian*, *Java*, and *Frolic*.'[49] While he was very concerned by the defeats and loss of life, he felt that the national dialogue was out of control. According to the press, the 'charm is broken,' 'and the trident is, according to their ideas, already snatched from our hands, – by what? By a navy so small we scarcely know where to find it, consisting of *three sail of the line*, three frigates, and about as many sloops.'[50] Part of the reason why these defeats, in J.C.'s mind, were inconsequential was the fact that the British ships were outmatched in each

44 McCranie, *Utmost Gallantry*, p.89.
45 Latimer, *1812*, p.102.
46 Fitz-Enz, *Old Ironsides*, pp.163–164.
47 James, *Naval Occurrences*, p.v.
48 Latimer, *1812*, pp.103–106.
49 'J.C.' to the Editor, 25 March 1813, *Naval Chronicle*, Vol.29, p.288.
50 'J.C.' to the Editor, 25 March 1813, *Naval Chronicle*, Vol.29, p.288.

of the actions. He did not refer to *Constitution*, *United States*, and *President* as frigates, instead calling them ships of the line. Moreover, he stated that 'they have been victorious in four actions, in all of which they have been vastly superior in tonnage, weight of metal, and number of men (all of them picked) in the proportion of three to two.'[51] Victory against those odds, then, were near impossible.[52] Linking the crews of those British warships to Leonidas and his 300 Spartans, he instead argued that the British crew should be praised for their conduct in battle. Despite losing, they inflicted so much damage upon the enemy that they were compelled to return to port and abandon their missions. Their defeat was honourable and reflected well on the British spirit.

'R.''s letter of October 13, 1812 countered the sentiment that HMS *Guerriere*'s loss was a stain on national honour. While 'The loss of H.M. frigate *Guerriere* is no doubt much to be regretted; but she is not in possession of the enemy, she is not a trophy of victory – not a tarnish is to be found upon the trident of the seas.'[53] He criticised papers that asserted that Dacres's efforts were not sufficient and a stain on national honour; therefore deserving of punishment:

> Is the editor of the paper alluded to ignorant of the force of the *Constitution*? Does he know that she is as heavy as an English sixty-four? Has any person informed him that the upper deck of the *Constitution* is flush fore and aft, and that she thereby mounts a double tier of guns, like a line-of-battle ship? Does he not feel, does his conscience not tell him, that when a ship has been fought to the last extremity, until resistance is impotent, and perseverance vain, that the captain is responsible for the lives of his crew; and that had Captain Dacres obstinately persisted longer, the blood of every forfeited life would have been upon him, and their valuable services would have been taken from their country, to deck the funeral of the commander. Had the *Guerriere* gone down from such obstinacy as the Editor alluded to requires, Captain Dacres would have been an executioner.[54]

He went on to ask the editors of other papers if they would have fought to the death under such conditions. In one sense, his argument was similar to that employed by the defeated officers he was defending – once all hope of victory was gone, it was Dacres's duty to save the lives of his men. However, just as important for 'R.' was the fact that *Guerriere* had faced such tremendous odds in the first place. His letter highlighted the comparison of USS *Constitution* with a British ship of the line. Given those odds, 'R.' argued, the fact that *Guerriere* fought until she had effectively been destroyed was a triumph for Dacres and for Britain's honour.

Many commentators, such as 'Arion' and 'Britannicus,' both argued that the American warships were not frigates at all, but instead fast two-decked

51 'J.C'. to the Editor, 25 March 1813, *Naval Chronicle*, Vol.29, p.289.
52 'J.C.' to the Editor, 25 March 1813, *Naval Chronicle*, Vol.29, p.289.
53 'R.' to the Editor, October 13 1812, *Naval Chronicle*, Vol.28, p.381.
54 'R.' to the Editor, October 13 1812, *Naval Chronicle*, Vol.28, pp.381–382.

ships of the line.[55] As such, Britain's frigates were simply outmatched by the American heavy frigates.[56] Because of this, the *Guerriere* and *Macedonian* did not stand a chance. 'Arion' believed that the superior broadside of the enemy was the one crucial factor – if the American ships had been manned by Frenchmen, they still would have won, and if the British had had the heavy frigates and the Americans the lighter ones, the heavier ships would have prevailed. It was a sentiment with which both Dacres and Carden would have firmly disagreed, just as they would have disagreed with 'Arion's' speculation that the British may have had a better chance if they had fought at long range due to the heavy but short-range carronades that made up the American frigates' forecastle and quarterdeck batteries. 'British officers have not been accustomed to find any disadvantage from close action, but the contrary; but here they have evidently a new species of force to contend with.'[57]

This new 'species of force' was reported to be quite extraordinary. Many commentators in the *Naval Chronicle* stated that the *Constitution*'s broadside was reported at 777 lbs and *Guerriere*'s at 526 lbs, and the USS *United States*' broadside was 'one hundred and eighty-eight pounds more than an English sixty-four gun ship!'[58] They were reported to effectively be 60-gun ships in terms of armament, with the hull and scantlings of English 74-gun ships of the line.[59] In truth, all three of the heavy frigates carried over 50 guns, all of a higher calibre than their British counterparts. While many commentators in the *Chronicle* were quick to point this out, few bothered to mention that *Guerriere*, *Macedonian*, and *Java* all carried more than 38 guns; each carried closer to 50 but were never referred to by the commentators as 50-gun ships. The first edition of the *Naval Chronicle* for 1813 included an overview of the naval strength of various powers, including the United States, as of November 1812. Each American ship was listed, including both its official rate and the actual number of guns mounted. British ships stationed in North America were also included, but while their official rates were detailed, there was no account of the actual number of carriage guns on board. Other specifications that were generally more important in the official dispatches of the 1812 losses, such as the size, length, tonnage, and broadside weight, were detailed. By pointing out that the American frigates carried more guns that their rate but omitting the same detail about many (though not all) British frigates, the *Chronicle* exaggerated the disparity between the forces available to the British and American navies in North America. The comparison's purpose, after all, was to 'enable the reader to appreciate the heroism with which our officers and seamen have defended themselves in the recent actions with our trans-Atlantic descendants.'[60]

---

55 'Arion' to the Editor, *Naval Chronicle*, Vol.29, pp.206–207; 'Naval Patriot' to the Editor, May 1813, *Naval Chronicle*, Vol.29, pp.466–468; 'Impartial' to the Editor, London, 23 May 1813, *Naval Chronicle*, Vol.29, pp.470–472.

56 'Arion' to the Editor, *Naval Chronicle*, Vol.29, pp.206–207.

57 'Arion' to the Editor, *Naval Chronicle*, Vol.29, p.207.

58 *Naval Chronicle*, Vol.28, p.314; *Naval Chronicle*, Vol.29, p.74.

59 'Albion' to the Editor, 14 January, *Naval Chronicle*, Vol.29, p.115; 'Naval Patriot' to the Editor, May 1813, *Naval Chronicle*, Vol.29, pp.466–468.

60 'General Maritime Force of Europe', *Naval Chronicle*, Vol.29, pp.37–38.

According to David Hannay, a prominent early twentieth century historian, 'it was long our uncandid practice, when comparing the forces of our ships to those of foreigners, to count all their pieces of ordnance, but to only give the official armament of our own. Thus we were made to appear victorious over greatly superior forces.'[61] This practice of giving a ships official armament that did not reflect the actual number of guns originated with the adoption of carronades, which for a time were not considered 'guns' for the purposes of rating. As the number of carronades carried by ships increased, and as other navies adopted them, this practice was somewhat modified, and some ships began to count some of their carronades; *Guerriere*, for instance, counted about half of her carronades towards the 38-gun rating.

Like the *Chronicle*, both the *Recorder* and the *Gazette* in Halifax commented on the superior size and strength of the American frigates, arguing that it provided sufficient justification for the losses, however shocking. When discussing the *Guerriere*'s loss, the *Recorder* assured its readers that the *Constitution* far outclassed the *Guerriere*, and added that it was rumoured to have had a large portion of Royal Navy veterans serving on board.[62] In the *Gazette*'s account of the loss of *Java*, the editor pointed out that HMS '*Java* was but a 36-gun frigate.'[63] The editors of the Halifax papers wanted to assure their readers of the superior strength of the American frigates so as not to diminish the reputation of the naval heroes so respected in Halifax society. Haligonians were also well aware of the debate beginning in Britain on the importance of the disparity in force on the recent losses.[64] Interestingly, the Halifax papers in 1812 and 1813 did not blame any party for the losses; the disparity in force was sufficient on its own. This was in stark contrast to British-based papers, many of which directed much of their anger at one party in particular: the Board of Admiralty.

'Had common precaution been taken': scapegoating the Board of Admiralty

In the wake of these losses, there were many calls for a reassessment of naval strategy in North America and the requisition of new heavy frigates for service there. Several voices in the *Chronicle* echoed the calls for the construction of new heavy frigates and for them to be stationed in North America to oppose America's three.[65] The Admiralty was in fact constructing several heavy frigates with 24-pounder main batteries, but for some this was not enough. 'An Iron Gun' questioned why HMS *Culloden*, a 74-gun ship being cut down into a frigate, was being armed with a battery of 24-pounders when she currently carried one battery of 32-pounders. 'Why deprive her

61 David Hannay, *Naval Courts Martial* (Cambridge: CUP, 1914), p.185.

62 McCranie, *Utmost Gallantry*, p, 89.

63 NSA, Microfilm Reel 8172, *Royal Gazette*, Wednesday 3 March1813, 13:635.

64 Mercer, 'Colonial patriotism', p.46.

65 'Albion' to the Editor, *Naval Chronicle*, Vol.29, p.292; 'Britannicus' to the Editor, *Naval Chronicle*, Vol.28, p.467.

of the advantage of retaining the 32-pounder guns already on board, as it is asserted that, after the intended alterations are completed, she will then be scarcely equal to the American frigates?' Additionally, he suggested that 68-pounder carronades be placed on the fore and quarterdecks to further give the British an advantage in strength. He also considered retaining her as a 74, as 'It is not usual to reduce one's strength when going to fight an enemy.'[66] Despite his confidence in the superiority of British sailors given equal conditions, he had no interest in giving the Americans a fair fight in which to test that confidence. Instead, he suggested that the ideal strategy for the destruction of the American frigates was to bring as much force to bear against them as possible.

The fact that there were not more heavy frigates available at the outbreak of war seemed egregious to many. 'M.' criticised the Admiralty for failing to station adequate forces on the North American squadron: 'I do not know what information the government may have possessed respecting the largest class of American ships of war, called by them frigates; but I remember being told, twenty years ago, by one who had been in their service, that if ever we should have war with that country, our frigates could be no match for them. ... Recent events have proved the correctness of the observations.'[67] This particular claim is easily disprovable; the frigates were not even ordered until 1794, so the commentator could not have discussed them 20 years previous. Still, he criticised the Admiralty for failing to acquire and act on the information he claimed he had learned of years before. He suggested this might be because, after so many years of success, the impossible was expected from British warships. However, it was still a serious blunder, one in which there was no retribution for the seamen 'who have fallen contending against a superior foe.'[68] 'Oceanus' wrote to the *Chronicle* to question pre-war Admiralty naval policy regarding North America and its inability to prevent the naval disasters that occurred in 1812:

> Though I am convinced that clever men are selected to form the board of Admiralty, I am at a loss to determine their motive for not employing our largest frigates on the American station. Had common precaution been taken, previously to the declaration of war against us, we should, in all probability, have been spared the mortification that was felt at the loss of the *Guerriere*.[69]

There were not enough ships on station as a precaution in case of war with the United States, and to 'Oceanus' it did not appear that enough was being done to rectify the situation and prevent another frigate from being overpowered by a superior foe. It was the government officials who should be blamed, according to 'Oceanus.' The solution, in his mind, was to send every one of Britain's heavy frigates 'which carry, or are capable of carrying, twenty-four pounders on their main decks ... as a flying squadron, under the

66 'An iron Gun of a Large Calibre' to the Editor, 28 January 1813, *Naval Chronicle*, Vol.29, p.114.
67 'M.' to the Editor, *Naval Chronicle*, Vol.29, p.469.
68 'M.' to the Editor, *Naval Chronicle*, Vol.29, p.469.
69 'Oceanus' to the Editor, 1 December 1812, *Naval Chronicle*, Vol.29, pp.12–13.

command of an enterprising officer' to hunt down and destroy the American squadron.[70]

'Albion' outright stated that he was not looking for a fair show-down with the American navy – he wanted it obliterated through overwhelming force:

> But the victory will be dearly bought: we cannot expect an easy conquest: the American frigates are much larger, loftier, carry more guns and men, (many, I lament to say, British sailors amongst them), and the Americans themselves, are second to none, but British tars. Under these circumstances, it is in vain to look for the conquest of the American navy by our frigates, without a sacrifice of lives, which I think ought to be avoided, by employing a few ships of the line.[71]

Another 'Albion' expressed that he wanted the Admiralty to dispatch large squadrons, including a ship of the line, to North America with the aim of catching and destroying America's frigates through overwhelming firepower.[72]

Some vehemently argued that powerful squadrons centred around ships of the line should have been stationed in North America to ensure that the United States Navy never posed a threat. These arguments called, not for fair contests, but for applying the overwhelming superiority of the Royal Navy in an effort to drive the United States Navy back into port, and if possible to destroy it outright. At the very least, Britain's own existing heavy frigates, carrying 24-pounder main batteries, should have been stationed at Halifax and Bermuda when relations with the United States began to sour. Overall, Britain's wider popular press agreed with the *Chronicle* that the Liverpool ministry and the Admiralty were to blame for the disasters in 1812, in part by not stationing sufficient naval forces in North America to counter the Americans. According to McCranie, predictions that the naval losses in 1812 would outweigh news of successes in Canada in the popular press proved true. Papers such as *The Morning Chronicle*, 'the mouthpiece of those in opposition to the current British government,' relentlessly attacked the Liverpool ministry and the Admiralty for the policies that lead to the disastrous course of the naval war with the United States.[73] Even less radical papers like *The Times* blamed the government and the Admiralty for the Navy's losses. A significant proportion of the *Naval Chronicle*'s commentators acknowledged and commented on the disparity in strength between the American heavy frigates and their British 18-pounder opponents. Segments of the general press did as well, including *The Morning Chronicle*, which argued that the disparity in force vindicated the defeated officers and sailors of guilt, but did not vindicate the policymakers in Whitehall.[74] So, why did Britain not station heavier frigates in North America prior to the outbreak of war? There were two main reasons for this.

70 'Oceanus' to the Editor, 1 December 1812, *Naval Chronicle*, Vol.29, pp.12–13.
71 'Albion' to the Editor, 10 November 1812, *Naval Chronicle*, Vol.29, p.387.
72 'Albion' to the Editor, 4 April 1813, *Naval Chronicle*, Vol.29, p.292.
73 McCranie, *Utmost Gallantry*, p.89.
74 McCranie, *Utmost Gallantry*, p.89.

Firstly, as there were very few naval threats in North American waters during the wars with Revolutionary and Napoleonic France, the North American squadron was a low priority. The bulk of the fleet was concentrated in European waters to blockade French, Spanish, and Dutch forces. In 1811, the North American squadron included a 64-gun ship, seven frigates, eight sloops, one gun-brig, and five schooners. It was the largest it had been since war broke out in 1793, though much smaller than in 1774, prior to the Revolutionary War. At that time, British Admiral Sir Hugh Palliser, who had extensive experience in those waters, estimated that 50 ships were needed to conduct a blockade of the 13 colonies. In 1814, Vice Admiral Alexander Cochrane estimated that the operation would require 90 ships.[75] Vice Admiral Sawyer and Admiral Warren both immediately realised that they needed far more ships to achieve their objectives of protecting Britain's extensive trade and operating against enemy trade and cruisers.[76] However, until such a war broke out, the Admiralty placed its available ships on more important stations. It was hoped, after all, that conflict with the United States could be avoided.

Secondly, the Admiralty did not place any 24-pounder frigates in North America to counter America's three heavy frigates because it was not thought to be necessary. During the French Revolutionary Wars, it quickly became apparent that Britain's smaller 18-pounder frigates were able to cope with their French cousins.[77] Of the 45 single-ship frigate duels fought between British and French frigates between 1793 and 1814, nine of Britain's 35 victories were against French ships with superior broadsides (up to 250 percent the firepower of the victorious British frigates), and Britain won every frigate duel where the two sides were evenly matched.[78] By the early 1800s, the Admiralty no longer felt that the French naval threat warranted the continued effort required to build and man the larger frigates. Admiral Sir John Jervis, Lord St Vincent, had concluded by 1797 that Britain's newer frigates were of excessive size, and remarked that in his time at sea he had never found himself in need of larger ships; instead, his concern as a serving admiral was that there were never enough frigates. The cheapest way to address the shortage of frigates was to build smaller fifth-rates: they were easier to build, maintain, and man. When St Vincent became First Lord of the Admiralty in 1802, he shifted the ship-building programme to focus on quantity rather than quality.[79] Larger numbers of smaller frigates, including 18-pounders and even 12-pounder designs, were constructed. Britain's existing heavy frigates were given a lower priority, and lighter frigates were armed and put to sea before heavier ones. A handful of Britain's heavier frigates, such as HMS *Endymion*, had their main batteries reduced from 24-pounders to 18-pounders.[80]

75 Gywn, *Frigates and Foremasts*, p.134.

76 Gwyn, *Frigates and Foremasts*, pp.134–140; Lambert, 'British Grand Strategy', pp.17–39, 21; Daughan, *1812*, p.125; Roger Morriss, *Cockburn and the British Navy in Transition: Admiral Sir George Cockburn, 1772–1853* (Columbia, SC: University of South Carolina Press, 1997), 87; Dudley, *Splintering the Wooden Wall*, 68–78.

77 Lardas, *British Frigate vs French Frigate*, p.69.

78 Lardas, *British Frigate vs French Frigate*, pp.69–40.

79 Gardner, *Frigates of the Napoleonic Wars*, pp.9–20.

80 Gardner, *Frigates of the Napoleonic Wars*, pp.9–20.

As Gardiner points out, the British public had been 'brought up on a diet of almost uninterrupted naval victories against apparently any odds.'[81] The Admiralty had consumed much of the same diet themselves, and over the course of the wars with France had concluded that heavier ships were not required. Smaller British frigates, which were cheaper to build and maintain, could do the same job as Britain's heaviest frigates. When the winning streak ended in 1812, there was a storm of outrage against the Admiralty. Gardiner points out 'That the American ships were about 40 percent larger and carried fifty percent more firepower was ignored by the journalistic clamor, and the public and parliamentary pressure forced the Admiralty to review its North American strategy.'[82]

Of course, the journalist clamour did not manifest itself in Halifax. There was none of the fervent antagonism towards the Admiralty that was seen in British papers, and British policymakers were not blamed for the losses at all. The reporting in the Halifax papers was more reserved and careful, although over time that caution began to waver. This was likely due to the political – and physical – distance from the policymakers in London. It also better reflected the respectful, event-focused, and sorrowful reports that came from naval officers in the Royal Navy. There was little else about the press's coverage of the naval losses that reflected the attitudes of the serving officers of the Royal Navy. A clear difference between the focus and general theme of the *Chronicle*'s coverage of the naval losses in 1812, and the correspondence and courts martial evidence from the officers involved, was the importance of the disparity in force between the ships involved in the single-ship actions. Carden and Chads described their shock at the enemy's firepower and the physical characteristics of their ships; they were beyond anything that the Royal Navy had that could be called a frigate. Yet neither officer leaned on these facts in their defence to the extent that the commentators in the *Chronicle* did. Dacres dismissed the *Constitution*'s superior firepower as a crucial factor in his loss altogether. While many in the *Chronicle* suggested that overwhelming forces should be applied to the American theatre to overpower America's super frigates, Dacres stated in his court martial that he would like to fight *Constitution* again with a ship of *Guerriere*'s class.

That the views of the wider press contrasted with those of the Royal Navy is not surprising, but the *Chronicle*'s viewpoints being so at odds is interesting. Among the editors were two naval men – a former chaplain and purser who entered the literary world after leaving the Royal Navy – but they were not commissioned officers themselves, and not linked as closely to that same culture. However, its contributors were, after all, supposed to have been naval officers. If the majority of the *Chronicle*'s commentators were naval officers, then why did their commentary differ so wildly from the officers examined in the previous chapter? The more likely explanation is that the commentators who wrote to the *Chronicle* were not mostly serving naval officers – indeed, it seems that very few were. It is more likely that civilians

81 Gardner, *Frigates of the Napoleonic Wars*, p.35.
82 Gardner, *Frigates of the Napoleonic Wars*, p.35.

and long-retired (either by choice or by the failure to secure appointments) naval officers sent in most of the letters to the *Chronicle*. Their opinions of strategy, honour, and means of retribution were markedly different from those displayed by the serving officers of the Royal Navy. All they shared was a mutual love of the Royal Navy and an urge for vengeance.

4

'Very happy to meet any American frigate': Crisis for the Admiralty and the officers of the North American squadron

The five losses in 1812 were deeply troubling to navy men at all levels and, after the events of the previous year, it might have appeared that 1813 would be just as bleak. However, while the public was coming to grips with the losses and the Admiralty began reassessing strategy in the American war, the officers and admirals of the North American squadron had to adapt quickly and continue pressing the fight. A conflict emerged between the squadron's leadership and the captains and officers throughout the fleet's ships regarding how to respond to the American victories. For Warren and his admirals, the primary duty was to protect the overall strategic situation for the United Kingdom. Britain's extensive trade needed to be protected to keep the economy and wider war effort afloat. The continued defence of Canada required the waters around Nova Scotia and the St Lawrence to be kept clear of American warships and privateers. This required extensive convoy networks and an ever-increasing strategy of blockades of the kind that were so effective in Europe against the French. It also meant preventing further single-ship losses; the morale impact alone had sent tremors throughout the fleet and the government, and the Royal Navy wanted to avoid such losses at all costs.

By contrast, vengeance was principally on the minds of many of the North American squadron's officers and captains. Their focus was on the honour of the Royal Navy, and Britain's strategic interests seemed to come second. Five of their comrades had been defeated over the last year – this was unthinkable and unacceptable for the Navy's officers. Personal accounts from these officers are scarce; the best examples are that of Captain Philip Broke, whose extensive correspondence with his wife Louisa has survived, and the 1814 journal of Lieutenant Henry Edward Napier, which is an excellent personal account. Beyond these accounts, there were the actions of the commanders on the station, several of whom violated orders and took matters into their own hands to bring about even contests with the enemy. These events and accounts illuminate the general trends of naval discourse and attitudes within the North American squadron following the losses of 1812.

Hornet–Peacock action, 24 February 1813

At the start of 1813, the American frigate USS *Constellation* was ordered to proceed to sea under the command of Captain Charles Stewart, but she was quickly blockaded by a powerful Royal Navy squadron and forced to anchor under the guns of local forts. Even as Warren began to organise blockading squadrons to patrol several important American ports, however, several American warships were already at sea, continuing cruises that had begun the previous year.[1] One of those warships was USS *Hornet*, under Master Commandment James Lawrence, operating under the command of Commodore Bainbridge. The two made a rendezvous in late October, not long after having first put to sea, and proceeded to San Salvador in Brazil. There they found the British sloop HMS *Bonne Citoyenne* under Commander Pitt Burnaby Greene. Bainbridge and Lawrence decided to issue a challenge to Greene through the American counsel, offering single combat between his sloop and Lawrence's *Hornet* with an assurance that should the British prevail Bainbridge would not intervene. Though given an opportunity of fighting an equally matched opponent, Greene declined the challenge owing to his cargo; he was carrying half a million pounds of gold and silver bound for Britain, and risking such a fortune in addition to his ship would have been a clear violation of his duty.[2]

Lawrence was particularly upset by the refusal. The 31-year old American officer was well known – and respected – in the service for his refined manners and 'heightened sense of personal and professional honour.' Indeed, Lawrence was obsessed with notions of glory, both in terms of its importance to his public recognition and to his career.[3] Like most officers in the United States Navy, Lawrence struggled in a small service for recognition and promotion. He had been frustrated earlier in the year when Lieutenant Charles Moriss, First Lieutenant of *Constitution* when she took *Guerriere*, had been promoted straight from lieutenant to captain. Lawrence had fought for such a promotion for years to no avail. He was also aware that his own promotion from lieutenant to master commandment was thanks to previous demonstrations of bravery in action, and knew that his only hope of reaching the rank of captain and being given command of one of America's crack frigates was to win some victory against the Royal Navy.[4] Thus far he had only taken prizes of vastly inferior strength, and his first chance at an equal combat had eluded him.

1 Roosevelt, *Naval War of 1812*, pp.160–163.
2 Latimer, *1812*, p.153; Roosevelt, *Naval War of 1812*, 118.
3 Voelcker, 'Victories or distractions', p.70.
4 Lambert, *The Challenge*, Chapter 4.

After Bainbridge departed, on route for his show-down with Captain Lambert far to the south, Lawrence remained off Salvador for over two months, hoping that Greene might reconsider or at least attempt to escape. He was frustrated yet again in late January, when a British ship of the line, HMS *Montagu*, arrived, forcing the vastly outmatched American to weigh anchor and flee.[5] Over the next month, Lawrence continued his cruise, taking a British merchant brig in the process and heading towards the British trade outpost near Georgetown, situated on the east bank of the Demerara River, where he expected to find rich commerce pickings and with any luck a British sloop protecting it. Sure enough, on the 24th his lookouts spotted a brig-rigged man of war anchored in the shallows at the mouth of the river, and he determined to close. The ship in question was HMS *Espiegle*, an 18-gun *Cruizer*-class brig-sloop, and most of her officers and crew were ashore, blissfully unaware of any danger. Early in the morning lookouts had sighted *Hornet*, but her lieutenant was somehow convinced that she was either a British warship or a merchant. Amazingly, all through the morning and into the afternoon, her officers had no idea that *Hornet* was an American sloop of war and was concocting a plan of attack. What saved *Espiegle* from a surprise attack was the arrival of yet another ship. She was another *Cruizer*-class brig-sloop, HMS *Peacock*, commanded by Commander William Peake.[6]

Lawrence kept his sloop close to the wind so as to secure the weather gauge. Around 5:00 p.m., having got to windward, he tacked through the wind and bore down on the approaching British sloop. Both ships hoisted their ensigns, and *Peacock* responded by baring up 'with the intention of bringing [*Hornet*] to close action.'[7] The two vessels quickly approached the other on opposite tacks, and at 5:25 p.m. their bows passed each other and their first guns opened fire. Continuing in opposite directions, the ships passed each other, each gun firing as it bore. Quickly, it became apparent that *Hornet*'s gunnery was superior. *Peacock*'s hull was smashed by the first broadside, and in response her smaller guns had done little but cut away some of her opponent's rigging and a handful of men aloft. *Peacock*'s fire was woefully ineffective. Beyond firing smaller shot, the shorter ship rolled more in the waves than her opponent, making aiming more difficult, and her crew were dangerously underprepared for action, having hardly exercised with the guns at all.[8]

As the ships passed each other, commander Peake resolved to wear ship to surprise the enemy and attempt to secure a raking position. Lawrence spotted this and bore up into the wind in response, managing to place his ship on the enemy's quarter. *Peacock*, with a damaged rudder and rigging, was slow to come around and found herself trapped under the enemy's

5 Latimer, *1812*, p.153.
6 McCranie, *Utmost Gallantry*, p.83.
7 LAC, MG12 ADM 1 1/503 Admiral's Dispatches, 1812–1813, North America, C-12854, Lieutenant Frederick Wright to Admiral Warren, New York, 26 March 1813.
8 McCranie, *Utmost Gallantry*, p.83; Roosevelt, *Naval War of 1812*, pp.166–169.

raking broadside 10 minutes into the action. At this point the brig practically disintegrated as a fighting vessel.[9]

Hornet's short-range gunnery wiped *Peacock*'s decks clean; scores of men were cut down by enemy round shot and grape as the bulwarks fell to pieces, the brig's topsails were ripped from the masts and collapsed, and the mainsail's sheets and other running rigging were ripped apart. Only moments into the exchange Peake was hit by a musket ball and a splinter. The wounded commander remained on the quarterdeck until, in the words of his lieutenant, 'he gallantly fell nobly defending his Ship by a Cannon Shot which instantly deprived him of Life.'[10] Lieutenant Frederick Wright inherited command of the shattered ship; nearly 40 men of her 130-some crew were dead or wounded, the rigging was completely torn apart, and the ship was quickly taking on water and appeared to be sinking. Fourteen minutes after the first gun was fired, Wright surrendered and signalled to the enemy that his ship was in a state of distress.[11]

Upon taking possession, Lawrence came to the same conclusion; *Peacock* was indeed sinking. He initially set to work trying to save the prize but quickly abandoned the idea. Despite the efforts, *Peacock* was gaining water faster than it could be pumped out, and even throwing supplies and guns overboard did not slow her. Worse, within sight was *Espiegle*, a brig of the same force as *Hornet* and untouched, and Lawrence was anxious to get away. He therefore ordered the prize evacuated. Men scrambled to get off as the ship quickly sank; her descent was so quick that four Hornets and nine Peacocks were trapped below. Those unable to make one of the boats as the ship's decks plunged underwater scrambled up the shrouds to the foretop, which remained just above the waves as the brig settled on the shallow ocean floor, and were rescued.[12]

Now carrying far more men than she was designed to, *Hornet* set sail back to America. Her officers still feared that *Espiegle* would come to challenge her in her wounded state and made every effort to put distance between them and the Demerara River. Yet to Lawrence's utter amazement, *Espiegle* never even weighed anchor. His fears were for naught.[13] *Espiegle* had every opportunity to come to her friend's aid, or at the very least to avenge her by attacking *Hornet*. Unlike *Peacock*, which carried a main battery of 24-pound carronades, *Espiegle* was armed with the standard 32s of the class and was evenly matched with *Hornet* – even in a lightly wounded state such an action would have posed a great danger to Lawrence. A later court martial determined that *Espiegle*'s officers had only determined that *Hornet* was a threat late into the action and by that time had quickly lost sight of them. This was an odd excuse, as she was only four miles away from the action, and it is surprising that her lookouts lost sight of the *Hornet* when she was plainly

9 Ibid; McCranie, *Utmost Gallantry*, p.83; Roosevelt, *Naval War of 1812*, pp.166–169.
10 LAC, MG12 ADM 1 1/503, C-12854, Wright to Warren, 26 March 1813.
11 LAC, MG12 ADM 1 1/503, C-12854, Wright to Warren, 26 March 1813; McCranie, *Utmost Gallantry*, p.83; Roosevelt, *Naval War of 1812*, pp.166–169.
12 McCranie, *Utmost Gallantry*, p.83; Roosevelt, *Naval War of 1812*, pp.166–169.
13 McCranie, *Utmost Gallantry*, p.83.

within sight of the Americans.[14] Whatever happened, *Espiegle* failed to come to *Peacock*'s aid, meaning Lieutenant Wright was placed 'in the painful situation of announcing … the Capture of His Majesty's Brig *Peacock*.'[15]

Wright's report to Admiral Warren, composed a month after the action, justified the loss in the same manner as had those in 1812. He began by asserting that the brig quickly moved to bring about a close action, but that 10 minutes into the fight they had been raked with the enemy on their starboard quarter. He detailed the actions and death of Peake, whose determination to bring the ship into close action and refusal to quit the deck after being wounded were praised, and Wright particularly mourned his death:

> at this period of the Action Captain Peake was wounded by a Musquet Shot and by a Splinter which knocked him down he continued however to retain the Command of the Ship for some Minutes longer when he gallantly fell nobly defending his Ship by a Cannon Shot which instantly deprived him of Life, and the Service of a Meritorious and brave Officer.[16]

Having given due credit to his fallen commander, Wright then detailed the condition of the brig when he took command. The situation was dire, as most of the gun crews had been killed or wounded, four guns were out of action, the rigging was virtually destroyed, and the ship was slowly sinking. Still, Wright asserted that he was not immediately ready to surrender:

> yet as the fire was briskly kept up by the Waist Guns I was determined to support the honor of the British Flag as long as defense was practicable but the Main Mast going close by the board a few minutes afterwards and the Enemy again taking up his raking position and the Vessel an unmanageable and sinking wreck, I was at length to save the lives of the remaining Crew however reluctant and painful it was compelled to wave my hat in acknowledgment of having struck the ensign having fallen with the Gaff into the water.[17]

Wright asserted that he initially wanted to continue the action, 'with an ardour characteristic of British Seamen,' but as he came to realise the unmanageable state of the ship and his inability to mount an effective resistance to the enemy off his quarter, he concluded that victory was no longer a possibility.[18]

In his account, Wright emphasised the enemy's superiority in men, but only referenced the disparity in broadside weight in passing:

> we came to compare the disparity of Force between the two Vessels with the extraordinary Number of Men on board the Enemy which allowed them to keep

14 McCranie, *Utmost Gallantry*, pp.83–84; Roosevelt, *Naval War of 1812*, pp.169–170.
15 LAC, MG12 ADM 1 1/503, C-12854, Wright to Warren, 26 March 1813.
16 LAC, MG12 ADM 1 1/503, C-12854, Wright to Warren, 26 March 1813.
17 LAC, MG12 ADM 1 1/503, C-12854, Wright to Warren, 26 March 1813.
18 LAC, MG12 ADM 1 1/503, C-12854, Wright to Warren, 26 March 1813.

> a large number in their Tops who supported an incessant galling and destructive Fire.[19]

By contrast, nowhere in his report did Wright discuss the disparity in gunnery, either in terms of speed, accuracy, or weight. In the postscript he did state that *Peacock* was armed with sixteen 24-pounder carronades, whereas *Hornet* carried eighteen 32-pounder carronades, but did not directly attribute this as a factor of the loss in the letter.[20] He did state that his crew would have prevailed had they 'not been opposed to an overwhelming force under more favorable circumstances and with anything like equality of Guns or Men have ensured success.'[21] In the court martial it was revealed that *Peacock*'s fire was very poor and often overshot, doing little damage to *Hornet*. One officer attributed this to the rough conditions of the waves, although the gunner attributed it to a poor gunnery training regime.[22] It was well known that under Commander Peake *Peacock* was an exceptionally tidy ship, earning herself the nickname 'Yacht' for her dedication to decoration and polish, but in consequence her crew had rarely ever fired live guns in practice.[23]

Coverage of the capture of *Peacock* in the *Naval Chronicle* was sparse, as it had been for the losses of *Frolic* and *Alert*. One individual did send in a letter that explained away the great carnage and loss of life by saying it was inevitable in any close action, and further implored the *Chronicle* to uphold the spirits of their naval heroes instead of 'magnifying the prowess' of the Americans by discussing their victories.[24] People were weary after six British vessels had been defeated in action without a single victory. As McCranie points out:

> The *Guerriere*, *Macedonian*, *Java*, *Frolic*, and *Peacock* made five warships defeated in single combat by what many considered ships of their class. Though these losses did little to diminish Britain's ability to command the sea, they gave the United States Navy honor and glory that the Royal Navy was not in the habit of conceding.[25]

If the British public, government, and naval community were dismayed by the events of 1812, then the first events of 1813 must have dimmed spirits even more. It appeared that the year was on track to shape up like the last, and the Admiralty resolved to try and change this.

19 LAC, MG12 ADM 1 1/503, C-12854, Wright to Warren, 26 March 1813.
20 McCranie, *Utmost Gallantry*, p.83; Roosevelt, *Naval War of 1812*, p.166.
21 LAC, MG12 ADM 1 1/503, C-12854, Wright to Warren, 26 March 1813.
22 McCranie, *Utmost Gallantry*, p.83.
23 James, *Naval Occurrences*, p.202.
24 'A Sailor' to the Editor, Bath, 18 June 1813, *Naval Chronicle*, Vol.30, pp.126–127.
25 McCranie, *Utmost Gallantry*, p.84.

'Their Lordships trust': changing naval policy in North America

The British strategic situation in North America was already complex and strained, and this was not helped by the fact that trust between the Admiralty and the commander-in-chief was slowly breaking down. Over 1813, the Admiralty grew increasingly frustrated with Warren. They resented what they saw as his inability to carry out their orders, to act decisively, and to communicate with them adequately.[26] There was some truth in their criticisms, but the Admiralty too were to blame for the disjointed British response to the Americans. Much like the modern defence departments in both the United Kingdom and Canada, the Admiralty was a government department, headed by parliamentarians serving as Cabinet Ministers. Occasionally professional sailors with a seat in Parliament were appointed to key roles, such as Lord St Vincent and Lord Barham, but for the most part these posts were filled by civilians. During the War of 1812, Lord Melville, the First Lord of the Admiralty, and his secretary, John Croker, were both civilians in parliament. Neither had ever commanded a warship and they found it difficult to properly consider the realities of managing a war front from across the Atlantic.

Rodgers, Decatur, and Bainbridge had all escaped to sea in October 1812, and this caused much stir at the Admiralty. Bainbridge and Decatur had both captured a British frigate, which sent shockwaves of resentment throughout Britain that were particularly damaging to the government. Rodgers was still at sea with a handful of other American warships, and Melville blamed Warren for failing to contain and apprehend the Americans.[27] What Melville and Croker never realised, however, was that the three American commodores had already escaped into the Atlantic when Warren arrived. While the politicians were frustrated by a perceived lack of decisive action taken by the new commander-in-chief in the months that followed, it should be remembered that Warren's original mission was to attempt to negotiate an armistice with the United States; taking an aggressive stance was hardly conducive to a quick end to hostilities. Further, it took Warren some time to properly consolidate his new command.

The British priority was to carry out the war in the manner they had done in Europe: through a close blockade of principal enemy ports.[28] It was a proactive but still defensive strategy designed to bottle up America's warships

26 First Lord of the Admiralty Robert, Viscount Melville to Admiral Sir John Warren, Admiralty, 3 December 1812, in Brian Vale (ed.), *The Naval Miscellany, Volume VIII* (London: Navy Records Society, 2017), pp.230–231; First Secretary of the Admiralty John W. Croker to Admiral Sir John Warren, RN, 20 March 1813, *Naval War of 1812*, Vol.2, pp.76–78; Robert, Viscount Melville to Admiral Sir John Warren, 26 March 1813, *Naval War of 1812*, Vol.2, pp.78–79; McCranie, *Utmost Gallantry*, pp.89–93; Drolet, 'North American squadron', pp.176–185.

27 Melville to Warren, 3 December 1812, in Vale (ed.), *Naval Miscellany, Volume VIII*, pp.230–231; Croker to Warren, 20 March 1813, *Naval War of 1812*, Vol.2, pp.76–78; Melville to Warren, 26 March 1813, *Naval War of 1812*, Vol.2, pp.78–79; McCranie, *Utmost Gallantry*, pp.89–93; Drolet, 'North American squadron', pp.176–185.

28 Lambert, *The Challenge*, Chapter 4; McCranie, *Utmost Gallantry*, pp.95–96.

in port and prevent them from carrying out attacks on British shipping. The logic was sound, as Melville explained to Warren:

> it must be to our endeavour by blockading some & stationing cruisers along other parts of the coast, to make it such a hazardous enterprize as … to produce the same affect [sic] upon the Americans as upon the French, viz, that their Line of Battle Ships & Frigates rarely attempt it, & that their expectations by Sea are chiefly confined to their small privateers in the Channel.[29]

Melville also replaced Sawyer with Rear Admiral George Cockburn, and informed Warren that he hoped:

> you will find some more active employment for the former than merely attending to the Port Duties of Bermuda or Halifax. He is understood to be a very intelligent & enterprising Officer, & I shall be sorry if you cannot find occupation for him, such as I have described.[30]

Melville's message to Warren was clear: the Admiralty would not tolerate what they had perceived as inactivity on the part of Sawyer, and Warren was to conduct the blockade of the United States to the utmost of his ability. To help and indeed to encourage him, Rear Admiral Cockburn had been dispatched to serve under him as the commander of a portion of the North American squadron. Cockburn had a well-known reputation as a fighting man and ambitious officer, and the Admiralty expected him to be put to good use. Their preferred strategy called for the organisation of powerful squadrons – forces powerful enough to overwhelm America's heavy frigates without endangering their own, often including at least one ship of the line.[31] For the first time since the war had begun, Britain's naval strategy in North America was properly established and consistent.

Only three days later, however, further orders were issued from the Admiralty which complicated the situation. The new orders specified that the blockade was to extend to American ports which were not naval bases and did not offer the facilities to service America's warships. Whereas the initial orders had implied that Warren's priority was to conduct a naval blockade – which necessitated large, powerful squadrons that would keep the enemy from attempting to get to sea – these new orders implied that he was being asked to conduct an economic blockade as well. Such blockades required larger numbers of smaller warships to prevent enemy commerce from entering or leaving America's principal ports. Further, Warren had to see to the protection of Britain's own commerce. This required sloops and frigates for convoy escorts as well as dedicated squadrons to patrol the sea lanes in the Atlantic to hunt down enemy cruisers at sea.[32] On paper it was

29 Melville to Warren, 3 December 1812, *Naval Miscellany, Volume VIII*, pp.230–231.
30 Melville to Warren, 3 December 1812, *Naval Miscellany, Volume VIII*, p.231.
31 *Utmost Gallantry*, pp.116–117; Croker to Warren, 20 March 1813, *Naval War of 1812*, Vol.2, p.76.
32 McCranie, *Utmost Gallantry*, pp.95–96.

an effective strategy, but Warren had to prioritise: he did not have enough ships to manage all three objectives in the vast area he commanded.[33] As Morriss pointed out, 'At least for the time being, war with America was to mean unlimited demands to which the response had to be at the smallest possible cost to the British effort in Europe.'[34]

Warren quickly appealed to the Admiralty for reinforcements, and throughout the next year he remained at odds with the Admiralty. Warren consistently insisted that he did not have enough ships to carry out his orders, and the Admiralty consistently pushed back, reminding Warren that the Royal Navy was overstretched around the world and that they had already given him what they considered to be adequate:

> My Lords are glad to think that you will consider the amount of force now under your orders as most ample – It exceeds very much what on a mere comparison with the means of the Enemy would appear necessary.[35]

On paper it was a dominating force, but given the realities of the theatre it never seemed that way to the Royal Navy commanders in North America. If the Admiralty can be blamed for not understanding this, Warren should also be blamed for failing to properly explain this to Melville. One reason that his forces were stretched too thinly was that at any one time there were many ships detached, under refit, or simply destroyed; Warren's effective strength was never what it was on paper. However, Warren did not keep the Admiralty informed of these details and so they relied on his paper strength, which to their mind seemed adequate.[36]

Sufficient or not, the size of the North American squadron was significantly increased in 1812 and 1813. This demonstrated the Admiralty's concern about the United States Navy and particularly its heavy frigates. Their priority was always Napoleonic France, yet ships were taken from the Channel and Mediterranean fleets to reinforce the North American squadron following the American victories in 1812.

The Admiralty should not have been as shocked by the heavy frigates as they were, as they were fully aware of the danger posed by the Americans – before the outbreak of hostilities *Constitution* had even visited Portsmouth.[37] Before the war Sawyer had expressed his fears that one of his frigates might be taken by one of the American heavy frigates, as well as his concern about the public and political fallout of such a loss.[38] However, no real efforts were undertaken to prepare the North American squadron for the American naval threat. As previously discussed, this was the result of the Admiralty's evidence-based conclusion that a British frigate armed with 18-pounders could cope with enemy frigates armed with 24-pounders. Nearly 20 years

33 Gwyn, *Frigates and Foremasts*, pp.138–139; Drolet, 'North American squadron', pp.176–181.

34 Morriss, *Cockburn*, p.84.

35 Croker to Warren, 20 March 1813, *Naval War of 1812*, Vol.2, p.76.

36 McCranie, *Utmost Gallantry*, p.92; Drolet, 'North American squadron', pp.177–178.

37 McCranie, *Utmost Gallantry*, p.85.

38 Gwyn, *Frigates and Foremasts*, p.135.

of war had instilled that impression into the Navy. If heavy frigates such as *Endymion* were not even a priority upon re-armament in 1803, it is not surprising that those expensive and important naval assets were not sent to a relatively calm theatre like North America.

As Sawyer had predicted, the losses had a major impact on the public and on the government, which precipitated a major policy shift in the Admiralty. For the first time in over a decade, enemy 24-pounder frigates were perceived as a threat to the Royal Navy's fifth-rates, and efforts were undertaken to expand the number of heavy frigates available. The process of downsizing the batteries of Britain's few heavy frigates was halted, and ships like *Cambrian* and *Endymion* were prepared for service in North America. There was also another round of cutting down old ships of the line into *razée* frigates, armed with 24-pounder batteries. As with the programme in the 1790s, obsolete 64-gun ships of the line were cut down, but so too were 74-gun ships. The Admiralty also ordered new frigates; these were massive ships, with designs varying between 50-gun and 60-gun frigate-built ships, some superior in size and broadside weight to the three American heavy frigates.[39] The fourth-rate ship of the line, long obsolete, had effectively been resurrected as the heaviest frigates in the world.

The Admiralty took two other policy decisions in response to the 1812 losses. They issued a series of directives aimed at improving gunnery in Royal Navy warships in response to the poor practising habits of several of the defeated commanders. In March, Warren issued this message to his captains in a memorandum to the North American squadron:

> Their Lordships trust that all of the Officers of His Majesty's Naval Service must be convinced that upon the good discipline and the proper training of their Ships Companies to the expert management of the Guns, the preservation of the high character of the British navy most essentially depends, and that other works on which it is not unusual to employ the Men are of very trifling importance, when Compared with a due Preparation (by instruction and practice) for the effectual Services on the day of Battle.[40]

This reminded captains that success in battle depended on handling of the guns; Royal Navy captains had to take gunnery drills seriously to keep up a rate of fire and accuracy needed to compete with the Americans, and to that end were ordered to instil regular gunnery drill and to record exercises in the ship's logs.[41]

Surprisingly, the Admiralty had always taken a hands-off approach to naval gunnery in the past. Official regulations required that Royal Navy captains would carry out gunnery drills but had never mandated specific

39 Gardner, *Frigates of the Napoleonic Wars*, pp.110–115.

40 Admiral Sir John Warren, RN, Standing Order on the North American station, Bermuda, 6 March 1813, *Naval War of 1812*, Vol.2, p.59.

41 Martin Bibbins, 'A gunnery zealot: Broke's scientific contribution to naval warfare', in Tim Voelcker (ed.), *Broke of the Shannon and the War of 1812* (Barnsley: Seaforth Publishing, 2013), p.114.

requirements as to how often or in what matter that gunnery drill was instituted, and often included vague language that gave captains leeway to neglect gunnery drill whenever conditions were not 'convenient.' As such, different ships under different captains were kept to different states of readiness for action. Some, like Commander Peake of HMS *Peacock*, had relied on pantomime exercises – carrying out all of the moves of loading and firing a gun without actually burning any of their limited and expensive supply of gunpowder. This often meant that inexperienced sailors would go into action and be shocked by the noise and commotion of a gunnery duel, which hampered their morale and effectiveness in action. Confusion on board a ship in as cramped a space as a gun deck was not conducive to safety or efficiency.[42] Others, like Philip Broke or Cuthbert Collingwood, insisted on regular, efficient, and meticulous gunnery practice in their ships, meaning that their crews were always in top fighting shape. Most Royal Navy officers existed somewhere between the two, which meant that the actual effectiveness of British gun crews varied widely from ship to ship. *Peacock*'s abysmal gunnery had proved a decisive factor in her defeat, and the fact that Lambert in *Java* had been unable to properly exercise his men (with the overcrowding and the difficulty of training the new hands in seamanship, he had probably judged it was not 'convenient' to carry out regular drills) may not have helped her in action against *Constitution*. The sub-standard gunnery that could be found in ships of the fleet had not been much of a problem over the last two decades; however bad some Royal Navy ships' crews were in gunnery, the average performance from the French and Spanish navies were even worse. Even in the close approach to the Franco-Spanish fleet at Trafalgar, where the allies arguably performed at their best, the leading British ships suffered little damage.[43] The United States Navy, however, was not the navy of Revolutionary and Napoleonic France; men like Philip Broke recognised this, and hoped that the American Navy would prove a more difficult and therefore honourable opponent. In addition to their larger crews with more sea training and their larger ships with heavier guns, the young United States Navy took gunnery training and preparation very seriously.[44] They did not have an established reputation of victory and invincibility; but they did have lots of powder and guns to fire.

In response to myriad attacks on the government from the press and from the opposition in Parliament, Melville issued a series of directives to change naval policy in North America. Warren was ordered to do his utmost to effectively destroy the American Navy, either through the use of overwhelming force in the form of powerful squadrons or through blockades. He was to avoid risking the loss of additional frigates and to conduct naval

42 Michael Duffy, 'The gunnery at Trafalgar: training, tactics, or temperament?', *Journal for Maritime Research*, 7:1 (2005), pp.140–145.

43 Duffy, 'Gunnery at Trafalgar', p.145.

44 Robert W. Neeser, 'American naval gunnery: past and present', *The North American Review*, 196:685 (1912), pp.780–782.

operations only where he judged that success was 'a reasonable prospect.'[45] Simple enough, but the Admiralty had also ordered Warren to do his utmost to harass and disrupt the enemy's shipping and operations, which in itself required an amount of risk that the Admiralty was not willing to take.[46] Frigates were no longer expected to sail alone, and squadrons were to include ships of the line as often as possible.[47]

This established an unofficial directive that Royal Navy frigate captains were not to challenge the enemy's heavy frigates alone, a sentiment later clarified in March through correspondence between Melville and Warren. The First Lord wrote to Warren to state that British frigate captains should be aware that they were

> not only not expected to attack those large American Ships, but that their voluntarily engaging in such an encounter would be considered here in the same light as if they did not avoid an action with a Line of Battle Ship.[48]

This was followed by an order issued on 10 July in which the Admiralty stated that under no circumstances should any frigate captains 'attempt to engage, single handed, the larger Class of American Ships, which though they may be called Frigates, are of a size, Complement and weight of Metal much beyond that Class, and more resembling Line of Battle Ships.'[49] From March onwards, Admiralty policy was that British frigate captains should consider the three heavy American frigates as ships of the line and avoid combat with them. One-on-one fights against USS *Constitution*, USS *President*, and USS *United States* like the ones fought by *Guerriere*, *Macedonian*, and *Java* were forbidden to Britain's frigate captains. In the wake of events over the previous year this policy was necessary, but that did not make it palatable to the Royal Navy. It ran counter to its fighting spirit and counter to the confidence and perception of invincibility that had developed over the last two decades of conflict.[50] Just the accusation against a Royal Navy captain of failing to bring an enemy to action was enough to tarnish a career; an anonymous accusation against Captain Philip Carteret of this sort was enough for Carteret to request a formal court martial to clear him of the anonymous charge.[51]

45 Morriss, *Cockburn*, pp.87–88; McCranie, *Utmost Gallantry*, p.87.

46 McCranie, *Utmost Gallantry*, p.87.

47 Admiral John Warren to Secretary John Croker, *San Domingo*, at Sea, 5 January 1813, *The Naval War of 1812*, Vol.2, p.16; Dudley, *Splintering the Wooden Wall*, pp.80–81.

48 Melville to Warren, 23 March 1813, NMM, WAR/82/56–64: quoted in McCranie, *Utmost Gallantry*, p.121.

49 First Secretary of the Admiralty John Croker to Station Commanders in Chief, 10 July 1813, *Naval War of 1812*, Vol.2, p.183.

50 McCranie, *Utmost Gallantry*, p.122.

51 'S.T.' to the Editor, in *The Naval Chronicle for 1814: Containing a General and Biographical History of The Royal Navy of the United Kingdom; With a Variety of Original Papers on Nautical Subjects*, Vol.31: January to June (London: Joyce Gold, 1814), pp.39–41.

'We are all very angry': reactions of the captains of the North American squadron

Whereas the Admiralty, the flag officers in North America, and the wider press were deeply concerned about the firepower of America's heavy frigates, this anxiety did not seem as pressing within the community of naval officers, particularly those serving in the North American squadron. The dispatches and defences of the defeated commanders of *Guerriere*, *Macedonian*, *Java*, and *Peacock*, as well as the findings of their courts martial, indicate that the Navy's officers were more concerned about other factors relating to the Americans. Much was made of the importance of fighting at close action and of the superior complement of the Americans, those extra men giving them a significant advantage in small arms fire. Fortune was also pressing, as it was largely attributed by the defeated officers and their judges to the dismasting of the lost ships, placing them in a position where defeat was all but assured. Elements of this view can be seen in accounts from shipboard officers of the period, both within and outside the North American squadron.

In response to the press hysteria regarding the 1812 losses, Captain William Tremlett, a frigate captain whose career was cut short by the sinking of his ship after a very successful cruise, wrote to the *Chronicle* to set the record straight:

> Much has been said about their superior weight of metal, and size of the vessels, but in my opinion more than is necessary; although it certainly assists; but every naval officer must know, that in action one good active seaman is at least equal to three landsmen, or such poor creatures as are to be found in every one of our men of war.[52]

For Tremlett, the superior broadsides of the American frigates were only assisting factors in the losses; seamanship mattered far more. The larger and better trained crews of the American Navy were a decisive advantage, giving the Americans an edge in sailing, manoeuvring, gunnery, and small arms fire.[53] Captain Sir William Dillon, in his published narrative, emphasised the importance of the size and skill of the American crews:

> Accustomed as our Navy had been to triumph on all occasions where a foe was met on anything like equal terms—and sometimes when he was vastly superior—these measures were necessary. … But the American frigates were far superior in every respect: the hulls were larger, and they had heavier metal, with crews of at least 500 picked men—no boys—whereas the crew of one of our 46-gun frigates never exceeded 285, including boys. Consequently, we were obliged to improve the size of our ships and increase the number of their crews.[54]

52 William Henry Tremlett to the Editor, Bath, 21 May 1813, *Naval Chronicle*, Vol.28, p.465.

53 Tremlett to the Editor, 21 May 1813, *Naval Chronicle*, Vol.28, p.465.

54 Sir William Henry Dillon (ed. Michael A. Lewis), *A Narrative of My Professional Adventures* (London: Navy Records Society, 1953), Vol.2, p.278.

Dillon considered the heavier armament and hull size to both be important factors in the losses, as had Carden and Chads. Yet he also acknowledged that, against Britain's European foes, the Royal Navy had triumphed over enemies with 'vastly superior' armament. What the Americans had that their French counterparts did not were exceptionally trained 'picked' crews, manning ships superior in both size and armament.

The personal journal of Henry Edward Napier, a lieutenant on board the 38-gun HMS *Nymphe* during her blockading cruise off New England in 1814, also expressed the navy's view of greater importance of crew size and training over broadside weight. One entry examined the importance of crew size in depth, and he explained that whereas the complement of HMS *Nymphe* was only 300, the complement of the similarly armed USS *Congress* was upwards of 400. This advantage, he explained, allowed the Americans to deploy a much larger body of disposable men in action. In his view, this advantage was sufficient to explain the losses in 1812: 'I say when this is considered... people perhaps may cease to wonder at the Americans having capture so many of our ships, as, the *Java* excepted, none of those ships had even 300 men and officers.'[55]

Tremlett's letter also highlighted the importance of gunnery practice and its impact on the British losses. He asserted that in each case American gunnery was superior in accuracy and rapidity, since their

> seamen have been more exercised in firing at a mark than ours – their government having given their commanders leave to exercise whenever they think proper, and to fire away as much ammunition as they please. By the rules of our navy, we are not allowed a sufficient quantity of powder in one year to exercise the people one month (notwithstanding we try, by every means in our power, to add to this allowance).[56]

The superior gunnery was demonstrated by the fact that, in each action, the British suffered much higher casualties and more extensive rigging damage. He also highlighted that it was the heavy losses and dismasting of the ship that caused each surrender. Because of the enemy's advantage in gunnery, the British ships were reduced to a state where they could no longer mount an effective resistance: 'most of our ships have been obliged to surrender, in consequence of their having been dismasted, and not being able to avoid being *raked*.' His proposed solution was not for Britain's fifth-rate frigates to avoid action, but instead for them to be provided with sweeps to give them some ability to manoeuvre when dismasted.[57]

It should be noted that, at the time, Tremlett was on half-pay and likely eager for a further appointment into active service, so it was in his interest to engage in the public debate on the American frigates. He may also have

55 Henry Edward Napier (ed. Walter Muir Whitehill), *New England Blockaded in 1814: the Journal of Henry Edward Napier, Lieutenant in HMS* Nymphe (Salem, MA: Peabody Museum, 1939), p.13.

56 Tremlett to the Editor, 21 May 1813, *Naval Chronicle*, Vol.28, p.465.

57 Tremlett to the Editor, 21 May 1813, *Naval Chronicle*, Vol.28, p.465.

been motivated by frustration with the Admiralty, expressing this through an attack on the meagre allowance of gunpowder provided to Royal Navy ships. Dillon, on the other hand, published his narrative decades after the fact, and was interested in writing an interesting account which would cement his professional reputation. Unlike Tremlett and Dillon's examples, however, Napier's journal was a more personal account and therefore not intended for publication. This suggests that his words and viewpoints were unaccompanied by biases seen in other public works but accurately reflected his own views. In fact, he included a scathing rebuke of Admiral Warren, his commander-in-chief:

> We are, however, very apt to judge of the conduct of our commanders too hastily, without making any allowance for secret reasons, which frequently are the cause of many apparent absurdities. The conduct of Sir John Warren, since he has commanded on this station, has been so very inexplicable that *his* reasons must be *very secret* indeed, as there is no a person able to form a conjecture on the subject; so secret are these reasons, that some people even begin to fancy he never had any. The American papers assert upon good authority that *Lady Warren* is immediately expected out to supersede him in command.[58]

He also attacked his own captain, stating that he was 'ashamed' of his conduct for holding an American fisherman for ransom. Such remarks, if made public, would have been career-ending, even for an officer as well-connected as Napier. No naval officer in his right mind would have put such words to paper unless he intended that no one would see his journal.[59]

The attack on Admiral Warren further highlighted Napier's views on the merits of frigate size and armaments. In the first entry of the journal, Lieutenant Napier expressed his frustration that Warren has prioritised refitting sloops and schooners in Halifax while *Nymphe*, 'a frigate of fifty guns,' was left waiting in port while 'some of the larger American frigates were at sea.'[60] *Nymphe* was a 38-gun frigate armed with 18-pounders, but like *Guerriere* and *Macedonian* carried closer to 50 guns in all. Strangely, though, he also referred to the soon-to-be launched USS *Guerriere*, a heavy frigate armed like her namesake's captor and with over 50 guns, as 'a new fifty-gun frigate.'[61] *Nymphe* and *Guerriere* were not of the same class, yet Napier used the same terminology to refer to both.

Nowhere in Napier's journal did he distinguish, either in the number or in the calibre of guns, between the disparity in force of a standard British fifth-rate like *Nymphe* and the American heavy frigates like *Constitution* and *Guerriere*. The fact that *Constitution* was a formidable opponent was only mentioned in passing when he stated that the new HMS *Leander*, a purpose-built 58-gun frigate, was 'a great deal more than a match for the

58 Napier, *New England Blockaded in 1814*, p.3.
59 Napier, *New England Blockaded in 1814*, pp.38–49.
60 Napier, *New England Blockaded in 1814*, p.3.
61 Napier, *New England Blockaded in 1814*, p.9.

Constitution.'[62] Napier's frustration with the admiral stemmed itself from his view that *Nymphe* would be of more use to the service out searching for *Constitution* than waiting in port, and throughout the journal he stated that he was quite eager to bring a ship like *Constitution* to action.[63] His ship was frequently on the lookout for the American heavy frigates, particularly *Constitution*, of which he heard 'various reports concerning her and none to be depended on.'[64] Still, his journal showed that he followed the reports closely. Whether in company with another frigate or acting alone, Napier suggested that *Nymphe* was eager to bring *Constitution* to action. In response to one rumour that *Constitution* carried a furnace for producing heated shot, Napier reflected: 'if she comes out and uses them, we have got a Roland for her Oliver.'[65]

Over all, Napier was frustrated by the lack of action and the passive strategy his captain seemed to be taking. This frustration motivated his attack on Warren and is reflected throughout the journal, as he frequently complains about inactivity and bad weather on blockade. *Nymphe* could frequently observe American frigates in harbours under the protection of shore batteries and forts, and several times he complained that an attack by boats might be mounted if not for the current timid strategy. At one point *Nymphe*, in company with several other warships, did encounter *Constitution*, and her escape particularly irked him:

> By the American officers' accounts one of the frigates might easily succeeded in bringing her to action with advantage, while the other would have reached her on another tack. The Americans blame us much for not doing it, and it certainly seems extraordinary that they did not. Without some risk, some dash, very little will ever be done in the navy; prudence has never yet answered. Even if you fail, the attempt will gain you the applause of Englishmen.[66]

Napier was willing to take risks, seeing it as the way to win glory at home and professional advancement. Instead he saw little action in his cruise off New England. In the privacy of his journal he could vent his frustrations on the strategy and tactics employed by his commanders and their seeming unwillingness to take the sort of risks inherent to the Navy's fighting spirit.

The correspondence of Captain Philip Broke was similarly personal and not intended for publication. Throughout the period Broke kept up a constant correspondence with his wife, and to her he vented similar frustrations as Napier. Unlike Napier, though, Broke was closely connected to the events in 1812. He had served from the beginning, continuously obsessed with bringing an enemy frigate to action and with punishing the Americans for starting the war:

62 Napier, *New England Blockaded in 1814*, p.37.
63 Napier, *New England Blockaded in 1814*, pp.3, 23, 31.
64 Napier, *New England Blockaded in 1814*, p.35.
65 Napier, *New England Blockaded in 1814*, p.23.
66 Napier, *New England Blockaded in 1814*, pp.23–24.

> I would give all our prizes for an American frigate, they are fighting in a bad way my Loo, and I shall feel a satisfaction in beating them… every overture of kindness we make to them, they consider as a submission, and become the more insolent to us: a year's war will tame them much, they have not yet felt our naval power.[67]

The dismal progress of the war was personal for Broke; *Constitution* had escaped from his squadron early in the war, and in consequence of that escape she later captured *Guerriere*, a ship from Broke's squadron. After acting as a judge in Dacres's court martial, Broke told his wife that

> We are all very angry at hearing that the American frigate *Constitution*, whom our squadron hunted so lately has taken one of our frigates and burned her. However this will all forward the chance of *Shannon*'s making an honorable game of it as the enemy will be *saucy* now.[68]

He informed her that Dacres was 'wishing only another frigate to go to *take his revenge*.'[69] By the end of November, he informed his wife that 'now the unlucky events of *Guerriere* and *Frolic*'s actions bind us all to the service until we have restored the splendor of our flag.'[70] The collective anger among the naval officers had transformed into a drive for vengeance as the news of more defeats reached Halifax and the squadron. On 8 January, Broke told his wife that '*Macedonian* must be avenged, or the Americans will be *quite too saucy*.'[71] Initially, Broke considered the boldness that *Constitution*'s victory had generated in the American Navy to be an advantage to the British, as they would be more likely to seek action – with *Macedonian*'s loss, however, Broke had reconsidered. In his eyes, the Americans were growing more and more confident without any checks on their naval successes. As Broke saw that confidence grow, so too did his desire to avenge his fellow captains and to uphold British honour.

In December 1812, Broke drew attention to the value of Britain's honour: '*Honor* is a jewel of more value than whole fleets & armies & public prejudice waits not to enquire into the particulars of a defeat where the result is so mortifying.'[72] He added in February that, 'Had the Americans been as heartily beaten at sea as they have been by land, we might now have retired with honor.'[73] His sense of duty and honour was both underscored and complicated by his sense of duty to his family.[74] Broke was a deeply homesick man, torn between his desire to return home and notions of duty and honour. His letters in 1813 emphasised a caveat to his desire to return home – his

67 SRO, HA 93/9/112, Philip Broke to Louisa Broke, 14 September 1812.
68 SRO, HA 93/9/113, Philip Broke to Louisa Broke, 22 September 1812.
69 SRO, HA93/9/115, Philip Broke to Louisa Broke, 29 September 1812.
70 SRO, HA 93/9/124, Philip Broke to Louisa Broke, 26 November 1812.
71 SRO, HA 93/9/132, Philip Broke to Louisa Broke, 8 January 1813.
72 SRO, HA 93/9/128, Philip Broke to Louisa Broke, 14 December 1812.
73 SRO, HA 93/9134, Philip Broke to Louisa Broke, 4 February 1813.
74 Ellen Gill, 'Letters to his wife "Loo"', in Tim Voelcker (ed.), *Broke of the Shannon and the War of 1812* (Barnsley: Seaforth Publishing, 2013), pp.86–89.

Constitution vs *Guerriere*, 19 August 1812
USS *Constitution* (top); HMS *Guerriere* (bottom). *Constitution* and her sisters were designed to vastly overpower their European counterparts, but few in the British sphere considered these ships a real threat until the losses in 1812. Original Artwork by Florian Richter © Helion and Company.

Wasp versus *Frolic*, 18 October 1812
USS *Wasp* (top); HMS *Frolic* (bottom). Though mounting relatively equal armament, inefficient British gunnery and prior rigging damage gave the Americans a devastating advantage in the brief sloop action.
Original Artwork by Florian Richter © Helion and Company.

United States versus *Macedonian*, 25 October 1812
USS *United States* (top); HMS *Macedonian* (bottom). *Macedonian*'s captain, John Carden, once boasted to Stephen Decatur of *United States* that the 24-pounder guns of the American ship were unwieldy, and the smaller 18-pounders of the British ship were superior. A few hours on 25 October proved otherwise.
Original Artwork by Florian Richter © Helion and Company.

Shannon versus *Chesapeake*, 1 June 1813
USS *Chesapeake* (top); HMS *Shannon* (bottom). After six defeats, the British were desperate for a win. *Shannon* and *Chesapeake* were as evenly matched as one could hope, and the resulting victory reinvigorated a nation. Original Artwork by Florian Richter © Helion and Company.

Pelican versus *Argus*, 14 August 1813
USS *Argus* (top); HMS *Pelican* (bottom). Just two months after Broke's spectacular victory, Britons were greeted by another win, when *Pelican* captured an American warship in the heart of British waters.
Original Artwork by Florian Richter © Helion and Company.

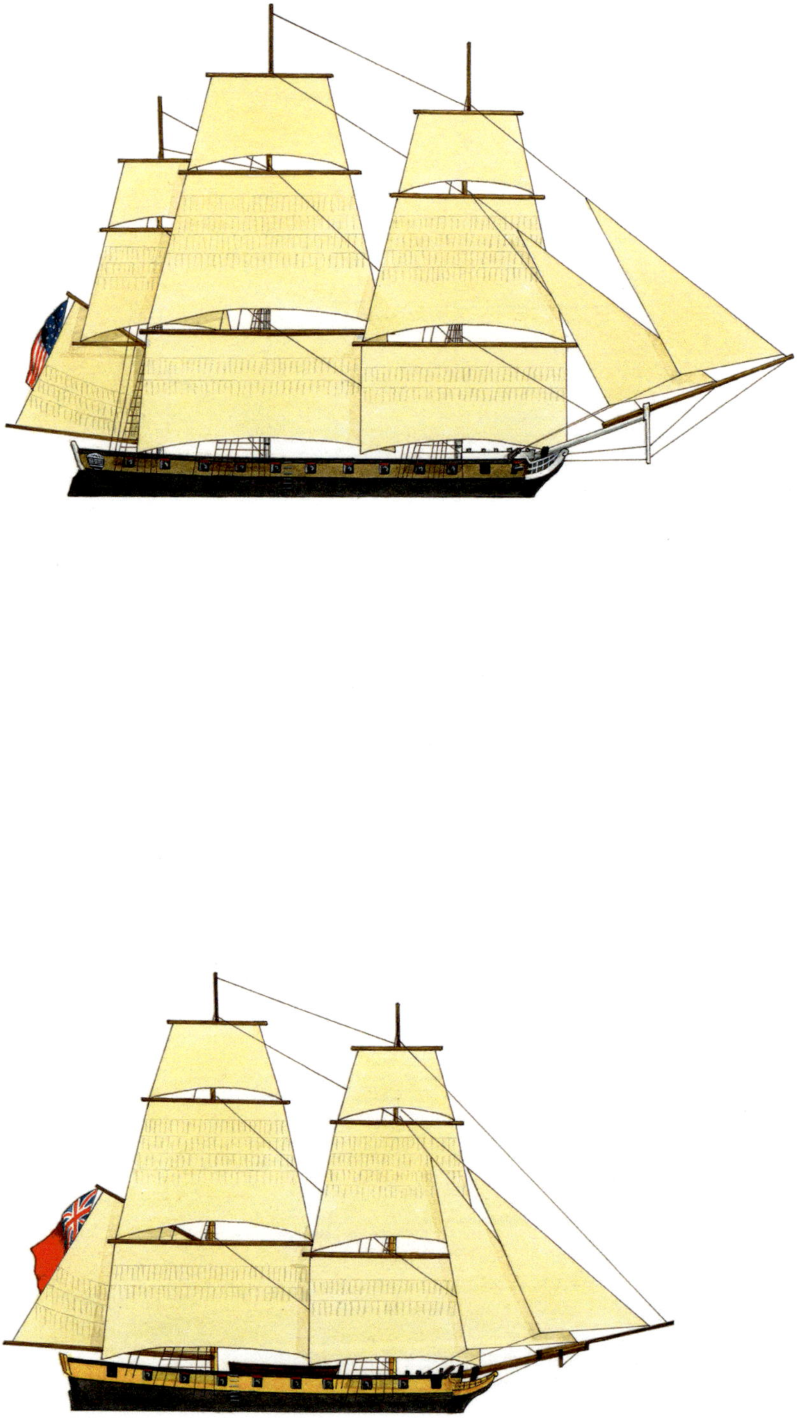

Wasp versus *Reindeer*, 28 June 1814
USS *Wasp* (top); HMS *Reindeer* (bottom). USS *Wasp*, built in 1813 and named after the victor over *Frolic*, captured two *Cruizer* class brig-sloops during her spectacular yet ill-fated European cruise.
Original Artwork by Florian Richter © Helion and Company.

Capture of the *President*, 15 January 1815
USS *President* (top); HMS *Endymion* (bottom). Nearly all of the action that led to *President*'s capture occurred between her and the all-black *Endymion*, whose crack gunnery smashed the prized American frigate to pieces. Original Artwork by Florian Richter © Helion and Company.

Constitution's last adversaries, action of 20 February 1815
HMS *Levant* (top); HMS *Cyane* (bottom); compare with profile of USS *Constitution* in Plate 1. The capture of *Levant* and *Cyane* was perhaps the most outmatched during the war. With her longer ranged guns, *Constitution* easily defeated each ship in detail. Original Artwork by Florian Richter © Helion and Company.

wish to retire home with honour: 'I shall at any time feel contented with the attainment of my only object when I first embarked – an opportunity of retiring honourably, with the consciousness of having done my duty as an Englishman.'[75] While searching for the *President*, he again emphasised the connection between honour and his desire to return home: 'They may prove our best friends yet, and favour me with an opportunity of retiring with honour to my gentle wife.'[76] His personal, professional, and familial duties were tied into his reputation in the Navy. As much as Broke wanted to return home, he sought an honourable action at sea before he could do so.[77] Only action against an evenly matched, or superior, opponent could provide that honour. The Royal Navy's culture and fighting spirit, and Broke's own honour, demanded it.

The grim events of 1812 only cemented this longing. His desire for personal honour was accompanied by a growing desire for vengeance and for restoring the honour of the Royal Navy as a whole. According to one source, Broke, in a conversation with a Halifax bookstore owner, proudly declared that he was going to Boston to challenge *Constitution*, saying he would counter her heavier armament by closing quickly and boarding.[78] It was no longer a personal matter of Broke's honour, but a matter of the honour of the entire British Navy. Philip Broke was an excellent example of an officer whose longing for a single-ship victory bordered on obsession, but he was hardly an exception. Other similarly minded officers, yearning for the chance for glory, prize money, reputation, and advancement, must also have been outraged by the losses in 1812.

Similar attitudes attributed to Captain Alexander Kerr were expressed in the *Naval Chronicle* edition for January and February 1813. In the account, Kerr, commanding the 40-gun, 18-pounder frigate HMS *Acasta*, was depicted assembling his men and demonstrating his determination to avenge the loss of *Guerriere*:

> Captain Kerr, placing a due confidence in the largest, the best officered, and the best manned frigate in the service, has been roaming about for his prey for several months, and we only wish him fairly alongside the *President*, *Constitution*, or the *United States*. On receiving the accounts of the capture of the *Guerriere*, Captain Kerr assembled his crew, and addressed them as follows; – 'My lads, it is with a distress which I cannot sufficiently depict to you, that I inform you of the capture of the *Guerriere*, by the *Constitution* American frigate. We are going to sea, and in the largest and best armed frigate in the service. Hear my determination – I am determined never to strike the colours of the *Acasta* – My mind is made up – What say you, my boys?' The exclamation of – 'To the bottom!' and three truly British cheers, followed his words.[79]

75 SRO, HA93/9/138, Philip Broke to Louisa Broke, 14 April 1813.

76 SRO, HA93/9/139, Philip Broke to Louisa Broke, 5 May 1813.

77 Voelcker, 'Victories or distractions', p.70; Gill, 'Letters to his wife', pp.86–89.

78 Thomas H. Raddall, *Halifax: Warden of the North* (Halifax, NS: Nimbus Publishing, 2010), p.141.

79 'Naval Anecdotes', *Naval Chronicle*, Vol.29, p.189.

Here Kerr was depicted as an officer determined to bring one of the heavy American frigates to action, with an equally enthusiastic crew. Without additional documents to verify the accuracy of the account, it is difficult to determine how well it reflected Kerr's own views. Even assuming some or all of it was inaccurate, one can conclude that this sort of boastful display of naval zeal was very appealing to the readers of the *Chronicle* and to members of the Royal Navy. The sentiment reflected that of Broke and Napier in their personal accounts, suggesting that Kerr's holding such an opinion was not entirely out of the realm of possibility.

There are also the letters submitted to newspapers in Halifax, and later to the *Chronicle*, from Captain Pigot and the crew of HMS *Orpheus* and Captain Hickey of HMS *Atalante*. *Orpheus*'s captain submitted a letter addressed by his crew to the senior lieutenant in response to a rumour that had appeared in Halifax:

> A report having been circulated, that the seamen and marines of HMS *Orpheus*, now lying at Halifax, commanded by Hugh Pigot, Esq. would act cowardly, they are very much hurt at the thought of such a representation respecting them, and they now beg the liberty to acquaint Mr. Fayrer, for the information of Captain Pigot, that they are anxious to have it in their power to shew their loyal disposition in defence of their King and Country... their determination is to fight against their enemies, to sustain the honour and glory of Great Britain, or die in the attempt.[80]

In their letter to Lieutenant Fayrer, the representatives (who stated they spoke for the entire crew) displayed their distress at being called cowards by the Americans and countered those rumours with a zealous assurance that they were determined to fight in the name of their country.

Captain Hickey of HMS *Atalante* also sent in a letter composed by non-commissioned members of his crew in response to that of *Orpheus*, expressing that 'the crew of the *Atalante* do most heartily coincide in their comrades' representation, and their loyal disposition for their King and country.'[81] Having read the letter composed on behalf of the crew of *Orpheus*, the Atalantes responded with their own letter that displayed their determination to fight. This account was seemingly intended to show a solidarity with the *Orpheus*'s crew, but it also may have been intended to exceed them in zeal. The Atalantes added that they would never surrender their ship, 'even to a superiority of force.'[82]

Both Captain Hickey and Pigot likely submitted these letters to demonstrate their gallantry and zeal to the Halifax community, and later sent them to the *Chronicle* to reach the naval audience back home. Officially they only wished to 'do justice to the character' of their respective crews, but

80 Collins *et al.* (crew of HMS *Orpheus*) to Lieutenant Fayrer, *Naval Chronicle*, Vol.29, pp.195–196; NSA, Microfilm Reel 8172, *Royal Gazette*, Wednesday 3 February 1813, 13:631; NSA, *Acadian Recorder*, Saturday 23 January 1813, 1:2 https://novascotia.ca/archives/newspapers/archives.asp?ID=753.

81 NSA, Microfilm Reel 8172, *Royal Gazette*, Wednesday 3 February 1813, 13:631.

82 NSA, Microfilm Reel 8172, *Royal Gazette*, Wednesday 3 February 1813, 13:631.

nonetheless displaying the determination, patriotism, and zeal of their crew in response to the loss of *Guerriere* reflected well on their own leadership. Their British crews responded to the threat posed by the heavy American frigates with the fighting spirit of the Royal Navy, which demonstrated to newsreaders that Hickey and Pigot had imposed a culture on their crew that reflected that of their officers; the men of *Orpheus* and *Atalante* were anxious to get into action with the enemy, and that reflected the determination of their captains and officers to fight the enemy in fair combat, to avenge their fellow captains and their Navy as a whole.

Fair combat in single-ship actions were very rare opportunities for naval officers, and that rarity only made them more enticing. Winning single-ship actions was one of the great motivators of naval officers; they provided honour and glory in the public sphere, increased chances of promotion and appointments professionally, and provided fortunes in prize money. Broke was not alone in his obsession with fighting such an action.[83] The officers in the North American squadron were no exception, but their chances were frustrated by Admiralty policy. Being ordered to cruise in pairs of small squadrons made finding a lone enemy and bringing them to battle virtually impossible. To count as a single-ship victory, all other ships had to be out of sight when the enemy struck their colours. After all, even the presence of an additional enemy on the horizon could impact the decisions and options available to a captain in an action. With the change in policy, captains were awarded fewer opportunities for the coveted independent cruise, and so had fewer opportunities of taking rich prizes or fighting lone enemies one-on-one.[84] There was no glory in capturing a vastly outmatched enemy, either for the Americans or the British, but the evenly matched fights that zealous officers so coveted were increasingly rare.

As the War of 1812 developed, single-ship action was increasingly linked to matters of honour and (for the British) professional vengeance. However, seeking this revenge came at the expense of explicit Admiralty instructions, as the captains of fifth-rates were forbidden from engaging the American heavy frigates – but this mattered little to the Royal Navy. Yet, as John Marshall, a half-pay lieutenant following the war, stated in the preface to his seminal *Royal Naval Biography*:

> Every person is aware that it is not always in the events most important to the country, that the greatest skill and courage have been exhibited; and yet, it is only when bravery and superior tactics have been displayed in acts of great public interest, that the reputation they deserved has been bestowed.[85]

It was understood in the Royal Navy that the acts of great public interest which displayed the 'greatest skill and courage' were not necessarily those that best served the country's strategic interests. The Royal Navy itself was

83 Wareham, *Star Captains*, p.160; Wareham, 'Duration of frigate command', p.420; Allen, 'British Navy rules', pp.204–230.

84 Wareham, 'Duration of frigate command', p.420; Allen, 'British Navy rules', pp.204–230.

85 *Royal Naval Biography*, Vol.1, Part I, p.xi.

built around this contradiction: the system of incentives in the Navy, such as the honours and prize money associated with single-ship actions, were balanced by the competitive market for appointments and promotions. Officers were expected to be zealous and active in the service, and seeking action and raiding enemy shipping provided professional, societal, and financial enrichment. At the same time, seeking action and prize money at the expense of one's orders was discouraged and punished. Wartime officers had to navigate the contradictory values of duty and honour inherent in the King's service.[86]

In the United States Navy, too, success in single-ship actions was particularly important. Given the fact that the United States Navy was dwarfed by the North American squadron and could not compete with the Royal Navy as a whole, its officers turned to commerce raiding and single-ship actions to carry out the war. Both had some strategic merit, but only victory in single-ship actions could satisfy the American officers' need for recognition and honour. Given the rarity of encountering lone enemies at sea, captains from both navies turned to issuing formal challenges in an attempt to 'propagate or redeem their personal or national honour through engagements between similar warships.'[87] In many ways it was an extension of the duelling culture prominent in both naval communities. While technically illegal, both the Royal Navy and United States Navy overlooked duellists even in cases when officers were killed. Prearranged duels over matters of honour had long been established in military and naval culture in Europe and the European New World, and in the conditions of the Napoleonic Wars and the War of 1812, these traditions were translated into the theatre of war.[88]

In 1793, American papers had been fascinated by a challenge issued by the captain of HMS *Boston* to the captain of the French frigate *Embuscade* and the action that followed. Over a decade later, American papers speculated on a possible similar challenge again involving *Boston*. This unique occurrence took on a life of its own in the Anglo-American conflict that followed, and several high-profile challenges were issued throughout the war.

Almost immediately upon the outbreak of war, American papers began excitedly reporting on challenges issued by British frigate captains. In August, a paper reported a challenge issued by Captain James Dacres, sent ashore via American merchantman, challenging 'any frigate in the American navy to single combat.'[89] Soon afterwards, another paper reported a challenge from Dacres directly to John Rodgers of USS *President*.[90] The provenance of either challenge is not entirely clear, and some contemporaries doubted the validity of the first challenge that appeared. But the second one appeared more plausible.[91] Such an act certainly fits with Dacres's behaviour in the

86 Allen, 'British Navy rules', pp.204–230.

87 Kevin D. McCranie, 'Dueling with warships to satisfy honour: the use of naval challenges in the War of 1812', *International Journal of Maritime History*, 25:2 (2013), p.61.

88 McCranie, 'Dueling with warships', pp.66–67.

89 *Columbian Phoenix* (Providence, RI), 12 September 1812, quoted in McCranie, 'Dueling with warships', pp.61–62.

90 McCranie, 'Dueling with warships', pp.61–63.

91 McCranie, 'Dueling with warships', p.63.

first months of the conflict; Dacres had 'Not the Little Belt' painted onto his fore topsail, wearing this badge into action due to his animosity towards USS *President*'s firing on *Little Belt* before the outbreak of war. It was reported that Rodgers had mistaken the 20-gun ship for Dacres's *Guerriere*, and so Dacres firmly believed he had a score to settle.

The American papers loved the story, especially as it appeared just before *Guerriere* was destroyed by USS *Constitution*, and before long another such challenge had appeared. Captain James Yeo of HMS *Southampton*, according to the *Philadelphia Democratic Press*, sent a message into Philadelphia to Captain Porter of USS *Essex*, declaring that 'he would be glad to have a *tête-à-tête* anywhere between the Capes Delaware and Havanna, where he would have the pleasure to break his own sword over his damn'd head, and put him down forward in irons.'[92] It has been suggested that the challenge stemmed either from Yeo's outrage over *Alert*'s capture by the vastly larger *Essex*, or from an incident in New York harbour just after the outbreak of war: Porter had allowed his crew to seize a British sailor on board *Essex*, who was promptly tarred and feathered before fleeing to the protection of the local police. Porter's actions were sternly rebuked by the Secretary of the Navy, among others, and several historians have suggested that Yeo's outrage at the treatment of a British subject motivated the challenge.[93]

Porter's acceptance of the duel was reported by the same paper, but no such action ever occurred. Whether this challenge was genuine is ambiguous. McCranie argues that the challenge itself was likely fraudulent, issued by Porter in an attempt to repair his reputation after he was officially rebuked for the tarring and feathering incident. Some of the particulars of the challenge itself suggest it may not be authentic; for one thing, *Southampton* appeared to be operating much further south than Porter was, and the wording of the challenge was suspiciously similar to an earlier one issued by Dacres.[94] Others, however, assert that it was a genuine challenge issued by Yeo. *Southampton* was escorting prizes to Bermuda at the time Porter finally set sail from Philadelphia, and so was unable to intercept *Essex* and carry out the duel as a result of poor planning.[95] It was certainly very convenient for Porter, whose reputation and honour had been tarnished by the incident, and the appearance of an angry British foil suited his interests. Most likely the challenge did not come from Yeo, at least not in such a harsh and direct fashion. The genesis of the 'challenge' may have been comments passed between Yeo and passengers on the American merchantman *Lion* that he hoped to encounter the American frigate, and either through the concoction of an overly excited press or by Porter alone his wish was transformed into

92 'Naval defiance: from the *Philadelphia Democratic Press*', *Naval Chronicle*, Vol.28, 372.

93 McCranie, 'Dueling with warships', pp.61–63; William James, *Naval History of Great Britain: From the Declaration of War by France in 1793 to the Accession of George IV* (London: Macmillan and Co., 1902), Vol.6, pp.363–364; David F. Long, *Nothing too Daring: A Life of Commodore David Porter, 1780–1843* (Annapolis: Naval Institute Press, 1970), pp.69–70. Ben Hughes, *In Pursuit of the Essex: Heroism and Hubris on the High Seas in the War of 1812* (Annapolis, MD: Naval Institute Press, 2016), p.12.

94 McCranie, 'Dueling with warships', pp.65–66.

95 Hughes, *In Pursuit of the Essex*, pp.12–13.

that of the bullying Englishman attacking one of America's gallant captains.[96] In either case, Porter was later able to slip away from local Royal Navy forces undetected.

The next commander to issue such a challenge was Master Commandment James Lawrence, to his counterpart Greene of HMS *Bonne Citoyenne*. Bainbridge, Lawrence's superior, encouraged Lawrence's challenge as the British sloop was secure in a neutral port. Both were ship-rigged sloops carrying eighteen 32-pounder carronades, as equal of an action as either Lawrence or Greene could have wished for. However, Greene was anxious. He knew that USS *Constitution* was nearby, and while Lawrence issued an assurance that his ship would not get involved, he could not be sure that Lawrence was not setting a trap. Nor was it just his ship that was at stake; he was carrying half a million pounds worth of gold and silver that he could not risk falling into enemy hands.[97] Reluctantly, Greene formally declined the challenge, informing Lawrence that

> The result could not be long dubious and would terminate favourably to the ship which I have the honour to command, but I am equally convinced that Comm. Bainbridge could not swerve so much from the paramount duty he owes his country as to become an inactive spectator, and see a ship belonging to the very squadron under his orders fall into the hands of an enemy.[98]

In declining the challenge, Greene could not appear to be shrinking from a fair fight. His reputation, and that of the Royal Navy, was at stake. Questioning Bainbridge's intention was very clever; refusing such an invitation opened Greene to accusations of cowardice, but his refusal turned the question to Bainbridge's honour.[99] The reality, of course, was that issuing or accepting challenges always posed some danger. Greene risked not only the loss of his sloop, but also a fortune in British gold. Still, that risk came with the potential for great rewards.

In both the Royal Navy and the United States Navy, promotion was hard to come by – there were always more officers than positions available. Achieving the rank of captain became a challenge for officers in both navies, and it was widely recognised that the best way to earn promotion was through displays of gallantry through fighting an opponent of equal or greater force.[100] Lawrence understood this when he was passed over for promotion by *Constitution*'s first lieutenant, and that motivated his challenge to Greene. While he was frustrated by the refusal, he did earn the step to captain following his victory over *Peacock*. Further promotion was impossible in the United States Navy – the rank of commodore was only nominal and there were no admirals in the navy until the American Civil War – but recognition

96 McCranie, 'Dueling with warships', pp.65–66.

97 McCranie, 'Dueling with warships', pp.70–71; Lambert, *The Challenge*, Chapter Four; Daughan, *1812*, pp.140–141.

98 Green in Consul Hill to Captain Lawrence, 29 Dec 1812, quoted in McCranie, 'Dueling with warships', p.77.

99 McCranie, 'Dueling with warships', p.71.

100 McCranie, 'Dueling with warships', p.69.

and honour were no less important for Lawrence as a captain. Lawrence was frustrated at being given command over the 38-gun USS *Chesapeake* rather than one of the crack heavy frigates, and as a zealous officer he continued to seek public acknowledgement as a man of honour.

Curiously, by this period, personal honour was increasingly linked with the collective honour of the two navies at war. It was becoming a collective virtue as well as a personal one. Officers issued challenges not only to satisfy and propagate their own honour, but also to uphold the glory of their respective naval service as a whole. This was universally recognised, but the practice of issuing and accepting challenges was technically forbidden by both navies.[101] This was largely because of the great risk involved; the United States only had a handful of ships, and risking them in such a manner was dangerous, even if the Navy Department and the public loved the spoils of victory. The Royal Navy, too, was desperate to avoid further embarrassing losses to the Americans. Issuing and accepting challenges not only risked the loss of important ships but also jeopardised Britain's strategic mission. The Royal Navy's task was to neutralise the United States Navy. Yet more than one British officer during the course of the war violated their orders to issue such a challenge, and the most notable cases occurred off Boston in 1813.

101 McCranie, 'Dueling with warships', pp.67–69.

5

'Hope yet of an honourable encounter': Philip Broke, Thomas Capel, and the blockade of Boston

When Warren arrived in Halifax to assume command of the North American squadron, he did so with the intention of opening negotiations to end hostilities. These efforts proved fruitless, but still Warren and the Admiralty were eager to limit the scope of the conflict. Britain had not chosen to fight this war, and many in America were as unenthusiastic about the conflict as the British. New England, whose trade was closely linked with the British North American colonies and the wider British empire, was particularly angered by the conflict, and the British hoped that this distaste might lead to civil strife or even secessionism. For that reason, most of New England was untouched by British blockading forces early in the conflict.[1] Elsewhere along the American coasts, the Royal Navy's blockades began to take shape and take effect. In January, USS *Constellation* was forced to anchor in Norfolk after being trapped by the blockading squadron in the Hampton Roads, and remained there for the entire war. On 1 June, a squadron trapped Commodore Decatur with *United States*, *Macedonian*, and *Hornet* in New London, where they would remain for the rest of the war.[2] Where resources and geography allowed, the blockades proved very effective against American commerce, privateering, and warships, but the Royal Navy's success was not repeated everywhere.[3] The extent of America's coastline and the number of her ports made conducting a thorough blockade nearly impossible, allowing American privateers to continue operating.[4]

---

1 Dudley, *Splintering the Wooden Wall*, p.79.

2 McCranie, *Utmost Gallantry*, pp.96, 140–141.

3 Dudley, *Splintering the Wooden Wall*, p.72; Brian Arthur, *How Britain Won the War of 1812: The Royal Navy's Blockade of the United States, 1812–1815* (Woodbridge: Boydell Press, 2011), p.5; Drolet, 'North American squadron', pp.177–181.

4 Rodger, *Command of the Ocean*, p.569; Dudley, *Splintering the Wooden Wall*, p.72; Arthur, *How Britain*, p.5; Drolet, 'North American squadron', pp.177–181.

Numerous as they were, though, not every port along America's coast had the infrastructure or logistics to provide a base for the United States Navy effectively. Ports like Norfolk, Portsmouth, New York, and Boston contained the yards and supplies necessary to keep American naval vessels in operation. The Admiralty ordered Warren to conduct his forces to blockade those ports with the goal of bringing the United States Navy's operations to a halt. Just as it had done in Europe, the Admiralty wanted the Royal Navy to trap the enemy in their own bases.[5] By March 1813, Warren had been reinforced with additional ships, including fast 74s, that allowed him to station powerful blockading squadrons off Delaware, New York, Rhode Island, Boston, and the Chesapeake. Efforts off New York and New London proved effective, as did blockading squadrons operating off Norfolk in the Chesapeake, though other ports, such as Boston, proved more difficult to blockade.[6]

While Boston was situated in the heart of New England, which in 1812 and 1813 was virtually free from blockading forces, it was one of the United States' primary naval bases and so Britain's strategy demanded that the port be blockaded. In 1812, forces operating in the area conducted a blockade that was distant, ineffectual, and occasional; as a result, the port virtually remained open. The geography and weather patterns of Massachusetts Bay made blockading Boston difficult, and during the winter the problems were only exacerbated.[7] In their correspondence with Warren the Admiralty acknowledged the difficulties involved, but stressed the importance of watching the port nonetheless:

> it was not possible perhaps to have maintained a permanent watch on that Port, yet having as you state in your letter of the 5 Novr last precise information that Commodore Bainbridge was to sail at a given time, my Lords regret that it was not deemed practicable to proceed off that Port at a reasonable and safe distance from the land) and to have taken the chance at least of intercepting the Enemy if the weather should not have permitted you to blockade him.[8]

Accordingly, a squadron was dispatched to watch the area in February, but it failed to intercept USS *Constitution* as she returned from her victory over *Java*.[9]

Captain Broke, with *Shannon* and *Tenedos*, another 38-gun fifth-rate, were the first to arrive on station, followed soon after by the senior captain Thomas Bladen Capel, an experienced frigate captain who now commanded a remarkably fast 74, HMS *La Hogue*. Capel had enjoyed an active career and rapid promotion in his youth; he was first commissioned as a lieutenant in 1797 and was a post captain a year and a half later after serving on Nelson's

5 McCranie, *Utmost Gallantry*, pp.95–96, 116–117.
6 Dudley, *Splintering the Wooden Wall*, pp.79–89.
7 Drolet, 'North American squadron', pp.177–181; Dudley, *Splintering the Wooden Wall*, p.79; Lambert, *The Challenge*, Chapter 3.
8 'Croker to Warren, 20 March 1813', *Naval War of 1812*, Vol.2, pp.76–78.
9 Lambert, *The Challenge*, Chapter 3.

flagship at the Battle of the Nile.[10] In addition to serving with Nelson at his first independent victory, Capel served under him again as a frigate captain at Trafalgar, and so twice witnessed the devastating effectiveness of Nelson's aggressive efforts to seek action and his ferocious tactics. In addition to *Hogue*, *Shannon*, and *Tenedos*, Capel commanded another 74, another frigate, and two sloops.

The squadron kept a close watch on the activity inside Boston harbour and found there were four frigates anchored inside. Broke, who along with *Tenedos* kept watch on the harbour, observed that USS *Chesapeake*, which had just returned to port in April, was some time away from being ready for sea, and so was not judged an immediate threat. He also observed that USS *Constitution* was dismasted, undergoing extensive repair work following her recent return in March, and probably would not be ready for sea for many months. But two frigates did appear ready for sea – *President* and *Congress* – which were both preparing to sail under the command of Commodore John Rodgers. Capel's mission was to maintain his blockade of the port and oppose any attempt by the Americans to leave. Rather than follow the Admiralty's directives and prioritise the shutting down of American shipping, however, Capel and his captains opted for a riskier strategy.[11]

Blockade and Challenges off Boston

As Broke's reconnoitre of the port took shape, he began to formulate a plan. On 8 April, Broke told Captain Robert Oliver of HMS *Valiant*, the second ship of the line on station, that he thought 'if two of us show off Boston for a few days, *President* and *Congress* will turn out, provided no 74s are seen from the capes or pilot boats.'[12] Broke's excitement at such a prospect continued to build, and on the 14th he informed his wife that he was 'keeping now close with the land, we are constantly chasing or reconnoitering our enemy, or exercising ourselves in readiness to play our part well when he meets us,' adding that he hoped 'Shannon's campaign will soon be honourably terminated, though perhaps, the fear of our friends in the offing (*La Hogue* and *Valiant*) may render our antagonists cautious of meeting us.'[13] Broke's idea quickly took hold with the captains of the squadron, and most importantly with Capel himself. It was decided that *Shannon* and *Tenedos* would continue operating close inshore, and that the rest of the squadron would keep well out into the Bay of Massachusetts in the hopes that Commodore Rodgers would be induced to venture out with *President* and *Congress* to confront *Shannon* and *Tenedos*. While the genesis of the plan resided in Broke and his

---

10 Syrett and DiNardo, *Commissioned Sea Officers*, p.72; T.A. Heathcote, *Nelson's Trafalgar: Captains and Their Battles* (Barnsley: Pen and Sword Books, 2005), p.21.

11 McCranie, *Utmost Gallantry*, p.117; Toll, *Six Frigates*, p.402.

12 Captain Philip Broke to Captain Oliver of the *Valiant*, *Shannon*, 8 April 1813, quoted in J.G. Brighton, *Admiral Sir P.B.V. Broke: Chiefly from Journals and Letters in the possession of Rear-Admiral Sir George Broke-Middleton* (London: Sampson, Low, Son, and Marson, 1867), 151.

13 SRO, HA 93/9/138, Philip Broke to Louisa Broke, 14 April 1813.

own determination for revenge,[14] the nature of the plan sat well with Capel; his early career had been shaped under Nelson, and he knew first-hand the effectiveness and rewards of victory under such ambitious circumstances. The captain of *Tenedos*, too, must have been delighted. Hyde Parker III was the son of the Hyde Parker who commanded the British fleet at the Battle of Copenhagen (1801), and his grandfather had won fame after capturing a rich Spanish galleon. His heritage was steeped in the fighting tradition of the Royal Navy. Rather than sit and maintain the blockade, these men decided to adopt a Nelsonian approach and tempt the enemy out.

Shannon and *Tenedos* continued to cruise off Boston, purposefully keeping in sight of the anchored ships in the harbour. The British captains hoped that the presence of two lone frigates, stopping merchants and fishermen trying to enter and leave the harbour, would anger the Americans and tempt them to come out and offer battle. By the end of the month, Broke decided formally to send a challenge to Commodore Rodgers to make it clear he was offering two-on-two combat. Various verbal messages were sent ashore by fishing vessels and pilot boats, and eventually an 'elegantly written' public letter was sent ashore as well.[15]

The prospect of combat between his two frigates and Broke's was very tempting for Rodgers, who initially accepted the proposal. *President* was the only one of the three heavy frigates not to have defeated an enemy in action so far, and while Rodgers had succeeded in running wild throughout the North Atlantic and had taken several prizes, he had not yet had a chance to properly fight the enemy. Yet accepting such a challenge was risky and in violation of his instructions, and Rodgers knew it. His mission was to carry out commerce raiding operations. As much as the United States Navy prized its single-ship victories, it understood that the losses had very little impact on the Royal Navy's ability to carry out the war. For little strategic benefit, such single-ship actions were not really worth the risk they posed; and as much as Rodgers wanted action, he understood that his duty was to carry out the mission and not to engage enemy frigates off Boston harbour.[16] His final decision came after he learned from a merchant ship that had just anchored in Boston that there were two ships of the line and other warships out of sight. This dramatically increased the risk, and Rodgers feared that if he accepted the challenge he would be sailing into a trap. Instead, Rodgers decided to try and escape. On 30 April, *President* and *Congress* took advantage of a shift in the wind and put to sea. Just as *Shannon* and *Tenedos* were driven off station, *President* and *Congress* sailed clear away from Boston. One of Capel's sloops spotted them on 2 May, but the rest of the squadron was nowhere in sight.[17] Broke, still unaware that Rodgers had left, wrote that 'the enemy have sent no frigate yet … but they seem by their papers to have been much annoyed

14 McCranie, *Utmost Gallantry*, p.117; Toll, *Six Frigates*, p.402.

15 Lambert, *The Challenge*: Chapter 4; Captain Philip Broke to Captain James Lawrence, HMS *Shannon* off Boston, 31 May 1813 [dated only 1813], in *Naval War of 1812*, Vol.2: 1813, pp.126–129; Toll, *Six Frigates*, p.402.

16 Toll, *Six Frigates*, p.408; Commodore John Rodgers to Secretary of the Navy Jones, *President*, 22 April 1813, *Naval War of 1812*, Vol.2, p.105.

17 McCranie, *Utmost Gallantry*, p.117.

at our being so familiar with their harbor lately. They may prove our best friends yet, and favour me with an opportunity of retiring with honour.'[18] By the time that the letter was completed and sent, Broke had learned that Rodgers was at sea, and added that 'I flatter myself that they are not gone away, but merely parading themselves to prepare for a field day.'[19]

Capel and Broke still believed that Rodgers intended to honour the challenge for over a week after he first sailed. The weather during the first days of May had been very poor, and so even as Capel dispatched his ships to look for the Americans he sent *Shannon* and *Tenedos* back to the *rendezvous* to wait for Rodgers.[20] Broke complained that 'the day those rogues sailed it was thick weather, we must have been very close to them but they did not seek us.'[21] Capel held out hope until the 11th, when he finally concluded that Rodgers had in fact eluded him. His report to Admiral Warren reflected the stakes of what had occurred:

> It is with great mortification I am to acquaint you, that since my letter of the 25 of April last, two of the Enemy's Frigates (the *President* and *Congress*) have escaped from Boston. I deeply lament the circumstance, but trust you will be satisfied that every exertion was made by the Ships under my orders to prevent the Enemy putting to Sea – indeed it is impossible for more zeal and perseverance to have been shewn by any Officer than by Captain Broke, who with the *Tenedos* has been invariably as close as possible off the Port of Boston as the circumstances of the weather would permit, but the long continued Fogs that prevail on this part of the Coast at this Season of the year give the Enemy great advantage.[22]

His letter was not a report of a ship lost in action, but it certainly seemed like one. He had failed to contain the American frigates in Boston or bring them to battle, and now two frigates were loose. In his effort to bring about an action between his frigates and Rodgers's he had failed in his duty and mission to blockade Boston. It was nothing short of a disaster.

Capel had not just failed to carry out the blockade; he had agreed to a course of action that placed two of his frigates in danger. The match, by Admiralty standards, was not fair. *Congress* was a 38-gun 18-pounder frigate and could match either *Shannon* or *Tenedos* in terms of weight of metal, but *President* was a sister of *United States* and *Constitution* – the 24-pounder frigates that had triumphed in the previous year and which the Admiralty had forbidden their 18-pounders to challenge. Technically, none of the Admiralty's directives forbade this sort of two-on-two action, so such a challenge may not have been a violation of orders in and of itself; but it did violate the spirit and intentions of the Admiralty's orders. Whatever advantage Broke and Parker might have gained from mutual cooperation could easily

18 SRO, HA 93/9/139, Philip Broke to Louisa Broke, HMS *Shannon*, 5 May 1813.
19 SRO, HA 93/9/139, Philip Broke to Louisa Broke, HMS *Shannon*, 5 May 1813.
20 McCranie, *Utmost Gallantry*, p.118.
21 SRO, HA 93/9/140, Philip Broke to Louisa Broke, HMS *Shannon*, 9 May 1813.
22 Captain Thomas Bladen Capel to Admiral Sir John Warren, HMS *La Hogue*, at sea, 11 May 1813, *Naval War of 1812*, Vol.2, pp.105–106.

have been countered by mutual support between the two American frigates, who retained the advantage in broadside strength and range. Had the action taken place and the British triumphed, then in all likelihood the British captains would have been praised. Instead, their blockade had failed in an attempt to bring about an action of the sort the Admiralty had no interest in risking.

Despite Rodgers's fears, it is unlikely that Capel had planned an ambush. While it is not explicitly clear from the surviving documents whether the British plan was to engineer a two-on-two action or to lead Rodgers into a trap, the former is more likely. For one thing, Capel's ships were far off Boston during the weeks leading up to Rodgers escape, and as the First Lord, Melville, later concluded, it did not appear any British ships of the line ever ventured within 150 miles of the port.[23] Given the realities of sailing and the average speeds of large vessels like Capel's ships of the line, it was not realistic for Broke and Parker to rely on support from ships that might be over 20 hours away. Finding ships at sea is no easy task, and this difficulty was demonstrated by Capel's inability to locate *President* and *Congress*. His squadron's only duty was to maintain a distant blockade and to try and intercept any American warships that slipped past Broke – this proved an easy obstacle for Rodgers to evade. If the plan of Capel and Broke was to trap the Americans, they must have been prepared for *Shannon* and *Tenedos* to fight the American frigates alone, as help could not be guaranteed.

Further, Broke's attitudes suggest that his intention was always a two-on-two fight. He had been obsessed with winning a frigate action for years, an obsession only stoked by his feeling of frustration and anger at the course of the war with America. Early in the blockade, Broke told his wife that he would 'at any time feel contented with the attainment of my only object when I first embarked – an opportunity of retiring honourably, and with the consciousness of having done my duty as an Englishman.'[24] On the 5th, while still hoping that the Americans intended to fight, Broke emphasised his hope that they would 'favour me with an opportunity of retiring with honour to my gentle wife (if the Admiralty do not remove me before they are decided upon meeting us).'[25] Honour was a key virtue to Broke. It underscored his understanding of his duty, his patriotism, and his self-perception as a naval officer. Britain's honour had been stained by the Americans, and Broke saw working to restore that honour as central to his duty. Broke was also increasingly homesick and wanted to return home; but to return home 'with honour' required some act of gallantry, a tangible event that would uphold Broke's reputation:

> I shall at any time feel contented with the attainment of my only object when I first embarked – an opportunity of retiring honourably, with the consciousness of having done my duty as an Englishman… Surely no man deserves to enjoy an

23 McCranie, *Utmost Gallantry*, p.148.
24 SRO, HA 93/9/138, Philip Broke to Louisa Broke, 14 April 1813.
25 SRO, HA 93/9/139, Philip Broke to Louisa Broke, 5 May 1813.

> estate in England who will not sacrifice some of his prospects to his country's welfare.[26]

As much as Broke wanted to return home, his sense of duty and honour compelled him to seek some act of honour; and destroying two American frigates as part of a squadron of two 74s and three frigates was hardly an honourable or valiant act. It may have pleased the commentators of the *Naval Chronicle*, but it would not have satisfied Broke's desire for personal and professional honour, nor would it have been seen as such by the Royal Navy. Winning against inferior foes was not a pathway to glory in the British Navy; frigate captains like Broke coveted victories in event combat, or against superior foes.

The escape of *President* and *Congress* and the events leading up to it have been sparsely covered in historical literature, but the event was important both for its impact and for what it reveals about the culture of the Royal Navy.[27] Broke and Parker risked everything – their ships, their mission, and their careers – for an action they had no guarantee of winning. In the end, there was no action, yet the enemy still escaped. Capel had failed to blockade Boston, and now two American frigates were loose, and most of the squadron dispersed to search for them. Capel and most of his squadron left their posts off Boston and spent the better part of May searching for the Americans. For the most part, Warren was left in the dark. Not until mid-June did the Admiralty learn of the events, by which time *President* was operating in European waters.[28] Weeks before, the Admiralty had issued orders to strengthen the blockading force off Boston, 'where the greatest number of Ships of War appear at present to be.'[29] Not only had Capel weakened the blockade in that time, but two of the four frigates had escaped. The news of *President*'s escape into the North Atlantic, and her subsequent cruise which took her deep into British waters, sent the Admiralty and British world into a panic. While *President* only took a handful of prizes, Rodgers managed to sail as far as the Shetlands and caused disruption throughout the Atlantic, from Halifax to Gibraltar. In fear of the American frigates, naval forces throughout the Atlantic were directed to search for her, insurance prices spiked, and the government went into a state of panic.[30] From that panic came the order on 10 July expressly forbidding Britain's fifth-rate frigates from engaging in single-ship combat with the American heavy frigates.[31]

26 SRO, HA 93/9/138, Philip Broke to Louisa Broke 14 April 1813.

27 Nicholas James Kaizer, 'Regret, determination, and honour: the impact of the single ship losses in North American waters on the British Royal Navy, 1812–1813' (MA thesis, Dalhousie University, 2018), pp.125–126.

28 McCranie, *Utmost Gallantry*, p.121.

29 First Secretary of the Admiralty John Croker to Admiral Sr John Warren, 3 June 1813, *Naval War of 1812*, Vol 2, pp.139–140.

30 NSA, *Acadian Recorder*, 22 May 1813, 1:19, https://novascotia.ca/archives/newspapers/archives.asp?ID=771; Lambert, *The Challenge*, Chapter 3; Latimer, *1812*, p.164; McCranie, *Utmost Gallantry*, pp.120–127; Toll, *Six Frigates*, pp.403–420.

31 McCranie, *Utmost Gallantry*, pp.121–122.

The Admiralty was incensed by what had happened but, owing to the slowness of communications, it took some time to figure out what exactly had occurred off Boston. Reports of *President* trickled into London through the month of June, and speculation ran wild in Whitehall – at one point the Admiralty suspected all three of America's heavy frigates were at sea. While it later became clear that only one heavy frigate, *President*, was loose, her presence in northern waters severely alarmed the Admiralty. In a desperate attempt to avoid a repeat of the losses in 1812, a significant force, including two ships of the line and accompanying frigates and sloops, was dispatched to find her.[32] Slowly, the Admiralty began to question Capel's conduct, particularly his deployment during the blockade. Why had the ships of the line seemingly never been closer than 150 miles off Boston? How were *President* and *Congress* able to slip away? Broke and Capel faced professional ruin, and thus far had only been protected by the slowness of communication.[33] Broke's best course of action may have been to lay low and stick to orders – or perhaps to throw the dice one more time.

Shannon–Chesapeake action, 1 June 1813

As the squadron dispersed to look for Rodgers, Broke and Parker remained off Boston for the rest of May, keeping watch on the two remaining frigates in the harbour. *Constitution* was still dismasted, but by now *Chesapeake* appeared ready for sea. Meanwhile, both *Shannon* and *Tenedos* were short on provisions and could not remain on station for long. Broke, now the senior officer on station, decided to send Parker back home:

> Having every reason to expect that the American frigate *Chesapeake* will sail from Boston in a few days, and thinking there is more chance of her being intercepted by our frigates cruising separately than if they keep together, I have to direct that during the absence of the Hon. Captain Capel, the senior officer, you will proceed to cruise upon the range lately occupied by *La Hogue* viz., from Cape Sable to the latitude of 42.10 N., to watch for the *Chesapeake*, should she pass by the *Shannon* in nighttime or thick weather. You are to take an opportunity, in such winds as you think less likely to favour the enemy's escape, to procure water enough to last out your provisions at Shelbourne, or any other port which you may find most convenient, joining the *Shannon*, off Boston, on the 14 June, unless otherwise ordered by the senior officer.[34]

Broke took on some of *Tenedos*'s stores before dispatching her to sea, enabling *Shannon* to continue off Boston. *Tenedos*'s operating range was vast, stretching from the northern boundary of Massachusetts Bay to Cape Sable, Nova Scotia. With the lack of stores, *Tenedos* would have to make port before too long, and so *Shannon* was left alone operating off Boston harbour. Half

32 McCranie, *Utmost Gallantry*, pp.120–127; Toll, *Six Frigates*, pp.419–420.

33 McCranie, *Utmost Gallantry*, p.148; Dudley, *Splintering the Wooden Wall*, pp.94–95.

34 SRO, HA 93/6/2/8/98, Philip Broke to Hyde Parker, *Shannon*, off Boston, 25 May 1813.

a year earlier a *Naval Chronicle* commentator had written 'it is not usual to reduce one's strength when going to fight an enemy' – and yet Broke had done so a second time.[35]

Remarkably, Broke was once again hoping to tempt the enemy out for a show-down by reducing the blockading squadron to a single 38-gun frigate. By instructing *Tenedos* to return on the 14th, Broke had given himself a window to try and tempt the enemy out before he would be forced to return for supplies himself. Given that this ploy had failed just a month earlier, resulting in the escape of two frigates, the fact that he tried it again demonstrates Broke's determination to bring about an action with the Americans. He had been very distressed by Rodgers's escape, but there was hope yet that Captain Lawrence of USS *Chesapeake* may prove more accommodating:

> Since Rodgers escaped we have rarely hunted our game far from his den, which still contains another large wild beast; if all the nobler prey elude us, we must chase the vermin, but have great hopes yet of an honourable encounter. My constant comrade, Parker, I detached two days ago on a separate range, that we might show an even more inviting appearance to our enemy, now a single frigate of our own size; we shall do a grand service if we can get hold of him, preventing all the mischief he would do if he escaped out; and I trust in God and our brave crew in brightening up the honor of our flag and soothing the feelings of our countrymen for their late mortifications.[36]

Risky though it was, Broke was desperate for action with the enemy, and time was running out. Upon *Tenedos*'s return, *Shannon* would need to return to port for provisions, and upon returning to Halifax Broke knew *Shannon* would need a refit.[37] His concern had been mounting for months, as on the 14th of April he wrote: 'My Wooden wife is very weak and crazy, and must soon be sent home.'[38] *Shannon* had always been a light and leaky ship, and during her eight years under the perfectionist Captain Broke she had been driven hard. Beyond the normal weathering and straining of a ship at sea, she had recently suffered damage; on 5 May, *Shannon*'s mainmast had been struck by lightning, which lit the fighting top on fire.[39] If Broke returned to Halifax than he might not be able to get back to sea for some months. This was his best chance at action and Broke seized the moment, penning a formal written challenge to Captain Lawrence:

> As the *Chesapeake* appears now ready for Sea, I request you will do me the favor to meet the *Shannon* with her, Ship to Ship, to try the fortune of our respective Flags; to an officer of your character, it requires some apology for proceeding

35 'An Iron Gun of a Large Calibre' to the Editor, 28 January 1813, *Naval Chronicle*, Vol.29, p.114.

36 SRO, HA 93/9/141, Broke to Louisa, 28 May 1813.

37 Martin Bibbins, 'The battle', in Tim Voelcker (ed.), *Broke of the Shannon and the War of 1812* (Barnsley: Seaforth Publishing, 2013), pp.127–128; McCranie, *Utmost Gallantry*, p.148.

38 SRO HA 93/9/138, Philip Broke to Louisa Broke, 14 April 1813.

39 Bibbins, 'The battle', p.129.

> to further particulars, be assured Sir, that it is not from any doubt that I can entertain of your wishing to close with my proposal, but merely to provide an answer to any objection which might be made, and very reasonably, upon the chance of our receiving an unfair support.
>
> After the diligent attention which we had paid to Commodore Rodgers, the pains I took to detach all force, but *Shannon* and *Tenedos*, to such a distance that they could not possibly join in any Action fought in sight of the Capes, and the various Verbal messages which had been sent into Boston to that effect, we were much disappointed to find that the Commodore had eluded us, … he, perhaps, wished for some stronger assurance of a fair meeting; I am therefore induced to address you more particularly, and to assure you that what I write I pledge my honour to perform to the utmost of my power.[40]

The uniqueness of this phenomenon has already been attested to – the fact that Broke issued two such challenges was remarkable. Indeed, Broke admitted that his frustration over the failure of the first challenge motivated his decision to issue a second one. This time, Broke left no loose ends. He made sure to thoroughly explain his reasoning for offering combat, to set out the conditions under which they might meet, and to appeal to his opponent's sense of honour and gallantry. Such formality was an effort to rectify what had happened with Rodgers. Broke did not accuse Rodgers of cowardice, and instead suggested that Rodgers's decision to escape rather than accept the challenge had been disappointing but inherently Broke's fault due to a lack of steadfast assurance that a fair challenge was being offered. To rectify this, Broke made sure that this challenge could not be interpreted as a trick or half-hearted promise.

To this end, Broke described the force under his command; the number of guns and men were specified, and he was careful to point out that a significant proportion of his crew were boys, and included an additional 30 men, boys, and passengers recently taken from recaptured ships and who were not drilled members of *Shannon*'s crew. He explained that *La Hogue* and the rest of Capel's squadron had left for provisions, and that he would 'send all other Ships beyond the power of interfering with us,' and would warn Lawrence if any additional British ships should arrive.[41] Broke was playing to Lawrence's sense of honour, hitting the same virtue that was so important in the Royal Navy. Victory in combat against an opponent of equal force was professionally and personally coveted by officers from both the Royal and the United States Navy. The match proposed was between two ships rated 38 guns, carrying approximately the same number of armaments in total, and of very similar broadside weight. *Shannon* had two additional guns compared to *Chesapeake*, though *Chesapeake* was of heavier tonnage and overall broadside weight.[42] Lawrence, in the same vein as his fellow Captain

40 Philip Broke to James Lawrence, HMS *Shannon*, off Boston, 31 May [only dated 1813] 1813, *Naval War of 1812*, Vol.2, pp.126–128.

41 Broke to Lawrence, 31 May 1813, *Naval War of 1812*, Vol.2, pp.126–128.

42 Bibbins, 'The battle', pp.133–134.

Porter, coveted glory in one-on-one combat perhaps as much as Broke, as Broke had hoped would be the case:

> You must, Sir, be aware that my proposals are highly advantageous to you, as you cannot proceed to Sea singly in *Chesapeake* without imminent risqué of being crushed by the superior force of the numerous British squadrons which are now abroad, where all your efforts, in case of a rencontre, would, however gallant, be perfectly hopeless;
>
> I entreat you, Sir, not to imagine that I am urged by mere personal vanity to the wish of meeting *Chesapeake*, or that I depend only upon your personal ambition for you acceding to this Invitation, we have both nobler motives – you will feel it as a compliment if I say that they result of our meeting may be the most grateful Service I can render to my Country – and I doubt not that you, equally confident of success, will feel convinced that it is only by continued triumphs in even combats that your little Navy can now hope to console your Country for the loss of that Trade it can no longer protect.[43]

Broke issued the call as a gentleman to another gentleman: two naval officers with similar notions of duty and honour, though different underlying motivations.[44] Both were to some degree in violation of standing orders. Broke was driven by his personal desire for combat, but also by a belief that vindicating his nation's honour in combat with the navy that had humbled his in the previous year was worth the risk. He had hoped to bring about an action earlier with Rodgers, who was either too wary of the British intentions or driven to adhere to his orders to go along with the plan. Broke bet successfully that Lawrence would offer him the even combat he craved.

Broke's tone was designed both to treat Lawrence with a great deal of personal respect and to inflame his patriotism by dismissing the value of Lawrence's ability to serve his country outside of single combat due to the vast power of the Royal Navy. It is very likely this challenge would have inflamed the deeply patriotic and ambitious Lawrence. Lawrence had sent a formal challenge to single combat once himself, encouraged by his commodore, and he must have been as frustrated by Captain Greene's refusal as Broke had been by Rodgers's escape. Despite having received similar orders to Broke warning against initiating single-ship actions (to mitigate the risk of losing one of America's few ships in combat), Lawrence was obsessed with winning a frigate action. Lawrence had won promotion following his victory over *Peacock* but was disappointed by being denied command of *Constitution*, in which he had once served as First Lieutenant and acting captain, or one of the other heavy frigates. In what he perceived as a slight, he had been given command of *Chesapeake*, one of the smaller three of the Navy's original frigates.[45] As such, the victory he had won did not satisfy Lawrence's personal and professional desire for glory: 'He wanted glory; the public recognition that he was an outstanding officer, a hero, who would go down in history as

43 Bibbins, 'The battle', pp.133–134.

44 Voelcker, 'Victories or distractions', pp.69–71.

45 Voelcker, 'Victories or distractions', pp.62–71; Bibbins, 'The battle', pp.127–128.

the man who had defeated the arrogant Briton who had sailed up to Boston light and fired a challenging gun.'[46]

Where Lawrence was motivated by his ambition and notions of public glory, Broke sought personal recognition. Honour and duty were tied more closely with his personal sense of honour. While his reputation mattered, so too did his own self-image.[47] In the end, the contrasting motivations played well together; both captains sought action with the enemy, an 'honourable encounter,' and both would have it. When *Shannon* appeared close in off Boston on 1 June, Lawrence seized the opportunity to win glory for himself and for the entire United States Navy. Without waiting long enough for the challenge to even reach his hands Lawrence ordered *Chesapeake* to weigh anchor and proceed to the open sea. *Shannon*'s continuous patrolling off Boston harbour, as she had been doing for months, was enough to goad Lawrence into seeking out action with the lone and vain British ship, under the vain Captain Broke.

HMS *Shannon* had stood in towards Boston the first morning in June to send the challenge ashore. Broke left the packet with an inbound fisherman and then stood in stood in close for Boston lighthouse, where her lookouts observed *Chesapeake* under weigh. In the early afternoon she rounded the lighthouse, accompanied by a plethora of small craft of well-wishers eager to witness the action. The keeper of the lighthouse himself came outside to witness what everyone in Boston presumed would be another thrashing victory. Just after 5:00 p.m., the splendid-looking *Chesapeake* cleared for action and hoisted her ensigns, along with a white flag from the foremast with 'Free Trades and Sailors Rights' emblazoned on either side. *Shannon* beat to quarters herself, though the ship had been cleared for action for hours. Next to *Chesapeake* and her captain, wearing the resplendent uniform of a United States Navy captain, *Shannon* appeared shabby and a little dirty. Her captain – the red haired 37-year-old – stood on the quarterdeck in a simple blue coat and top hat; even with the sword he did not look the part of a naval officer. Yet the appearance belied the truth. Broke was an aggressive commander and a perfectionist, who since 1806 had honed his ship's crew into a murderously efficient fighting force. He had drilled his men daily in firing, honing both their speed and accuracy. Where most Royal Navy captains were obsessed with cleanliness, Broke was obsessed with gunnery. He approached it as a scientist and an innovator, and among other things had developed new types of sights and tools for his gunners to improve their accuracy. His frigate was perhaps one of the best trained afloat, and yet during his time in command Broke had never had the opportunity of testing his crew nor his training regime against an equal opponent. After years of longing, his chance had finally come.[48]

The contest would be one between remarkably even forces. While *Chesapeake* was only rated 36 guns to *Shannon*'s 38, both carried effectively

---

46 Voelcker, 'Victories or distractions', pp.62–70.

47 Voelcker, 'Victories or distractions', pp.62–70.

48 Gwyn, *Frigates and Foremasts*, p.143; Bibbins, 'Gunnery zealot', pp.103–126; Bibbins, 'The battle', pp.127–128; McCranie, *Utmost Gallantry*, pp.150–151.

the same armament. Each had main batteries consisting of twenty-eight 18-pounders and secondary batteries of 32-pounder carronades. Thanks to a handful of lighter guns, *Shannon* had 52 in total to *Chesapeake*'s 50, but *Chesapeake* had the slight edge in broadside weight and hitting power. In size they were nearly identical, and for once the American advantage in manpower was almost negligible.[49] Ironically, Broke did not intend to use much of his meticulously studied theory and methodology of long-range gunnery in the coming action. He had concluded that the key to defeating the Americans was to bring about a close-range action and to fight murderously once there, but his training regime meant that he entered combat with a crew drilled to perfection and eager for action after many months of blockading Boston.[50] His opponent similarly intended to fight a direct battle, using the same tactics that had proved so effective against *Peacock*. *Chesapeake*'s crew were experienced and Lawrence was a very capable commander, but most of the officers were new to their positions and the crew's morale was very poor. Some hands were intoxicated at their action stations as the two ships approached.[51] Still the crew was enthusiastic, and as the two ships approached the Chesapeakes called out three cheers. The Shannons, ordered to remain quiet and at their stations, waited as the two ships closed.[52]

At 5:50 p.m., *Chesapeake* came alongside *Shannon*, and as her bows passed ahead of the stern-most gun port the first of the British 18-pounders fired. One by one, the guns fired in a rolling broadside stern to stem, answered quickly by the Americans. The two frigates were very close, and over the next few minutes *Chesapeake* was pushed slightly closer by the wind blowing across her side. In those few minutes both the British and the Americans managed to pour a murderous fire into each other. Round shot, grape, and cannister ripped through the wooden hulls, while musketry from both sides poured into the weather decks, inflicting heavy casualties on both frigates. *Chesapeake*'s master was shot dead and moments later Lawrence was shot in the knee. Bleeding and hobbling, he remained on deck directing his ship's fire and ordered his gunners to elevate their guns to cut away the enemy's rigging.[53]

Chesapeake's fire inflicted heavy damage on her opponent but was unable to deal out much of that damage aloft. Miraculously, neither Broke nor any of his officers had been hit, and his steering and rigging were mostly intact. The quartermaster – a Trafalgar veteran – was shot by an American marine but he kept to his post, holding *Shannon* on her course.[54] Broke and First Lieutenant Watt remained on the quarterdeck directing the ship, while Lieutenants Provo Wallis and Charles Falkiner commanded the 18-pounders below, which continued to pour fire into *Chesapeake*'s closely packed deck. Just four minutes after the firing had begun, British fire had cut away elements

49 Bibbins, 'The battle', p.134.

50 Bibbins, 'Gunnery zealot', pp.103–126; McCranie, *Utmost Gallantry*, pp.150–151.

51 McCranie, *Utmost Gallantry*, pp.150–151.

52 Bibbins, 'The battle', pp.127–133; McCranie, *Utmost Gallantry*, pp.150–151.

53 Bibbins, 'The battle', pp.134–137; McCranie, *Utmost Gallantry*, pp.150–152.

54 Toll, *Six Frigates*, p.412.

of *Chesapeake*'s running rigging and had smashed the ship's wheel to pieces, killing her quartermasters in the process. In consequence, Lawrence lost control of his ship's steering and she was left to the mercy of the wind. Sailing craft naturally are pulled towards the source of the wind, and without any ability to keep the ship on course that is exactly what *Chesapeake* did. The frigate drifted away from her opponent and was pulled into irons, leaving her sails flapping uselessly as her stern and larboard quarter were left facing the enemy. *Shannon*'s gun crews did not hesitate and continued firing quick and well-aimed shots from the 18-pounders and carronades. The raking fire smashed *Chesapeake*'s stern and reduced her gundeck to a state of chaos. Scores of men were cut down below as they fled from the aftermost guns, while on the quarterdeck grape shot and musketry continued to drive men away from the carronades. In the confusion a cask of musket cartridges caught fire and exploded, miraculously avoided lighting the nearby spanker sail aflame.[55]

Just moments into the raking broadside, Lawrence realised the wind was pushing the ship backwards, and that within another moment her stern would collide with *Shannon*'s starboard side. He called for a boarding party, hoping to rush onto *Shannon*'s deck in the confusion and even the odds, but the state of the crew was beginning to unravel and some men fled below in terror. One was the recently appointed bugler whose job was to alert the crew to prepare for boarding. The lieutenants managed to rally a handful of men, but just as they came aft, Lawrence was shot once again, a musket ball passing through his body and causing him to collapse. The Third Lieutenant, William Cox, carried the mortally wounded captain below with Lawrence screaming to the men: 'Don't give up the ship; fight her 'til she sinks!'[56]

While the American captain was being carried below, his ship collided against *Shannon*'s side. Men from the British frigate quickly lashed the ships together while the officers rallied a boarding party. Broke could see that the enemy quarterdeck was nearly empty – his gunnery and small arms fire had wreaked havoc while raking and had killed or driven the enemy sailors away. At 5:58 p.m., Captain Broke climbed up onto *Shannon*'s side, called for his men to follow, and leapt down onto an enemy quarterdeck carronade. Thirty men followed him armed with cutlasses, muskets, pikes, and tomahawks, and Broke led them in a mad dash forward across the enemy's torn-up quarterdeck, where the Americans were rallying on the gangways between the quarterdeck and forecastle. Lieutenants Watt and Falkiner followed with another 40 men, climbing on board *Chesapeake* just as the wind tore her off *Shannon*'s side. As the two frigates drifted apart again, a ferocious melee ensued on the American's weather deck. Watt was shot in the foot but continued to rush to his captain's aid, managing to smash through a party of men rushing up from the gundeck to help those trying to repel the British. The two American lieutenants on deck were both wounded in the fighting

55 Budiansky, *Perilous Fight*, p.232; Bibbins, 'The battle', pp.137–140; Roosevelt, *Naval War of 1812*, pp.183–184.

56 Budiansky, *Perilous Fight*, p.232; Bibbins, 'The battle', pp.137–140; Roosevelt, *Naval War of 1812*, pp.183–184.

and the American resistance collapsed. In the confusion, however, a handful of American sailors and marines rushed at Broke; two slashed his face with cutlasses, and the third knocked the captain over with the butt of his musket. Broke was saved by a marine who bayonetted his assailants, and around them the last of the American fighters were driven below. The decks were effectively under British control.[57]

Watt, though bleeding from his foot and limping, made his way aft with a small group of men with a spare blue ensign in hand. Flying the ensign of the captor over that of the defeated party was the universal sign of a prize, and so Watt and his men hauled down the American colours and went to re-hoist it underneath the British blue ensign.[58] Watt understood the gravity of the moment; his ship had triumphed, the first British victory yet in the conflict, and as the senior lieutenant he stood to receive promotion and approbation. In the overcrowded officer corps of the Royal Navy, it was a moment that could make his career.

In the confusion the British mistook the similarly coloured stars and stripes for their own flag and briefly hauled it up the mast before realising their error. As Watt reached back up to correct the mistake, a gun captain at one of *Shannon*'s carronades spotted the American ensign. For a few moments he had thought that the Americans were driven from the quarterdeck, but through the smoky haze he could clearly see a blue-coated officer re-hoisting their ensign. Without hesitating he fired his gun, packed with grape shot, into the crowd of men at *Chesapeake*'s stern. Lieutenant Provo Wallis, in command of *Shannon*, quickly realised what had happened and ordered his men to stand down, but not before Lieutenant Watt had been hit and instantly killed by his own ship's shot in his moment of triumph. Ahead, Broke lay wounded, dazed, and bleeding profusely, with one of the midshipmen attending to him. As the blue ensign was finally hoisted with the tattered stars and stripes below it, the midshipman excitedly informed his captain of the fact, moments before Broke collapsed unconscious.[59]

'Never can be excelled': celebrations of the *Shannon*'s victory

By Lieutenant Wallis's count the last shots were fired at 6:01 p.m., just 11 minutes after *Shannon* had first opened fire. During that time, the fighting had been ferocious from both sides. Both *Shannon* and *Chesapeake* had inflicted great damage and casualties on the other, but whereas *Shannon*'s fire had knocked away the Americans' steering and killed or wounded nearly every officer before the ships collided, *Shannon*'s steering remained intact and no officers had been cut down. The Shannons maintained their resolve throughout the action, but with the collapse of leadership and their already poor morale the Americans resolve unravelled quickly. Of the Shannons,

57 Budiansky, *Perilous Fight*, p.232; Bibbins, 'The battle', pp.137–140; Roosevelt, *Naval War of 1812*, pp.183–184.

58 Bibbins, 'The battle', pp.140–141.

59 Bibbins, 'The battle', pp.140–141; Toll, *Six Frigates*, p.415.

34 had been killed or mortally wounded, and another 49 were injured. Of the Chesapeakes, 69 had been killed, with another 77 wounded. Overall, *Chesapeake* suffered more casualties in the action than HMS *Victory* did at Trafalgar. Indeed, the rate of casualties per minute on both frigates exceeded the rate of casualties per minute in both Nelson and Villeneuve's fleets. Both sides had kept up a murderous rate of fire, and it showed.[60]

Lieutenant Provo Wallis, Nova Scotian-born senior surviving lieutenant of HMS *Shannon*, by Davey Fitzner. (Library and Archives Canada)

It took five days for Lieutenant Wallis (now acting captain of *Shannon*) and Falkiner (in command of the prize) to put their ships into a state of seaworthiness and sail the two battered frigates back to Halifax. The sick bays of both ships were crammed with British and American wounded, and both exhibited signs of battle: expansive structural damage and the gore of dozens of dead and wounded sailors. Upon their arrival, *Chesapeake* entered the mouth of the harbour first and hove to near McNab's Island, allowing Wallis in *Shannon* to lead the procession towards the town. Word quickly spread, and as much of the town was gathered in church, the service at St Paul's Church was interrupted by word that an American prize frigate was in the harbour. Soon, nearly all the town's 5,000 residents had gathered on the wharves and beach to greet and cheer *Shannon*'s arrival.[61]

The naval officers at Halifax, too, were overjoyed, and hastily put together a report of the action to send to the Admiralty. Capel, the senior officer in the port, quickly sent letters both to the Admiralty and to Admiral Warren, in which he praised Broke's victory as a 'brilliant achievement.' To Croker he praised Broke's determination to seek 'every opportunity of meeting the enemy on fair terms,'[62] while the report to Warren was more modest, though still reporting 'the glorious issue of a contest with the United States frigate *Chesapeake*.'[63] The letter to the Admiralty quickly found its way into various British papers, including the *London Gazette* and the *Naval Chronicle*. As this account was more likely to be made public, it was vested with the imagery befitting Broke's achievement.

Capel's report, of course, was simply an introduction to Broke's own dispatch to Capel, his senior officer, announcing his achievement. There

60 Bibbins, 'The battle', p.142.

61 Raddal, *Warden of the North*, p.141.

62 Copy of a letter from the Hon. Captain Capel of HMS *La Hogue* to John Wilson Croker, dated Halifax, 11 June 1813, in *The Naval Chronicle for 1813: Containing a General and Biographical History of The Royal Navy of the United Kingdom; With a Variety of Original Papers on Nautical Subjects*, Vol.30: July to December (London: Joyce Gold, 1813), p.83.

63 LAC, MG12 ADM 1/503 Admiral's Dispatches, 1812–1813, North America, C-12854, Captain Thomas Bladen Capel to Admiral John Warren, HMS *La Hogue*, Halifax, 11 June 1813.

was just one problem: upon their arrival in Halifax, Broke was in a serious condition and in no state to write anything. Rather than wait, Capel decided to pen a report himself, with the assistance of fellow captains Philip Wodehouse and Richard Byron. Lieutenant Wallis, who felt uneasy about putting words into his captain's mouth and preferred to wait for him to recover, later asserted that the report was inaccurate, but Capel wanted to send an official dispatch as soon as possible, no doubt motivated by the excitement of the victory and by Capel's own apprehensions about Rodgers's escape. If Capel feared repercussions from a potentially furious Admiralty, he was likely correct. Dispatching the news of this victory, then, was of great importance to the senior captain.

The account, fictitiously from Broke's perspective, was brief but powerful. The prose was boastful and patriotic in its description of the boarding and capture of the enemy frigate:

> I gave orders to prepare for boarding – Our gallant hands appointed to that Service immediately rushed in under their respective Officers, upon the enemys Decks driving every thing before them with irresistible fury... The American flag was hauled down and the proud old British Union floated triumphant over it... I have to lament the loss of many of my gallant Shipmates, but they fell exulting in their Conquest.[64]

The imagery of the 'gallant hands' rushing the enemy deck with 'irresistible fury' was potent, as was the image of the triumphant British flag being raised. Various officers who were wounded or killed were mentioned by name, as was customary with dispatches of the sort. Capel stated that Broke's 'brave first Lieutenant Mr. Watt' was killed in the act of hoisting the British colours – killed in the moment of victory.[65] Wallis and Falkiner were directly commended, and 'Broke' asked 'to recommend these Officers most strongly to the Commander in Chiefs patronage' for their role in the action and in sailing *Shannon* and her prize back to Halifax.[66] However, the account did not reference Broke's now famous challenge. Instead, Capel and his fellow captains only described that *Shannon* stood in when they observed *Chesapeake* 'coming out of the Harbour to engage the *Shannon*.'[67] The particulars of how this action came about were ignored completely, though they would soon become common knowledge anyway and were widely praised in naval circles. However, perhaps due to the current climate in the Admiralty, Capel and his fellow captains felt adding such a detail might inflame some perhaps-justified displeasure.

While Broke recovered in Halifax, the town celebrated. The residents responded with paintings, songs, and poems influenced by the victory. The post-battle literature reflected a deep sense of patriotism in Nova Scotia,

---

64 Captain Philip Broke to Captain Thomas Capel, HMS *Shannon*, Halifax, 6 June 1813, *Naval War of 1812*, Vol.2, pp.129–133.

65 Broke to Capel, 6 June 1813, *Naval War of 1812*, Vol.2, pp.129–133.

66 Broke to Capel, 6 June 1813, *Naval War of 1812*, Vol.2, pp.129–133.

67 Broke to Capel, 6 June 1813, *Naval War of 1812*, Vol.2, pp.129–133.

'which combined pride in Britishness with local concerns over the American maritime threat.'[68] When Broke had recovered enough to visit the town, he was welcomed by a public address and a piece of plate by the Haligonian merchants.[69] A prominent journalist, Joseph Howe, in an open letter to the British colonial secretary, described *Chesapeake* as the greatest trophy of the war, all the sweeter as she was brought in under a Nova Scotian.

The newspapers competed to cover the action through compelling editorials and interviews with the veterans of HMS *Shannon*.[70] The *Acadian Recorder* praised Broke's glorious achievement while regretting that 'instead of the *Chesapeake* it had not been the largest Frigate of the United States, commanded by their ablest Captain.' The editor had no doubt that Broke would have prevailed against any American foe, such was the ferocity of *Shannon*'s broadsides and his 'consummate skill combined with personal bravery.'[71] The highest praised was reserved for Broke:

> We have long witnessed the indefatigable zeal with which Capt. BROKE has sought after the American squadron, and we have beheld with admiration this gallant officer foregoing the enjoyments of affluence and domestic comfort to serve his country; an example most worthy imitation, less from the sacrifices he has made, great as they were, than from the skill he has manifested, it being at all points prepared to uphold and increase the glory of the British Navy – Truth cannot be flattery, not can aught we can write do justice to his merits or express the estimation in which we hold it; the ease with which he captured a frigate of equal force is proof to us, that the largest America can boast of, would have met a similar fate, and again we express our regret that his opponent was not of that class.[72]

Another issue reported on the particulars of the action, concluding: 'Thus ended in 13 minutes from the firing of the first gun, one of the fairest, shortest, severest, and most decisive actions that ever was fought between two-ships of equal force.'[73] Concerns over the remaining American frigates did not go away, but the victory offered Haligonians a sense of relief. It had vindicated the honour and prestige of their beloved naval service, giving the Haligonians the confidence to begin re-examining the previous losses. Motivated by *Shannon*'s victory, Halifax's papers declared that the previous losses had been attributed to luck. Surely, Broke's achievement had proved that Britain was the sovereign of the seas?[74]

---

68 Broke to Capel, 6 June 1813, *Naval War of 1812*, Vol.2, pp.129–133.

69 Raddall, *Warden of the North*, pp.142–143.

70 Mercer, 'Colonial patriotism', pp.45–46.

71 NSA, *Acadian Recorder*, 12 June 1813, 1:22, https://novascotia.ca/archives/newspapers/archives.asp?ID=774.

72 NSA, *Acadian Recorder*, 12 June 1813, 1:22, https://novascotia.ca/archives/newspapers/archives.asp?ID=774.

73 NSA, *Acadian Recorder*, 19 June 1813, 1:23 https://novascotia.ca/archives/newspapers/archives.asp?ID=775.

74 Mercer, 'Colonial patriotism', pp.45–46.

While Broke recovered, James Lawrence died on route to Halifax and was buried with full military honours. Some historians have criticised him for going into action with his ship in a poor state, although some argue this was not the case. Lawrence would not have disobeyed orders and risked his ship if he did not think he could win, and the butchers bill of *Shannon* following the action attested to the destructiveness of *Chesapeake*'s gunnery. While he lost the battle, in death Lawrence's memory and final words lived on – he won his glory on the deck of *Chesapeake*.[75] In homage his friend, Commodore Oliver Hazard Perry, had a banner emblazoned with Lawrence's famous words, 'Don't Give Up The Ship,' that was flown in action against the British on Lake Erie. The phrase itself has remained steadfast in the cultural memory of the United States Navy, and through it the memory of Captain Lawrence lives on. Yet, it is strange that 'Don't Give Up The Ship' should have struck such a cord and remained the Navy's unofficial slogan – it was the despairing cry of a dying captain, who, though resolute to fight to the last, could do nothing to prevent the capture of the ship in an action lasting just 11 minutes. Rather than heed his words, the demoralised and shattered crew *did* give up the ship. In issuing such a challenge, and in standing *Chesapeake* out to face *Shannon*, both captains disobeyed orders. The Admiralty, once they learned of the escape of *President* and *Congress*, were furious – had *Chesapeake* done the same, or worse, by defeating *Shannon* off Boston, both Capel and Broke would have faced blame for letting three frigates escape from what had originally been a tight blockade of overwhelming force. Dudley argued that 'Lawrence paid with his life for ignoring his orders; had he emerged victorious; however, death would have been Broke's only alternative to being condemned by court martial.'[76] Instead, Broke came home to public approbation.

The British public were overjoyed at the news of the victory, and celebrated it like a second Trafalgar.[77] William Cobbett, an infamous radical and editor of the *Political Register*, stated that as far as the public and press were concerned Broke's victory was 'of far greater importance than the victories of Lord Wellington, and as such the public appear to feel it… Why there is more boasting about the defeat of one American frigate than there used to be about the defeat of whole fleets.'[78] Broke received a baronetcy, the keys to London, and was showered with additional praise and gifts from the nation, in addition to being offered command of one of the new heavy frigates.[79] Lieutenants Wallis and Falkiner were both promoted to commander, and two of the midshipmen were commissioned as lieutenants. Falkiner had been a lieutenant for just over three years and was very junior: he struggled in the peacetime navy, never securing command of another ship and only reaching post rank in retirement.[80] Wallis would see active employment for

75 Voelcker, 'Victories or distractions', p.70.

76 Dudley, *Splintering the Wooden Wall*, p.95.

77 Latimer, *1812*, p.168.

78 William Cobbett, *Political Register*, 17 July 1813, quoted in Voelcker (ed.), *Broke of the Shannon*, p.102.

79 McCranie, *Utmost Gallantry*, p.154; Latimer, *1812*, p.164.

80 Syrett and DiNardo, *Commissioned Sea Officers*, p.150; 'Charles Leslie Falkiner, Esq.', *Royal Naval Biography*, Vol.4, Part I, p.116.

decades, eventually becoming admiral of the fleet and the longest serving naval officer in British history, refusing to retire until his death in 1892.[81] The promotions were typical of any notable victory, even with the overabundance of commanders and lieutenants in the Navy and generally difficult promotion prospects. The honours bestowed on Broke and his officers were remarkable; *Shannon* and *Chesapeake* were essentially evenly matched ships, and such a victory had rarely received such praise before by British society. Before the shock of the 1812 losses, a victory against an evenly matched foe was not a novelty, and was indeed expected.[82] 'Broke had indeed been correct when writing his challenge to Lawrence: "The result of our meeting may be the most grateful Service I can render to my Country".'[83] British society, shocked by loss and starved of victory, was overjoyed by Broke's triumph.

The *Chronicle*, too, praised the victory, with the editors proclaiming that 'the brilliant style in which the business was done, may perhaps be equaled, but we are sure will not be excelled, by any incident that can be quoted from British history.'[84] One commentator declared that

> too much cannot be said respecting the capture of our frigates by the Americans, although we had agreed that enough had already appeared. We have now, however, a most glorious winding up of the tale; and the gallant Shannon has shewn, that the food old tune of 'Britons strike home!' can still be sung in full chorus, and to the finest effect, as exemplified by the victorious Broke, and his brave crew. I most sincerely, Sir, congratulate you, and my countrymen, on this happy solution of all difficulties, although I never attributed our losses to one moment's want of personal valour or zeal in those brave fellows who were before less fortunate.[85]

The victory had wound 'up the tale,' in his mind. Broke's victory had seemingly proved Britain's naval mastery once and for all. Various other letters that were sent in over the following months praised the action and declared it affirmed the supremacy of Britain at sea. Broke's victory was a vindication for the readers and editors of the *Chronicle*.[86] While the war in the North American theatre continued throughout the year, the *Chronicle* began to lose interest in the American conflict, at least until the end of the 30th volume. Broke's victory was, for the time being, satisfactory to settle the wound caused by the shocking 1812 losses. For many, the action seemed to be a pure vindication of the Royal Navy's honour: a bandage to the shattered spell of invincibility.

---

81 Syrett and DiNardo, *Commissioned Sea Officers*, p.456; Ronald E. Hickey and Donald E. Graves, *Don't Give Up the Ship!: Myths of the War of 1812* (Montréal: R. Brass Studio, 2008), p.113; 'Provo William Parry Wallis, Esq.', *Royal Naval Biography*, Supplement, Part IV, pp.214.

82 Margaret Lincoln, *Representing the Royal Navy: British Sea Power, 1750–1815* (Aldershot: Ashgate and the National Maritime Museum, 2002), pp.17–18; McCranie, *Utmost Gallantry*, p.154.

83 McCranie, *Utmost Gallantry*, p.154.

84 *Naval Chronicle*, Vol.30, p.69.

85 'A.F.Y.' to the Editor, 22 June 1813, *Naval Chronicle*, Vol.30, p.130.

86 'A.F.Y.' to the Editor, 22 June 1813, *Naval Chronicle*, Vol.30, p.136; 'Albion' to the Editor, 16 August 1813, *Naval Chronicle*, Vol.30, pp.199–200.

6

'All I request is that both ships may quickly meet': Victory, defeat, and stagnation, 1813–1814

Just over a month after *Shannon*'s victory, HMS *Dominica*, a small British schooner commanded by Lieutenant Barrett, encountered the American privateer *Decatur*. Rather than try to run, as most privateers would when chased by a Royal Navy vessel, *Decatur*'s commander decided he would engage. He was Dominique Diron, an experienced French privateersman, as bold as he was cocky. The two engaged in a fierce, close-quarters action, and by the end 'not more than three men' still in fighting shape were left on the British schooner. Her lieutenant was killed and the midshipman next in command, Nichols, was badly wounded. The losses on board were so horrific, and the command team so thoroughly destroyed, that the crew had not even managed to throw their secret signal code book overboard before capture. Charles Simpson, a British official who worked to secure parole for Nichols and the surviving crewmen, blamed Lieutenant Barrett's inexperience with schooners (coupled with Diron's long privateering experience) for the embarrassing defeat.[1] It was a remarkable occurrence; privateers rarely fought naval vessels, let alone beat them so thoroughly. Just as remarkably, the event has been overlooked in nearly every account of the naval War of 1812, including Roosevelt's own seminal work.

When reading most histories of the War of 1812, one might think that little happened in the Atlantic following the *Shannon–Chesapeake* action. Yet, a lot happened in the naval theatres of the war in 1813 and 1814; the British blockade intensified and further strained the American economy, ships of the Royal Navy conducted raids and liberated thousands of enslaved African Americans, and the naval contest for the Great Lakes helped decide the fate of Upper and Lower Canada as British colonies. Some more general

1 Charles R Simpson to Thomas Barclay, 24 August 1813, *Naval War of 1812*, Vol.2, pp.216–217; Lambert, *The Challenge*, Chapter 6.

histories of the Royal Navy dismiss everything that occurred following the *Shannon–Chesapeake* action. The better works, like James Davey's excellent *In Nelson's Wake*, still do not discuss the single-ship actions and other events that occurred following the *Shannon–Chesapeake* action and the capture of USS *President* in 1815. The capture of *Dominica* is not an exception. Unlike the frigate actions that occurred in the first full year of the conflict and those that occurred in the last months, the victories and defeats of these British and American commanders and crews have been largely forgotten.[2]

Why were these actions neglected? Were the actions of less importance than the frigate actions, which had a profound impact on the respective navies, presses, and publics, and therefore not worth historical consideration? Certainly, these actions had little impact on the general course of the war. There were far more American privateers attacking British shipping than sloops of war operating throughout the Atlantic during the war, and the strategic impact of those which fought single-ship actions in 1813 and 1814 was minimal. But none of the American heavy frigates had a major impact on the broader war effort either; the fear and concern that *Constitution*, *United States*, *President*, and their new sisters under construction generated was relatively irrational, but it was potent. If the 1812 frigate actions are worthy of historical consideration, why are the 1813–1814 single-ship actions left out of most historical narratives? Largely, this was because frigates had a degree of star power attached to them. They were exciting and glamourous; the British public had always celebrated frigate victories, just as they were horrified by the frigate losses. The sloop losses, while distressing and a subject of conversation, did not have the same emotional attachment. As a result, the single-ship losses of 1813 and 1814 were not as impactful as the three lost frigates in 1812. With the tumultuous events and the welcome end to the Napoleonic Wars – so it seemed – in 1814, they were largely overshadowed, whereas memory of the frigate battles lived on due to their celebrity status.

Victory of the *Pelican* and loss of the *Boxer*, 14 August and 5 September 1813

Following *Shannon*'s victory, the North American squadron continued to expand the blockade. One of Warren's subordinates, Rear Admiral George Cockburn, was given command of the blockading forces in Chesapeake Bay, where several important American ports and cities, including the capital, were located and instituted an aggressive and successful strategy. Elsewhere along the coasts, the Royal Navy was still overstretched and unable to properly watch every port. With Capel's squadron dispersed in search of *President* and *Shannon* still in Halifax, Boston was left completely open. Even at New York, which still had its full blockading squadron protecting it, the Royal Navy had some trouble, and in early June the 18-gun brig-sloop USS *Argus* slipped past the squadron and proceeded to sea.

2 Rodger, *Command of the Ocean*, pp.567–572; Herman, *To Rules the Waves*, pp.409–411; Davey, *In Nelson's Wake*, pp.256–276.

She was commanded by William Henry Allen, recently promoted after having served as First Lieutenant of *United States* in her victory over *Macedonian*. Their mission was to carry the new American minister, William H. Crawford, to France across the Atlantic and the British blockade. Exceptionally cooperative weather and Allen's sailing abilities combined saw *Argus* make France in just four weeks, and after slipping past the British blockade and proceeding back to sea, Allen steered northwards to cruise within British waters and to destroy as much commerce as possible. It was the beginning of the new American strategy, which focused on sending out small lone cruises to wreak havoc on British trade. For four weeks Allen did so, cruising along the south west coast of Ireland, taking and burning over 20 prizes, many captured within just 60 miles of Cork, where the Royal Navy's Irish Station was headquartered. Her cruise generated a degree of panic, and several warships were dispatched to look for the unknown American cruiser, assumed by most to be a privateer. Among the ships out searching was the *Cruizer*-class 18-gun brig-sloop HMS *Pelican* under Commander John F. Maples.[3] After a brief period of searching, just before sunrise on 14 August her lookouts spotted a burning ship. She was a merchant called *Belford*, which had just been caught and burned by Allen, and it was not long before the morning light revealed the American warship herself.[4]

Upon spotting the lone British sloop, Allen was determined to fight. While his orders stated that he should prioritise commerce raiding and that destroying enemy warships was of little strategic benefit, they did not expressly forbid Allen from fighting a comparable enemy warship, at least as he understood it. Allen himself was very confident of victory; he had been second-in-command of one of the United States Navy's great victories in 1812 and had drilled his men thoroughly. However, they were also exhausted after long weeks of sailing and action, and some may have been hung over after having broken into wine stores on the captured *Belford*. Soon after spotting her, Maples had manoeuvred his brig to assume the weather gauge and hoisted his colours; Allen, determined to fight, hoisted his own.[5]

At 6:00 a.m. the two ships were alongside one another, and *Argus* opened fire with her portside 24-pounder carronades. *Pelican*'s crew immediately responded with a resounding cheer and her 32-pounder carronades, beginning a fierce cannonade yardarm to yardarm. Despite Allen's drilling, it was quickly apparent that his ship was outmatched. *Pelican*'s fire was fast, accurate, and deadly, and quickly cut *Argus*'s running rigging to pieces. Minutes after the first guns went off, a British round shattered Allen's leg, leaving the American commander bleeding profusely. Though badly wounded, he refused to be taken below, but shortly after collapsed from

3 McCranie, *Utmost Gallantry*, pp.132–137; Budiansky, *Perilous Fight*, pp.280–281; Latimer, *1812*, pp.238–239.

4 McCranie, *Utmost Gallantry*, pp.132–137; Budiansky, *Perilous Fight*, pp.280–281; Latimer, *1812*, pp.238–239.

5 McCranie, *Utmost Gallantry*, pp.132–137; Budiansky, *Perilous Fight*, pp.280–281; Latimer, *1812*, pp.238–239.

blood loss,[6] leaving the ship in the hands of lieutenant William Watson. Just as Watson took stock of the situation, he was himself hit; British grape shot had grazed his skull, and he collapsed and was taken below.[7]

On board *Pelican*, the British fire was kept up 'with great spirit' and she received very little damage. Thus far none of her officers had been hit, although Maples had a close encounter: a spent cannister shot struck one of his coat's buttons, rebounding harmlessly off.[8] By contrast, *Argus* was leaderless in the hands of her remaining officers, several of whom were themselves wounded. With her running rigging cut away, Maples seized an opportunity to come along and cross *Argus*'s stern and continued to sail up along her starboard side, firing furiously as she went. Watson returned on deck to find *Pelican* within pistol range and further destroying her rigging. He ordered the men to assemble into a boarding party, realising that in gunnery his ship was quickly losing the engagement. Within moments, however, he also realised that, with the rigging so disabled, *Argus* had no way of closing with the enemy to attempt a boarding. *Pelican* continued sailing and soon came about, taking position off *Argus*'s starboard bows and beginning a raking broadside. Watson was unable to respond with any guns and could only answer the British's nine 32-pounders with muskets. What remained of her rigging was shot away, and her bulwarks and decks were smashed around the men. Around 6:45 a.m., the *Pelican* had drifted close enough to board, and as men scrambled over the *Argus*'s bulwarks, waving cutlasses and pikes, Watson concluded that resisting was futile and struck the colours.[9]

In his report of the victory, Maples expressed his delight at the light loss of life and at having 'the good fortune' to learn of *Argus*'s whereabouts by the merchant brig. He praised the gallantry of his men, remarking that they commenced the action with cheers and commenced a cannonade that was 'kept up with great spirit on both sides.'[10] The victory saw Maples promoted to post captain by the end of the month, although he finished his career in retirement, promoted to rear admiral a year before his death.[11] His senior lieutenant, however, never reached the rank of commander, despite serving as the second-in-command in a victorious action and receiving his commander's praise in the following report.[12] This was highly unusual, as the senior lieutenant in such an action was almost invariably promoted. This was possibly because the event was overshadowed by Broke's victory, where two

6 John Hawker to William Allen, Plymouth, 19 August 1813, *Naval War of 1812*, Vol.2, p.224.

7 McCranie, *Utmost Gallantry*, pp.132–137; Budiansky, *Perilous Fight*, pp.280–281; Latimer, *1812*, pp.238–239.

8 Commander John F. Maples to Vice Admiral Sir Edward Thornborough, 14 August 1813, *Naval War of 1812*, Vol.2, p.223; 'John Fordyce Maples, Esq.', in *Royal Naval Biography*, Supplement, Part III, pp.149–153.

9 Maples to Thornborough, 14 August 1813, *Naval War of 1812*, Vol.2, p.223; 'John Fordyce Maples, Esq.', in *Royal Naval Biography*, Supplement, Part III, pp.149–153; Budiansky, *Perilous Fight*, pp.280–281; Latimer, *1812*, pp.238–239.

10 Maples to Thornborough, 14 August 1813, *Naval War of 1812*, Vol.2, p.223.

11 Syrett and DiNardo, *Commissioned Sea Officers*, p.298; 'John Fordyce Maples, Esq.', in *Royal Naval Biography*, Supplement, Part III, pp.149–153.

12 Maples to Thornborough, 14 August 1813, *Naval War of 1812*, Vol.2, p.223; Syrett and DiNardo, *Commissioned Sea Officers*, p.464.

lieutenants had been promoted to commander at a time when the number of commanders already far exceeded the available commands for them.

Promotion and career were the least of Allen's worries. He was gravely wounded during the action and was quickly carried to a hospital in Plymouth, where he died just four days later. Just like James Lawrence, Allen had brought an enemy to battle, confident of victory, despite orders to the contrary; and, again just like Lawrence, he had tackled an enemy whose seamanship and gunnery was impeccable and had paid for it with his life.[13]

By now President Madison was growing weary of single-ship losses. The victories in 1812 had provided the nation with a great boost to morale and had been seized upon by the administration, but they had been risky. The new Secretary of the Navy Jones was also worried about the risk; he only had a limited number of ships and recognised that, as embarrassing as the single-ship losses were for the Royal Navy, the United States Navy stood to lose much more. To that end, he adopted a shift in policy: rather than dispatch ships in small squadrons, as had occurred early in the war, he would focus on having the United States Navy's limited number of frigates and sloops cruise alone, operating in tandem with the hundreds of privateers to wreak havoc on Britain's commercial trade. *President*'s mission throughout 1813 and 1814 would be to harass British shipping; following her escape from Boston under Capel's nose, she managed to instil a disproportionate degree of panic throughout the Royal Navy and British government.[14] *Argus* was to have been an elusive wolf among the trading vessels in Britain's own backyard; instead she had been captured after a brief, albeit successful, cruise.

Like *Chesapeake*, *Argus* had disobeyed her orders to avoid single-ship combat with the enemy, and was subsequently taken. As such, the initial shock she had instilled in Britain soon gave way as news of the victory reached home. It was the second British victory in a row, and surely proof that the Royal Navy's spell of invincibility had been cast anew. Yet hopes that this signalled the beginning of a long-running trend proved premature: a reverse occurred just three weeks later.

* * *

Back on the American side of the Atlantic, another lone American cruiser was operating close inshore. USS *Enterprise* was a small brig-sloop under Lieutenant Commandment William Burrows – a veteran of *Constitution* in the Barbary War – and was patrolling the coastline north of Boston where important coastal trade and naval stores were being ferried from port to port. Armed with fourteen 18-pounder carronades packed into a small and weak frame, hardly built to accommodate such an armament, some in the navy had concerns about her putting to sea at all. On 5 September she was spotted by a British warship, which immediately gave chase, but by a stroke of luck she had happened upon one of the few British vessels in the area with a smaller armament than her – a brig-sloop mounting twelve 18-pounder

13 Lambert, *The Challenge*, Chapter 7.
14 McCranie, *Utmost Gallantry*, p.139.

carronades.[15] She was HMS *Boxer*, under the command of Samuel Blyth, a recently promoted commander and grandson of HMS *Barfleur*'s sailing master at the 1782 Battle of the Saintes. While unable to ascertain her exact armament, Burrows concluded he was facing a small brig and decided that the contest would be a relatively fair one. He had *Enterprise* come about to stand for *Boxer*.[16]

Over the morning, the two brigs slowly approached in light winds, both preparing for action. Blyth ordered the British ensign nailed to the mast and proclaimed to his crew that the colours would never be struck while he stood. Cheers erupted from both crews as the vessels approached. At just 40 yards, Blyth came about in the hopes of opening the engagement by raking *Enterprise*, but Burrows managed to counter and bring his vessel onto a parallel course, just a few yards apart at half-pistol range. At 3:15 p.m., both vessels opened fire. At such short range, the carronades were devastatingly effective, and both commanders fell in minutes. Blyth was reduced to 'a bloody pulp' by a carronade shot just before Burrows was struck by a musket ball.[17] Burrows collapsed onto the deck but refused to be taken below, shouting for his men to continue fighting. Still, Lieutenant Edward McCall effectively assumed command, and the two vessels fired seven or eight closely packed broadsides. Several of *Boxer*'s guns were ripped from their mounts and her main topmast yard and associated rigging was cut away, while much of *Boxer*'s own fire went high but did little damage.[18]

USS *Enterprise* against HMS *Boxer*, the latest in a series of shocking defeats for the British, painting by Michel Corne. (Naval History and Heritage Command)

15 McCranie, *Utmost Gallantry*, pp.191–192; Roosevelt, *Naval War of 1812*, pp.213–214.

16 McCranie, *Utmost Gallantry*, pp.191–192; Roosevelt, *Naval War of 1812*, pp.213–214.

17 McCranie, *Utmost Gallantry*, p.192.

18 McCranie, *Utmost Gallantry*, p.192; Roosevelt, *Naval War of 1812*, pp.214–215.

Emboldened, McCall ordered *Enterprise* to set further sail, and so ranged ahead of her opponent, assuming a raking position off *Boxer*'s starboard bow. The Americans continued to pour raking broadsides into *Boxer*, the crew of which began to unravel. Her remaining officers struggled to rally the men, some of whom fled their stations altogether. Meanwhile, the rigging was cut to shreds, and McCrery was unable to move the ship out of the dangerous position. Together with the remaining officers, he concluded that resistance was futile and decided to surrender. However, with the ensign nailed to the mast this could not be done by simply lowering the flag, so McCrery was forced to step forward, though the hail of round shot and cannister fire, and hail the enemy to report that he had surrendered.[19] As the guns fell silent, Burrows remained on deck, mortally wounded, until Lieutenant McCrery's sword was presented to him; according to Roosevelt, Burrows simply said 'I am satisfied. I die contented' before being taken below.[20]

Both William James and Theodore Roosevelt argued that *Enterprise*'s superior armament and crew size sufficiently explained her victory, and while James admitted that the American guns were handled with more skill, Roosevelt asserted the two forces fought with equal skill, pointing to the fact that the casualties on both sides were close to equal.[21] By contrast, the *Boxer*'s court martial took a different view:

> The court is of the opinion that the capture of HM brig *Boxer*, by the US vessel of war *Enterprise*, is to be attributed to a superiority in the enemy's force, principally in the number of men, as well as to a greater degree the skill in the direction of her fire, and the destructive effects of her first broadside.[22]

The addition of two extra carronades of the same calibre as the 12 on board *Boxer* was only treated as a minor factor in the defeat by the court. The impact of the superiority in force was 'principally' the much larger crew on board *Enterprise*, which went into action with nearly double the men. More importantly, as far as the court was concerned, the crew of *Enterprise* handled their guns with greater skill and accuracy, which saw *Boxer* suffer more damage than her opponent. Although her officers and most of her crew 'conducted themselves with courage, and [with] a determination not to surrender while any prospect of success remained,' due to the destructive fire of the enemy, *Boxer* was left unmanageable and that prospect of success vanished, making surrender the prudent course.[23] The verdict of the court was similar to that of the courts martial for *Guerriere*, *Macedonian*, and *Java*: each ship was acknowledged to have fought until the last moment that success was possible. However, while the state of the damage on board the three frigates had been attributed more or less to ill-fortune, here the court

19 McCranie, *Utmost Gallantry*, pp.192–193; Roosevelt, *Naval War of 1812*, pp.214–215.

20 Roosevelt, *Naval War of 1812*, p.215.

21 Latimer, *1812*, p.239; James, *Naval History*, Vol.6, pp.317–318; Roosevelt, *Naval War of 1812*, p.216.

22 ADM 1/5440, Verdict, CM *Boxer*, quoted in James, *Naval Occurrences*, pp.lxx–lxxii.

23 ADM 1/5440, Verdict, CM *Boxer*, quoted in James, *Naval Occurrences*, pp.lxx–lxxii.

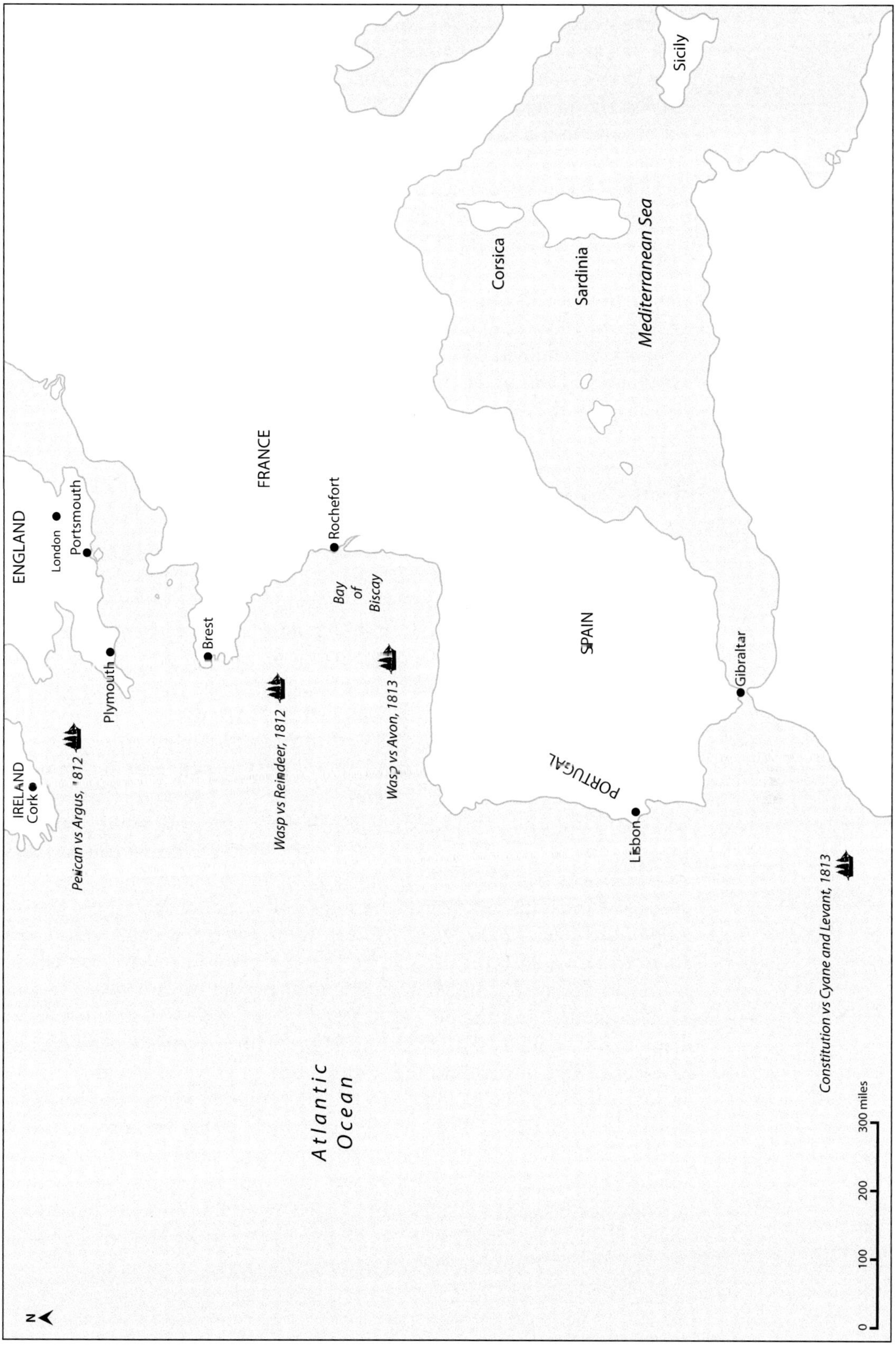

Map 3 Actions in European and West African Waters, 1812–1815.

expressly concluded that the Americans had fought their guns with greater skill. It was a striking admission by the Royal Navy officers in attendance; even in the *Macedonian* court martial, during which Carden and Hope were extensively questioned on the lack of proper gunnery training before the action, and in the case of *Java*, which had been unable to properly exercise her crew owing to her overcrowded state, the respective courts had not attributed the losses to a deficiency in the British gun handling.

McCrery and his fellow officers were not reprimanded for inadequate gun practice and were honourably acquitted. The court did severely reprimand and convict several members of his crew of cowardice, negligence, or disaffection' for having 'deserted their quarters during the action; and … withdrawn themselves from their duty in the engagement';[24] but, though honourably acquitted, McCrery fell victim to the post-war slump of available appointments and never reached the rank of commander, dying a half-pay lieutenant in 1831.[25]

Blockade and challenges off New London

In late spring of 1813, Commodore Decatur prepared to set sail. He had the newly repaired *United States* and the newly commissioned *Macedonian* which was now under the command of Jacob Jones, recently promoted after his victory over *Frolic* half a year earlier. With them was *Hornet*, and together Decatur hoped his squadron could elude the squadron blockading New York and escape into the Atlantic to join the other American cruisers in harassing British commerce. However, the British blockading squadron was well-organised. Captain Robert Oliver, who had previously served under Capel at Boston, held overall command from his exceptionally fast 74-gun ship of the line HMS *Valiant*. He was patrolling the entrance to Sandy Hook at the end of the southern passage out of New York, along with Captain Kerr's heavy frigate HMS *Acasta*. *Acasta* alone was more than a match for *Macedonian*, and Decatur recognised that his own frigate did not stand a chance against the British ship of the line. The slow *United States* was unlikely to be able to slip past them either, so Decatur decided he would slip out through Long Island sound to the north, which was defended by the much slower 74-gun HMS *Ramillies* and the 36-gun HMS *Orpheus*, under the command of Captain Sir Thomas Hardy, Nelson's flag captain at Trafalgar. However, as Decatur's ships moved into the sound, Captain Oliver ordered Hardy to move to Sandy Hook so that Oliver's ships could take over the northern blockade. Officially, Oliver wanted to switch places because his ships needed to take on water, and a convenient source was located just off the mouth at Block Island; but Oliver was also well aware that Decatur was moving northwards, and likely anticipated he would come out. In Oliver's mind, Hardy had already won his share of glory under Nelson; if anyone

24 ADM 1/5440, Verdict, CM *Boxer*, quoted in James, *Naval Occurrences*, pp.lxx–lxxii.

25 Syrett and DiNardo, *Commissioned Sea Officers*, p.288.

should confront Decatur and his squadron, it should be him. Reluctantly, then, Hardy set sail for Sandy Hook, and Oliver's two ships took over the northern blockade.[26]

Not until the morning of 1 June did Decatur's ships weigh anchor and proceed towards Montauk Point, where lookouts spotted *Valiant* and *Acasta*. The Americans steered northwards, hoping to slip past them, but Oliver quickly got his ships underway. As the Americans approached Block Island, however, calls from lookouts on all three ships reported warships in the distance past the island; the reports varied but all agreed that there was at least a ship of the line to northward. With Oliver's ship of the line and heavy frigate approaching from the south, Decatur was trapped. Proceeding to sea would likely mean being brought to action by the much superior British force. Unfortunately for Decatur, the northwards ship of the line did not exist – in the morning mist his lookouts might have spotted a large merchantman, but nothing that posed any threat to him. Still, his ships came about and instead proceeded to the nearest safe port, New London, Connecticut. Oliver immediately set out in pursuit. His ships were lighter, as they were only intended to operate in a small area and were not provisioned for a long voyage like Decatur's, and by noon they had nearly caught up to the Americans. *Acasta* and *United States* exchanged some ineffectual long-range fire as the American squadron passed into the Thames, eventually anchoring within range of local fortifications. Oliver was dismayed that he had not been able to catch the Americans, but he had managed to trap one of America's heavy frigates and two other warships in a relatively narrow harbour, where they could easily be blockaded by the Royal Navy. Along with the capture of USS *Chesapeake*, 1 June saw the Royal Navy remove nearly half of the United States' total operational warships from play. It was far from the gallant climax Oliver and his fellow captains would have hoped for, but it was exactly the sort of outcome that the Admiralty and Warren hoped the blockades would bring about.[27]

While the American warships in New London remained a threat, it was an impotent one. As the months dragged on into 1814, Decatur found no opportunity to slip away; the blockade conducted was too effective, and the weather and geographic conditions too cooperative. Worse still, the population in New London were bitterly against the war, and some turned to sending out reports to the British squadron about Decatur's activity.[28] Decatur and his fellow officers wanted a way out of the tedious boredom. They were of no use to their country sitting in a port town that was flirting with treason, and perhaps the only naval activity more boring and idle than blockading was being blockaded. All along the coastline, British officers too complained about boredom. Captain Robert Barrie stated that 'this Blockading affair is a sad disappointment,' frequently complaining about the tedium, cold weather, and lack of prize opportunities. As unhappy as he was blockading, he was

26 McCranie, *Utmost Gallantry*, pp.141–144; Budiansky, *Perilous Fight*, pp.236–237.
27 McCranie, *Utmost Gallantry*, pp.144–147; Budiansky, *Perilous Fight*, pp.236–237.
28 Budiansky, *Perilous Fight*, pp.346–247.

weary of peace, preferring the war to continue so that the Royal Navy could reduce the United States to 'proper insignificance as a maritime power.'[29]

By January 1814, Captain Oliver had moved on with *Valiant* and *Acasta*, leaving the tedium of blockading Decatur to Hardy, who had been reinforced by the fifth-rate HMS *Statira* commanded by Michael Stackpoole and the crack heavy frigate HMS *Endymion* under the young Captain Henry Hope. Hope had been appointed to command the frigate following an 1813 refit at the recommendation of his uncle, Admiral Sir William Hope – an influential parliamentarian and a member of the Board of Admiralty. It was a prestigious appointment, particularly given the times. HMS *Endymion* was one of two 24-pounder frigates built during the arms race of the 1790s. Newly daubed a full, menacing coat of black paint, her main battery had just been restored in 1813, after having been reduced to 18-pounders following the outbreak of war in 1803. She now once again carried her proper batteries of twenty-six 24-pounders and twenty 32-pound carronades, giving her a broadside weight just 200 short of the American heavy frigates she hoped to bring to action. While she was not as strongly built as the American heavy frigates, Hope had high hopes for her. Beyond her newly restored heavy battery, she was an exceptionally fast ship, able to reach 14 knots downwind and 11 knots close-hauled in an era when most ships averaged closer to six or seven knots.[30]

In mid-January, HMS *Endymion* stopped an American merchantman and Hope brought her master, Nicholas Moran, to a meeting with Captain Hardy. There, Hope expressed his desire for a challenge between his ship and Decatur's *United States*. After several long months of inaction, Hope was eager to come to grips with the enemy; *Endymion* had been ordered to North America and given back her 24-pounder battery for the sake of combating the American heavy frigates, and there was one anchored in the harbour alongside *Macedonian*, a former British ship. Hardy, perhaps motivated by the sting of a former British ship sitting within sight, also suggested a meeting between USS *Macedonian* and HMS *Statira*, both fifth-rates, but stated he would not issue a formal challenge himself. Instead, Moran was allowed ashore to carry the message to Decatur, who immediately responded.

If Hardy had some hesitation about issuing a formal challenge, then Decatur should have done as well. Following the loss of *Chesapeake*, the Madison administration had sought to ensure such a loss would not be repeated. The President and his Secretary of the Navy were uneasy about the preoccupation their officers seemed to have with 'naval chivalry' rather than with their duty. It was an unpopular opinion, as the American public

29 Captain Robert Barrie, RN, to Mrs George Clayton, 4 September 1813, in *Naval War of 1812*, Vol.2, p.384; Captain Robert Barrie, RN, to Dolly Gardner Clayton, 4 February 1814, in Michael J. Crawford, Christine F. Hughes, Charles E. Brodine, Carolyn M. Stallings (eds), *The Naval War of 1812: A Documentary History*, Vol.3: 1814–1815 (Washington: Naval Historical Center, Dept. of Navy, 2002), p.17; Captain Robert Barrie, RN, to Eliza Clayton, 14 March 1814, in *Naval War of 1812*, Vol.3, p.18.

30 Lambert, *The* Challenge, Chapter 7; Gardner, *Frigates of the Napoleonic Wars*, p.145; Morgan Kelly and Cormac Ó Gráda, 'Speed under sail during the early Industrial Revolution', VOX: CEPR Policy Portal (online), available at https://voxeu.org/article/speed-under-sail-during-early-industrial-revolution (accessed 29 January 2019).

were fascinated by their naval triumphs and the concept of challenges, but Secretary Jones initiated a press campaign to influence the public against the practice. In secret orders issued to Captain Stewart of USS *Constitution*, he explicitly stated that 'should any attempt be made to allure you by challenge to single combat, I am directed by the President to prohibit strictly the acceptance either directly or indirectly.'[31] A copy of those orders was also issued to Decatur, although the sailing orders for Decatur and *United States* itself did not include an explicit order against accepting challenges. Jones felt that a copy of his order to Captain Stewart would have been enough to dissuade Decatur, but Decatur was anything but dissuaded.[32] For one thing, the order was not addressed to him; as he saw it, that gave him a grey area in which to operate. Further, his situation was complicated by the fact that he saw no prospect of escaping to sea. Jones's preference may have been to harass enemy trade rather than risk defeat against the enemy, but Decatur's ships posed no threat at all to Britain's commerce from within New London.

On the 17th, then, Decatur wrote to Hardy and recounted the message he had received from Moran:

> Having been informed by Nicholas Moran, the master of a sloop recently captured by his Brittanic [sic] Majesty's ship *Endymion*, now lying before this port, that, whilst he was on board the *Ramillies*, and in your hearing, Captain Hope of the *Endymion* did ask him, whether the frigate *United States* would not avoid an action. He further states, that he heard you declare it to be your wish, that the US ship *Macedonian*, should have a meeting with HBS *Statira*; that you would furnish men, and give room for such meeting; but that you would not permit the challenge to come from your side…
>
> The only difficulty that appears to be in the way, is from whom the formal invitation is to come. If, sir, you admit Moran's statement to be correct, the difficulty will be removed, and you will be pleased to consider this as an invitation.[33]

This then became the American's formal challenge, and it bore some similarity to Broke's challenge to Lawrence the previous summer. Like Broke, Decatur laid out the force of the four frigates of the proposed match:

> The *Endymion*, I am informed, carries 24-pounders; and mounts 50 guns in all. This ship also carries 24-pounders, and mounts 48 guns; besides a 12-pound carronade, a boat gun… The *Statira* mounts 50; the *Macedonian*, 47; metal the same. So that the force on both sides is as nearly equal as we could expect to find.[34]

According to Decatur, the match was as fair as possible under the circumstances, as each ship mounted armaments that were relatively equal

31 Jones to Stewart, 19 September 1813, K. Jack Bauer (ed.), *The New American State Papers: Naval Affairs*, Vol.4 (Wilmington, DE: Scholarly Resources, 1981), pp.182–185, quoted in McCranie, 'Dueling with warships', p.77.

32 McCranie, 'Dueling with warships', p.77.

33 Decatur to Hardy, 17 January 1814, in James, *Naval Occurrences*, pp.c–ci.

34 Decatur to Hardy, 17 January 1814, in James, *Naval Occurrences*, pp.c–ci.

to their intended opponent. He also praised the 'laudable desire' of Hope and Stackpoole for wanting to get into action, and affirmed that he himself and Captain Jones of *Macedonian* were ready and 'equally desirous for such meeting.'[35] Like Broke, Decatur stated that the challenge was made in a good spirit: 'we beg you will assure Captains Hope and Stackpoole, that no personal feeling towards them, induces me to make this communication. They are solicitous to add to the renown of their country: we honor their motives.'[36] In Decatur's mind, with his squadron trapped in port, this matter of honour usurped the vague orders he had received. His duty, then, was to pursue this matter of honour, just as Broke had done months earlier when he disobeyed his orders to maintain the blockade of Boston.

The letter was delivered to the blockading squadron later that day by Master Commandment Biddle of USS *Hornet*, and the British captains immediately began deliberating on a response. Hardy took some time to come to a decision regarding whether to accept the challenge as he was the commanding officer – a commodore in all but name – and whatever happened was his ultimate responsibility, but he did allow Captain Stackpoole to pen an initial response to Decatur affirming that there was no question of a challenge between *Statira* and the former British frigate:

> Captain Sir Thomas Masterman Hardy Bart., and commodore off New London has this afternoon handed me a letter from you, expressing a desire that the United States Ship *Macedonian* commanded by Captain Jones should meet His Majesty's Ship *Statira* under my command: and that the United States Ship *United States* bearing your broad pendant would embrace the same opportunity of meeting the *Endymion* commanded by Captain Hope. In the event of Sir Thomas Hardy's permitting our joint acceptation of this rendezvous I, of course, must be the senior officer; but in the interim, I shall continue my reply to you obliging letter, as to the future acts of His Majesty's Ship I have the honour to command.[37]

Stackpoole stated that a meeting between *Statira* and *Macedonian* would give him, his 'officers, and Crew, the greatest pleasure.' In the same vein as Broke, Stackpoole described his previous frustration at never having had the chance to meet a single opponent, but he also made it clear that his intention to accept the challenge was 'not to vaunt or, in the more trifling degree, to enhance my own professional character, or take from what is so justly due to Captain Jones.' It was, instead, his wish to defend 'the honour of my King, defence of my country, engaged in a just and unprovoked war,' and to add 'to the glory of the British flag.'[38] To that end, he offered his assurance that he would do everything in his power to ensure a fair contest; as the most senior captain under Hardy in the area, he could order friendly ships to depart, and offered Captain Jones of *Macedonian* to select a time and location. It was a

35 Decatur to Hardy, 17 January 1814, in James, *Naval Occurrences*, pp.c–ci.
36 Decatur to Hardy, 17 January 1814, in James, *Naval Occurrences*, pp.c–ci.
37 LAC, MG12 ADM1/505, Admiral's Dispatches, North America, C 12855, Captain Hassard Stackpoole to Commodore Stephen Decatur, HMS *Statira*, off New London, 17 January 1814.
38 LAC, MG12 ADM1/505, Stackpoole to Decatur, 17 January 1814.

generous offer, and one that belied the nature of the Admiralty's blockading strategy.

Stackpoole did take one issue with Decatur's challenge, however, regarding Decatur's estimated statement of force:

> I fear you have been led into error, shall take this opportunity to say, the *Statira* carries only forty six guns instead of fifty with two little boat guns of more utility in exercising the men than any effect they may have in the hour of Battle; and without any external finery to recommend her, is simply a British man of war of her class.[39]

Still, the matter was a minor one; he explained that *Statira* and *Macedonian* were still remarkably close in weight of metal – though pointing out that his ship was the slightly lighter one, rather than *Macedonian* – and that 'a more fair and equal match, in ship and guns, may not soon occur.' They were as close as could be hoped; both fifth-rates, no different than the match between *Shannon* and *Chesapeake*. It was a fair contest of honour that Stackpoole and his commanding officer had no hesitation of accepting. Stackpoole concluded the letter simply: 'all I request is that both ships may quickly meet.'[40]

As Stackpoole's letter explained, the matter of whether *Endymion* would be allowed to accept the challenge was still being deliberated, even if *Statira* had officially accepted. The matter was up to Hardy, and it was not until the following day that he came to a conclusion and sent his response to Decatur ashore:

> I have no hesitation whatever in permitting Captain Stackpoole, in the *Statira*, to meet the *Macedonian*, as they are sister ships carrying the same number of guns and weight of metal; but, as it is my opinion the *Endymion* is not equal to the *United States* … I must consider it my duty (tho very contrary to the wishes of Captain Hope) to decline the invitation on his part.[41]

Hardy took issue with Decatur's statement of force; Decatur had stated that *United States* and *Endymion* were effectively equal, but Hardy did not believe so. Hardy explained that *Endymion* carried only twenty-six 24-pounders on her main deck to *United States*' 30, and that while *Endymion* had a secondary battery of 32-pounder carronades *United States* carried 42s. In all, the British frigate was 200 tons lighter. Hardy made no mention of Decatur's claim that *United States* carried two fewer guns than *Endymion*, but this too must have been difficult to believe. Reports of Decatur's capture of *Macedonian* were well known, and in that action *United States* had carried 54 guns. As it turned out, Decatur had in fact removed six of the forward carronades due to his concern about the already slow ship's hogging and so was telling the truth, but Hardy could not have known that. To him, it appeared that Decatur was

39 LAC, MG12 ADM1/505, Stackpoole to Decatur, 17 January 1814.
40 LAC, MG12 ADM1/505, Stackpoole to Decatur, 17 January 1814.
41 LAC, MG12 ADM1/505, Admiral's Dispatches, North America, C 12855, Captain Thomas Hardy to Commodore Stephen Decatur, HMS *Ramillies*, off New London, 18 January 1814.

not being completely truthful. In the course of the blockade, little had been done to cement trust between the respective commanders. Not long before, Decatur had sanctioned the use of an early form of torpedo in an attempt to sink HMS *Ramillies*; while the attempt failed, it had shocked the British squadron, who were appalled that Decatur had resorted to such 'cruel and unheard-of warfare.'[42] Hardy, whose notion of honour was as strong as any in the period, had little reason to trust Decatur's word. Further, the risk of engaging *United States*, one of the frigates the Admiralty had explicitly prohibited its captains from fighting, was too great.[43] Hardy may have remembered the panic that followed Rodgers's escape following Capel and Broke's challenge off Boston, and had no wish to make the same mistake. Broke's later victory was all that had saved Capel's career and reputation, and there was no guarantee Hardy would be so fortunate. As McCranie points out, 'Though he relished a glorious, honourable and fair fight for the prestige of the Royal Navy, he looked more closely at the potential results of such an engagement, and one could even argue that he considered the potential results on his career.'[44]

Still, it was a remarkable change in tone. Hardy declined a challenge between *Endymion* and *United States* over the risk posed by the enemy's superior broadside. The principal issue were the additional 24-pounders on *United States* and her heavier battery of carronades. Imagining Horatio Nelson coming to a similar conclusion during his lifetime is difficult, and just two years earlier John Carden had boasted to Decatur that a frigate armed with 18-pounders was simply superior to one with the heavier 24s. Decatur would come to realise that himself, Carden assured his friend, and so would the rest of the United States Navy. Instead, Carden and two fellow captains had found that the Americans were able to match their rate of fight, even surpass it, with their heavier guns, and three British frigates had been wrecked. Even if many in the Navy were willing to risk such a battle, the admirals and commanders of squadrons were less willing to take such risks; at the end of the day, they were responsible for losses.

Hope was deeply wounded; his chance to try the best of the British Navy against the *United States* had been denied. The challenge between the two fifth-rates, however, was still on, and Hardy offered his enthusiastic support:

> I have the honour to enclose a letter from Captain Stackpoole bearing your address; and I pledge my honour to facilitate, by every means in my power, the meeting on the rendezvous pointed out by him, and that none of the Captains of His Majesty's ships junior to me shall interfere.[45]

He further offered a guarantee that, should *Macedonian* prevail, he would allow her and the prize to proceed to any safe port, and added that:

42 Benson Lossing, *The Pictorial Field-Book of the War of 1812* (New York: Harper and Brothers, 1868), pp.240–243, 693.
43 Lambert, *The Challenge*, Chapter 7.
44 McCranie, 'Dueling with warships', p.79.
45 LAC, MG12 ADM1/505, Hardy to Decatur, 18 January 1814.

> The Captains of His Britannick Majesty's frigates under my orders as well as myself cannot too highly appreciate the gallant spirit that has led to the communication from you Sir, and are equally convinced, that no personal feeling towards each other can ever influence a laudable ambition to add to the naval Renown of our respective countries.[46]

The matter was now in Decatur's hands. Half of the challenge had been accepted, owing to Hardy's sense of duty and responsibility over engaging one of the heavy frigates with an inferior ship, albeit one close to *United States*' force. The two British captains and the American commodore demonstrated the same zeal and motivations for action, and a similar ambition to resolve the slow and unproductive blockade in a contest of personal and professional honour.

Decatur's response on the following day was not greeted kindly by the British captains. Decatur was annoyed that the initial offer had been rejected, and a proposal for an action between *Statira* and *Macedonian* left no role for him.[47] He also expressed his concern over the risk; *Statira*'s loss could be easily replenished, but if Decatur lost *Macedonian* than he would lose not only one of his frigates, but also a significant chunk of his trained sailors, which would inhibit his ability to carry out his orders to 'put to sea the first favourable opportunity that may occur.'[48] The stakes had been raised and the potential gain, both in terms of honour and material, had been lessened. He admitted that the initial assurances he had given may have been without sufficient caution and added that 'the guarantee against recapture in case the *Macedonian* should prove successful very far from satisfactory.' It was the same defence put forward by Greene in declining the late Captain Lawrence's challenge back in December 1812; assurances aside, could the defeated party be trusted not to come to the captured ship's defence? It was, after all, their duty.

Ultimately, neither commander wished to take the responsibility necessary for such a challenge. Both Decatur and Hardy had orders that more or less prohibited the actions they were considering, and losing even one ship in such a manner would put their respective commands and their mission – not to mention their careers – in jeopardy. They did their best to argue the case for declining in an effort to defend their honour. Decatur also stated he was declining the challenge against the wishes of Captain Jones, who was 'extremely desirous that a meeting should take place,' thereby taking on the responsibility and protecting Jones's honour from any accusations of cowardice.[49] Hardy had done the same in his previous letter by stating that his decision to decline a challenge between *Endymion* and *United States* was 'very contrary to the wishes of Captain Hope.'[50] Whatever practical and strategic reasons had caused the challenge to collapse, the honour

46 LAC, MG12 ADM1/505, Hardy to Decatur, 18 January 1814.

47 McCranie, 'Dueling with warships', p.79.

48 LAC, MG12 ADM1/505, Admiral's Dispatches, North America, C 12855, Commodore Stephen Decatur to Captain Thomas Hardy, HMS *Ramillies*, off New London, 19 January 1814.

49 LAC, MG12 ADM1/505, Decatur to Hardy, 19 January 1814.

50 LAC, MG12 ADM1/505, Hardy to Decatur, 18 January 1814.

and reputation of their captains had to be protected; and certainly Hope, Stackpoole, and Jones were deeply saddened that their chance at action had been denied. Not long after, Commander William Mends of HMS *Loup Cervier* – formerly the American *Wasp*, under Captain Jones's command – arrived and learned that, in the negotiations, Master Commandment Biddle of USS *Hornet* had issued a challenge between their ships. Mends offered to accept the challenge; but this, too, quickly fell apart; Mends and Biddle wished to modify their complement and armament to ensure the action would be as equal as possible, but while Decatur allowed Biddle to remove two of his guns to put her on par with the British sloop, he would not allow Biddle to sacrifice his advantage in crewmen. Because of this, Hardy again took it upon himself to decline the challenge, disappointing Mends while shielding him from responsibility.[51]

Subsequently, Hardy reported the exchange to Warren, and included copies of his, Stackpoole's, and Decatur's letters in the dispatch. Hardy admitted that he had taken extraordinary responsibility over discussing a potential encounter with the enemy, but argued that the matter was 'deeply interesting to the feelings of Captains Hope and Stackpoole and the honour of the British character' and hoped Warren would agree that the novel exchange merited a thorough consideration and 'most mature deliberation.'[52] Warren did not agree, and reported to the Admiralty that he was 'very glad the matter terminated in the manner it did.'[53] Warren wished to avoid further losses to the Americans, and he was shocked Hardy had considered so reckless of a course of action, particularly on the whim of personal honour, 'thinking it extremely improper private feeling should interfere … with the public service.' Personal honour, even professional honour, was not worth 'affording the enemy an opportunity to advance his small force upon an equality with ours in its present great superiority.' The Admiralty was entirely in agreement, and they subsequently issued orders to prohibit the issuing and accepting of challenges at all, as the United States Navy had after the loss of *Chesapeake*.[54]

Such challenges were indeed novel occurrences, and yet at least seven formal and informal challenges were issued during the conflict, with several more possibly authentic ones. As strange as this was, stranger still was that not a single one actually resulted in an action. Dacres's challenge to *President* or any of her sisters in revenge for *Little Belt* was likely never seen by Isaac Hull before he chanced upon the British frigate with 'Not the Little Belt' emblazoned on her topsail. Greene, faced with the risk of an American heavy frigate nearby and a fortune of gold he was duty-bound to deliver home, declined Lawrence's challenge. Broke and Capel's ploy off Boston nearly resulted in a challenge, but Rodger in the end decided his duty to carry

51 McCranie, 'Dueling with warships', p.80.

52 LAC, MG12 ADM1/505, Admiral's Dispatches, North America, C 12855, Captain Thomas Hardy to Admiral John Warren, HMS *Ramillies*, off New London, 21 January 1814.

53 LAC, MG12 ADM1/505, Admiral's Dispatches, North America, C 12855, Admiral John Warren, to Secretary John Croker, Bermuda, 2 February 1814.

54 LAC, MG12 ADM1/505, Admiral's Dispatches, North America, C 12855, Warren, to Croker, 2 February 1814.

out his mission was more important than his personal honour, particularly given the risk posed by Capel's ships of the line lying somewhere beyond the horizon. Even Broke's carefully crafted challenge to James Lawrence had been for nothing; the letter had not even reached the harbour by the time that *Chesapeake* was under weigh. The presence of a lone British frigate, defiantly parading within sight of Boston, was all the provocation Lawrence needed. The same conditions that made single-ship actions so rare – namely the conflict between duty and matters of chivalric honour and the frequency that ships cruised in groups rather than alone – made such challenges difficult to accept. Accepting a challenge depended upon a great deal of trust, near-perfect weather and situational conditions, and a willingness to disobey or deliberately misinterpret orders.

This aborted challenge was deeply disappointing for Hope and Stackpoole. Hope saw his mission in North America as being to confront one of the American heavy frigates, and perhaps his best chance at doing so had slipped him by. Stackpoole, meanwhile, was frustrated. Like Broke, his ship had not yet had the opportunity of encountering a lone enemy, but by a stroke of abysmal luck he had twice come across American squadrons and been forced to retreat. Now his chance to command a small squadron action against a superior enemy was seized from him. Just months later, an irritated Stackpoole got into an argument with one of the lieutenants in the blockading squadron. Having been denied his chance to fight a duel for honour at sea against the Americans, the two officers fought one ashore, and Stackpoole was shot and killed just weeks before his 45th birthday.

David Porter and USS *Essex* in the Pacific

Captain David Porter's experience during the first 18 months of the War of 1812 was full of activity. The young American captain of USS *Essex* had already captured nine merchant prizes by the time he captured HMS *Alert* in early August, 1812, marking the end of a brief but successful first cruise in the conflict. On route home to the Delaware, one night several of the captured *Alert* crewmen broke out of the hold, intending to slip overboard into one of the ship's boats and effect their escape. As the group, led by the former commander's coxswain, crept through the dark and silent berth deck, one of the midshipmen, feigning sleep, spotted the men creeping by and managed to sound the alarm. Porter responded by running throughout the ship bellowing 'Fire!' The well-rehearsed *Essex* crew sprang to their feet, ready to battle a shipboard fire; instead they found themselves surrounding a panicking group of escaped British prisoners who believed the ship actually to be aflame, and quickly rounded them up. Upon his return home, Porter had much to be proud of: he had taken over 400 British prisoners and captured prizes worth over $300,000. Yet Porter was still frustrated. He had missed his one chance at fighting an enemy frigate one-on-one when HMS *Minerva* avoided battle to protect the troop convoy under her care, her captain no doubt equally frustrated at having to decline action, and his victory over the tiny *Alert* carried no glory or satisfaction for the ambitious young naval captain.[55] Porter was unawares he had missed another chance; early in his cruise he encountered HMS *Shannon*, along with a merchant prize just captured, but mistaking the prize for a sloop of war he had prudently fled, much to Philip Broke's great annoyance.

Essex remained in port for less than two months. Despite his concerns over *Essex*'s armament, which consisted of carronades rather than long guns, Porter was eager to get into action, and in October 1812 he put to sea and began a voyage that would prove to be the most ambitious in American history to date. Initially, he was to sail to the Cape Verde Islands (3,500 miles away) to rendezvous with Commodore Bainbridge, his nominal commanding officer; but due to poor weather, the inevitable realities of sailing, and the vastness of the ocean, that rendezvous never took place, and early in January 1813 he learned from an American merchant vessel that Bainbridge had fought and defeated a British frigate and gone home. Alone in the South Atlantic, with provisions running low, and with attempts to sail back to the United States being virtually impossible due to the approaches to home ports being blocked by the Royal Navy, Porter needed a neutral port to take on provisions, and he judged that the nearest port that was safe from British cruisers was in Chile. Knowing he was deviating far from his orders but eager to strike out on his own, Porter drove his ship hard through the South Atlantic and around Cape Horn, and throughout the next year cruised in the heart of the territory of the British whaling fleet, snapping up a dozen rich whaler prizes. One particularly well-built and fast prize he converted into a small sloop of war armed with a small crew and 20 guns, affectionately named *Essex Junior*.[56] As the months stretched on and the prizes mounted, Porter anticipated – and indeed hoped – that the Royal Navy admiral commanding the fleet in the South Atlantic would hear of Porter's exploits and dispatch ships to hunt him down.[57] Provided *Essex* could find a fair and honourable match, it would prove a fitting victorious end to a long cruise.

As it turned out, a Royal Navy frigate had been dispatched by the Admiralty to operate in the Pacific under the command of the long-serving and distinguished Captain James Hillyar. Hillyar, in command of the fifth-rate HMS *Phoebe*, had been dispatched to assert British control into the area of what is now Oregon, where several American traders had set up work, much to the annoyance of the British Northwest Company.[58] In June 1813, *Phoebe* arrived in Rio de Janeiro, where the South American station under Rear Admiral Manley Dixon was based. Dixon was overjoyed at *Phoebe*'s arrival, especially upon learning she was bound for the Pacific. He had received reports of *Essex* running amok in the unprotected Pacific waters, but did not have enough ships to spare to send anyone after Porter. He was able to attach two sloops, *Cherub* and *Racoon*, under Hillyar's command for her voyage into the Pacific, and made it clear to Hillyar that, orders aside, hunting down *Essex* was now his most pressing concern. Once in the Pacific,

55 Daughan, *Shining Sea*, pp.4–6.

56 Daughan, *Shining Sea*, pp.87–160; McCranie, *Utmost Gallantry*, pp.176–181.

57 Daughan, *Shining Sea*, pp.143–144.

58 Daughan, *Shining Sea*, pp.164–165.

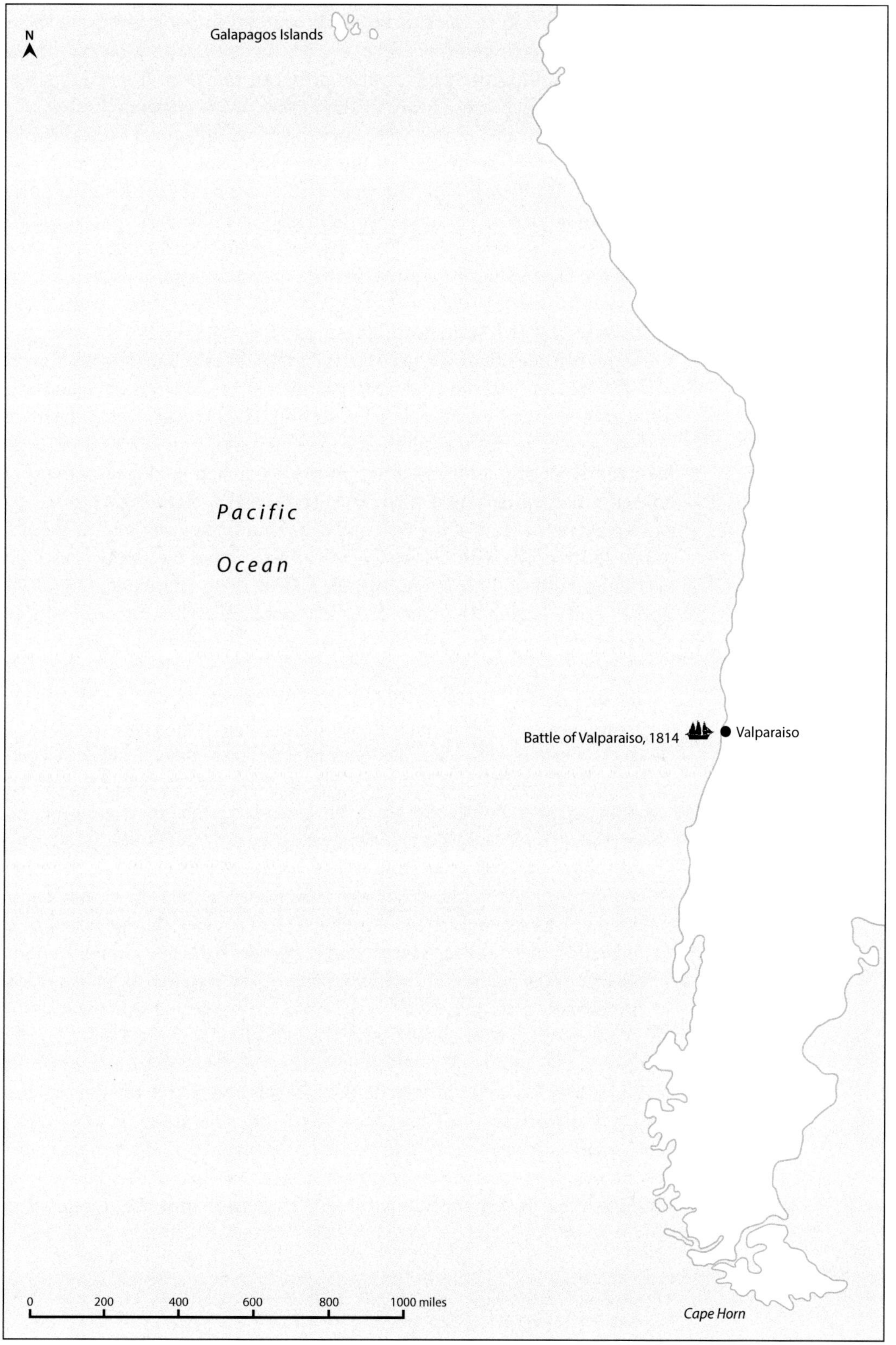

Map 4 Operations in the Pacific, 1814.

Hillyar dispatched *Racoon* to fulfil his original mission along the Oregon coast, while *Phoebe* and *Cherub* set out on the hunt for USS *Essex*. After long weeks of searching the vast expanse of ocean they found nothing, and the frustrated British put in towards Valparaiso to take on stores.[59]

Both Hillyar and Porter were spoiling for a fight, and unbeknownst to each other they were headed in the same direction. Upon their arrival off Valparaiso, the British lookouts were astounded to see an American frigate with a small consort anchored in the harbour. Hillyar was ecstatic; he had found his quarry *Essex* and *Essex Junior*. Inside the harbour, the men of *Essex* were alerted by a signalman firing a gun, and the crew began excitingly preparing for battle.[60] *Phoebe* and *Cherub* sailed into the port within hailing distance of the two American ships, and for several days the combatants stood off, neither side wishing to fire the first shot in a neutral port. The crews of both sides taunted the other with patriotic songs, chants, and jeers, hoping to goad their rivals into action or deserting. Hillyar and Porter, meanwhile, both sought to tempt the other captain into making the first move. Beyond their manoeuvring and posturing, they also turned to sloganeering. Porter hoisted a flag emblazoned with 'Free Trade and Sailors Rights', one he had carried since the start of the war, and the same slogan carried by *Chesapeake* in her show-down with *Shannon*. Hillyar responded by hastily hoisting one declaring 'God and Country; British Sailors' Best Rights; Traitors Offend Both.'[61] On 9 March, the crew of *Essex* even challenged the crew of *Phoebe* themselves:

> The sons of liberty and commerce on board the saucy *Essex*, whose motto is 'Free Trade and Sailor's Rights,' present their compliments to their oppressed brother tars, on board the ship whose motto is too tedious to mention, and hope they will put an end to all this nonsense of singing, sporting, hunting and writing, which we know less about than the use of our guns – Send the *Cherub* away, we will meet your frigate and fight you, then shake hands and be friends; and whether you take us or we take you, either will be to your advantage; as in the first case, you will not doubt, for the service you render in a cause every brave and free man detests, be turned over to Greenwich hospital, or to a new ship, on your arrival to England; and if we take you, we shall respect the rights of a sailor, hail you as brethren whom we have liberated from slavery, and place you in future beyond the reach of a press gang.[62]

The two forces opposing each other were similar but not quite equal. *Essex* carried a much heavier broadside than *Phoebe*, but her armament consisted mainly of carronades. This gave her a tremendous advantage in close-quarters action, but at longer range she was at a disadvantage. *Essex Junior*, on the other hand, was a warship hastily outfitted in the open ocean. She was vastly outnumbered in terms of crew by HMS *Cherub*, and only mounted guns

59 Daughan, *Shining Sea*, pp.166–169; McCranie, *Utmost Gallantry*, pp.184.

60 Daughan, *Shining Sea*, pp.219–221.

61 Daughan, *Shining Sea*, pp.221–223.

62 'The Crew of *Essex* to the Crew of *Phoebe*, 9 March 1814', in *Naval War of 1812*, Vol.3, p.721.

with half the broadside weight. The British then had a noteworthy advantage, particularly if the action was not fought at point-blank range. To rectify the situation and even the odds, both Porter and his crewmen openly challenged Hillyar and the crew of *Phoebe* to single combat, but Hillyar declined. He was under explicit orders to destroy *Essex*, and if he fought and lost without utilising his powerful consort, HMS *Cherub*, he risked serious penalties back home. After a long career during which Hillyar had established a steadfast reputation as a daring and zealous officer, he felt no particular need to prove himself. He had his orders and his duty, and he intended to see them through.[63] Porter, meanwhile, was motivated by 'personal chivalry and honour.'[64] If he was facing a younger opponent, like Broke or Henry Hope, or if Hillyar had not been specifically directed to neutralize *Essex*, then perhaps he would have got the fight he wanted. Instead, both British ships remained in the harbour, opposing the Americans.

After weeks of waiting, Porter finally accepted that Hillyar would not grant him a fight; on 28 March he weighed anchor and headed out to sea, hoping to draw the British after him and allow *Essex Junior* to escape. Once she was safely away, *Essex*, by far the better sailor of the ships in the harbour, could outrun the British and meet up with *Junior* later. Almost immediately the plan went awry, and *Essex* suffered damage in strong winds, which forced her to turn back. *Phoebe* and *Cherub* were at this time in pursuit, alarmed at *Essex*'s near escape. As the American limped back, Hillyar concluded he could not afford her attempting to escape again; neutrality within the port be damned, he was going to destroy the American frigate. Porter, his ship anchored and damaged, had no choice but to let the two British ships approach. *Essex* cleared for action and her crew rigged additional guns from her stern ports as the two British ships ranged alongside. *Phoebe* with her long 18-pounders took position off her stern and *Cherub* off her bow, and both opened fire just before 4:00 p.m. *Essex* was trapped and badly mauled during the firing, but despite only being able to respond with a handful of chase guns on the bow and stern, she put up a steady fight. Porter, despite his efforts, was unable to bring his ship around and place his broadside alongside the enemy, and so the action continued as the British ships drifted out of the range of the *Essex*'s chasers, hammering the American ship without receiving any shot in return.[65]

With no other option left, Porter's men hoisted a tattered jib from the wreckage of her forward rigging, cut her anchor cable and began drifting towards HMS *Phoebe*. He intended to crash into the other frigate and carry her by boarding, but in her crippled state she was not able to approach before Hillyar manoeuvred away, continuing to batter *Essex* with *Phoebe*'s long guns. The dead and wounded mounted on board *Essex*, and Porter decided that continuing to fight was fruitless. Rather than surrender, though, he pointed his ship towards the shore, where he intended to land the vessel and set her on fire to avoid capture. In the heavy winds, even in her crippled state,

63 Daughan, *Shining Sea*, pp.222–223.

64 McCranie, 'Dueling with warships', p.83.

65 Daughan, *Shining Sea*, pp.226–230.

he judged he could make it. Just as he was 100 feet away the wind shifted, and *Essex* was pushed back towards the British frigate, which was still firing ceaselessly. Finally, at 6:20 p.m., over two hours after the fighting had begun, Porter struck his colours. Miraculously, Porter and his senior lieutenant were unharmed, but few of their fellow officers or crew could say the same. Of the 255 men on board, 155 were dead, wounded, or missing.[66]

Hillyar proved a gracious victor, welcoming the distraught Porter 'delicately' and letting the defeated captain keep his sword. He acknowledged how bravely Porter's men had fought, and indeed, despite the odds and the limited guns *Essex* could bring to bear at any one time, they had done considerable damage, and the defeated crew were treated with great humanity and respect.[67] Still, the action had opened with *Essex* outnumbered and in a raking position, and the disparity in causalities and outcome of the battle were no surprise. Barring some stroke of luck that would have allowed Porter to escape or seriously disable one of his opponents, victory was impossible. Hillyar certainly acknowledged and appreciated that. While he praised the gallantry and zeal of his officers and crew (and the wounded Commander Thomas Tucker of *Cherub*), Hillyar's official dispatch was not boastful:

> The defence of the *Essex*, taking into consideration our Superiority of force; the very discouraging circumstance of her having lost her Main Topmast; and being twice on fire, did honor to her brave defenders, and most fully evinced the courage of Captain Porter and those under his command: Her Colours were not Struck until the loss in killed and wounded was So awfully great.[68]

He had simply done his duty to protect Britain's merchantmen and sailors in the Pacific, even initiating a fight in neutral waters against an outmatched opponent, whom he praised for fighting until their ship was in a 'condition so seriously bad as to render further resistance unavailing.'[69]

Not all of the officers involved were as content as Hillyar. His First Lieutenant, William Ingram – one of the few to be killed in the action – reportedly urged his captain to abandon the raking position during the action and instead to board the crippled ship. Ingram, described as 'a chivalrous young man,' maintained that standing off the enemy's stern when she was helpless was nothing but murder.[70] His notion of honour and chivalry contrasted sharply with that of the much older Hillyar during the action. Porter himself accused Hillyar of cowardice for not initiating the action until *Essex* was disabled and trapped by superior opponents. Curiously, though, Porter's own beloved foster son, David Farragut, later came to Hillyar's defence:

---

66 Daughan, *Shining Sea*, pp.230–234.

67 Lambert, *The Challenge*, Chapter 8; Daughan, *Shining Sea*, pp.238–240.

68 Captain James Hillyar, RN, to First Secretary of the Admiralty John W. Croker, 30 March 1814, in *Naval War of 1812*, Vol.3, p.729.

69 Hillyar to Croker, 30 March 1814, in *Naval War of 1812*, Vol.3, p.729.

70 David Glasgow Farragut, in Loyall Farragut, *The Life of David Glasgow Farragut: First Admiral of the United States Navy* (New York: D. Appleton and Company, 1879), p.39. Daughan, *Shining Sea*, p.239.

> It has been quite common to blame Captain Hillyar for his conduct in this affair; but, when we come to consider the characteristics of the two commanders, we may be inclined to judge more leniently, although Captain Porter's complaints in the matter will excite no surprise. Porter was about thirty-two years of age at the time, and the 'pink of chivalry,' of an ardent and impetuous temperament; while Hillyar was a cool and calculating man about fifty years old, and, as he said to his First Lieutenant, ' had gained his reputation by several single- ship combats, and only expected to retain it on the present occasion by an implicit obedience to his orders, viz., to capture the *Essex* with the least possible risk to his vessel and crew ; and, as he had a superior force, he had determined not to leave anything to chance, behoving any other course would call down on him the disapprobation of his government.[71]

Farragut, who was a midshipman on board during the cruise, was deeply attached to Porter but still defended Hillyar in this matter decades later. It was, quite simply, a conflict between the notion of chivalry and duty. For many of Hillyar's contemporaries in the Royal Navy, the two went hand in hand. Pursuing matters of honour and chivalry was considered to be within the interest of the service, even when officers neglected their orders and official duty to find them. Hillyar was no Broke – as a younger man, perhaps he had been, but he had nothing left to prove, a keen sense of his own duty, and a determination to follow his orders through to conclusion.

71 Farragut, *Life of Farragut*, p.39; Daughan, *Shining Sea*, p.239.

7

'Defended so long as she could be with any prospect of success': Lost sloops and elusive frigates, 1814

Even as the War of 1812 raged along the American–Canadian border, the inhabitants of Canada and Nova Scotia were well aware that the focus of the United Kingdom was on the titanic struggles in Europe rather than, as one Canadian journalist called it, 'our puny war.'[1] While the North American squadron swelled in size, the bulk of the Royal Navy was still needed to blockade the vast European coasts, where Napoleon Bonaparte was slowly rebuilding his battle fleet. The British Army, aside from scattered colonial garrisons and the few thousand men guarding the Canadian frontier, were fighting under Lord Wellington in the Peninsula. Strategy in North America always hinged on the state of the War of the Sixth Coalition in Europe, but by early 1814, the British (with their Spanish and Portuguese allies) had invaded across the Pyrenees into southern France. In Germany, Bonaparte's army had been shattered by a grand coalition of the Austrians, Prussians, and Russians, and he had been pushed back deep into France. On 4 April, he was confronted by his marshals, who informed him he had lost the support of the army. Just a few days later, he heard that the French Senate had dethroned him and that the allies had demanded his unconditional surrender. On 11 April 1814, Napoleon surrendered and abdicated, and after over 20 years of unprecedented continental conflict Europe was finally in a state of peace. In the United Kingdom, this meant that thousands of veteran soldiers were now available to be dispatched to North America, and the 'puny war' was about to take a dramatic turn.

The change in strategy began with Warren's replacement by Alexander Cochrane, a zealous though irritable Scottish peer with a deep loathing of

1 NSA, *Acadian Recorder*, Saturday 4 December 1813, 1:47 (online), available at https://novascotia.ca/archives/newspapers/archives.asp?ID=800.

the Americans.[2] Raising his flag on HMS *Tonnant*, an 80-gun ship of the line, Cochrane immediately petitioned for additional ships, much to the Admiralty's annoyance. Cochrane recognised he needed many more ships to properly carry out his orders and set to work on bringing the war to America. The blockade was expanded to include the entire American coastline and the Royal Navy conducted a series of campaigns in cooperation with the newly arrived British veterans to assault prominent targets along the American coast, including Baltimore and even Washington itself – a strategy Cochrane had envisioned since 1812 but had been impossible to conduct as long as resources were limited by the war in Europe.[3]

British campaigns were launched throughout the year – with mixed success – and the capital was seized and burned, with thousands of slaves liberated along the coast. America's trade was squeezed as the blockade tightened, and the limited number of American warships increasingly struggled to get to sea. *United States* and her consorts remained trapped in New London, and USS *President* was shut into New York harbour from February 1814 onwards by the blockading squadron. *Constitution* cruised (without much success) for the first few months of 1814 before being chased back into Boston in April by a pair of British frigates. Several more ships, including the small frigate USS *Adams* and the sloop *Rattlesnake*, got to sea but were unable to escape from the Royal Navy squadrons prowling the coastline. The United States Navy in 1814 was reduced to a handful of operational warships – all sloops – which continued the mission of preying on Britain's commerce. Two of those sloops fell in with the Royal Navy, and between them fought three British sloops into submission. Unlike the previous year, there were no single-ship victories to offset the losses.

Peacock–Epervier action, 28 April 1814

USS *Peacock*, named in honour of James Lawrence's victory over HMS *Peacock*, began her naval career uneventfully. A heavily-built sloop of war armed with twenty 32-pound carronades, she was launched in September of 1813, but due to the neglect of naval infrastructure throughout the country it took four months to fully rig, arm, and man her, so she only put to sea in March of the following year. While she evaded the squadron blockading New York, she spent the next month and a half searching in vain for British merchants, chasing but not catching the only three ships she spotted. It was not exactly what Master Commandment Lewis Warrington had hoped for upon putting to sea, but his luck changed on the 29 April when *Peacock*'s lookouts spotted a small British convoy off Florida under the protection of the 18-gun *Cruizer*-class brig-sloop HMS *Epervier*.

Epervier, under Commander Richard Wales, was not exactly a lucky ship. Her officers complained at length over the poor quality of their small

2 Budiansky, *Perilous Fight*, p.284.

3 Toll, *Six Frigates*, pp.431–437; Gwyn, *Frigates and Foremasts*, pp.145–149; Latimer, *1812*, pp.245–255; McCranie, *Utmost Gallantry*, pp.213–220.

crew and the defective state of the brig herself; she had once sunk at anchor during a hurricane in Halifax harbour, remaining under water for some time before being raised. In that time, the saltwater had corroded much of her equipment, further weakening the ship. The same morning that she encountered *Peacock*, her mainmast and bowsprit were badly sprung. Yet Wales had the weight of Royal Navy tradition and its urge for revenge upon his shoulders as well as his responsibility to protect the merchantmen under his protection, not to mention nearly $120,000 worth of specie on board his own ship. Though he carried a smaller armament – sixteen 32-pound carronades and a pair of lighter long guns to *Peacock*'s twenty 32s – and a much smaller crew, Wales knew his duty was to engage the enemy to allow his convoy to escape, and so stood on in between *Peacock* and the fleeing merchants and cleared for action.[4]

Peacock came down with the wind towards the enemy, clearing for action herself, and at 10:00 a.m. manoeuvred to get behind *Epervier* into a raking position. *Epervier* instead tacked and brought herself alongside the American. Both opened fire at close range with their starboard broadsides. *Epervier*'s opening broadsides posed as much danger to her crew as to the enemy, as several of the carronades snapped from the sides and went caravanning along the deck. Their fastenings were corroded, likely due to exposure to the saltwater while the ship was submerged, and the impact of recoil caused them to snap off. The close-range shot, round and grape, quickly cut away the running rigging on both vessels, and *Peacock* found herself effectively unable to manoeuvre quickly into the action; but Warrington still had the advantage in numbers and weight of shot, and his carronades continued to hammer *Epervier* hard. On board the British sloop, the situation slowly deteriorated. Her rigging was cut to pieces, and before long Wales had lost his one advantage of manoeuvrability over the enemy.

With every broadside, more of *Epervier*'s bolts were shook to pieces and carronades came loose, threatening to crush the sailors scrambling around her deck. Dozens of men were diverted with every broadside to catch and restrain the guns shaken loose, stretching the demoralised men to their limits as they tried to keep up with the Americans' rate of fire. The Eperviers' morale deteriorated over the next half-hour, many men fleeing their stations and taking refuge below. The senior lieutenant, John Hackett, attempted to rally the men, but was struck in the arm by enemy shot, which carried his elbow joint clean off. The crew were fleeing their stations, the mainmast collapsed over the side, and only one carronade was left in action on the engaged broadside; Wales thus 'deemed it prudent to surrender,' forced to be content with the fact that he had fought long enough to allow his convoy to escape.[5]

4 McCranie, *Utmost Gallantry*, p.204; Roosevelt, *Naval War of 1812*, p.313; Lambert, *The Challenge*, Chapter 6.

5 LAC, MG12 ADM1/506, Admiral's Dispatches, North America, C 12855, Commander Richard Wales to Vice Admiral Alexander Cochrane, 8 May 1814; McCranie, *Utmost Gallantry*, pp.204–205.

Warrington carried the battered prize and her small fortune in specie home to America. As of the end of August, Wales and his crew remained prisoners in Savannah, Georgia, where Wales reported the loss to the new commander-in-chief.[6] Wales explained that the defeat was principally owing to the damage to the rigging and to the disabled broadside. Over the course of the action, the carronades had been put out of action by their own restraining bolts snapping and by enemy shot, which eventually rendered the engaged broadside useless. Owing to the extensive rigging damage, however, Wales had been unable to come about and bring the other broadside to bear against the enemy, so *Epervier* was left unable to effectively respond while steadily taking on water. He also reported that Lieutenant Hackett was recovering in hospital but had been forced to have his shattered arm amputated.[7]

Wales remained a prisoner for some time. By this period in the war, the cordial system of prisoner exchanges and parole between the United States and United Kingdom had broken down, in large part over Britain's refusal to return escaped slaves to America and the overabundance of American prisoners of war held in British prisons.[8] Wales's court martial was then delayed until the following January, during the brief period between the signing and ratification of the Treaty of Ghent, which brought the war to an end. At the trial, Wales reiterated his argument that extensive damage had led to his defeat, further stating that the ship's wheel had been rendered useless by the wreckage of the boom and main sail that had covered it. Efforts to man the tiller proved impossible, and the ship had been dead in the water under enemy fire.[9] According to Second Lieutenant John Harvey, at the close of the action Wales summoned the remaining officers who concluded that getting the unengaged starboard battery to bear

> was thought impracticable, the Captain then asked if we were of opinion that we could carry the enemy by boarding and the officers were of opinion it was impossible, the colours were then ordered to be struck by the captain, we were then about half a cables length from the enemy.[10]

Neither officer commented on the advantage the Americans had in the additional carronades as several historians have done, but instead focused on the disparity in the quality of the respective crews. Wales complained of the boatswain's 'want of activity and exertion,' while Harvey stated that for the most part the Eperviers 'were not strong men.'[11] This was reiterated by Lieutenant Hackett, the master, and the quartermasters, who all complained at length about the poor state of the crew, among whom not even 'twenty men in the ship … had been in action before; they were a weak crew and not

6 LAC, MG12 ADM1/506, Admiral's Dispatches, North America, C 12855, Vice Admiral Alexander Cochrane to Secretary John Croker, 29 August 1814.

7 LAC, MG12 ADM1/506, Admiral's Dispatches, North America, C 12855, Wales to Cochrane, 8 May 1814.

8 Dietz, *For Their Safekeeping*, pp.371–386; Latimer, *1812*, p.397.

9 TNA, ADM 1/5447, Testimony of Commander Richard Wales, CM *Epervier*.

10 TNA, ADM 1/5447, Testimony of Lt. John Harvey, CM *Epervier*.

11 TNA, ADM 1/5447, CM *Epervier*: Testimonies of Wales, Harvey.

bred as seamen.' One of the quartermasters even stated that 'if we had been well manned we should have taken her I think.'[12]

The crewmen were described as weak and as poor seamen, and their incompetence was a major feature of the defence of the officers of *Epervier*. Nevertheless, this defence offered by the command team (from the commander to the lowly quartermasters) belies the fact that, as officers, they were responsible for instructing, training, and leading the crew. The court martial questioned on this extensively, particularly regarding gunnery. Wales reported that the crew was 'frequently exercised, but there were many who were not so expert as I thought they ought to have been, from the time they had been exercised.'[13] Lieutenant Hackett was later asked if the carronade fastening bolts, which had been shaken loose by the recoil of the guns, had showed any sign of damage or had previously failed during gunnery practice, and made a startling admission: 'no, as we never exercised with powder.'[14] Instead, the men ran through the motions of loading, aiming, and firing the guns without actually loading and firing.[15] In fact, in the time since Wales had taken command, the ship had only ever fired one gun with live ammunition. No wonder, then, that the men were so inadequate at gunnery; pantomime drill was no substitute for proper practice. Because of this, the men performed slowly in the heat of battle, and many were shocked and demoralised by the fighting, which only added to the confusion. It is likely also that the decayed carronade bolts, which had proved defective and shattered with the impact of recoil, would have been identified before the action if the guns had been regularly fired with powder, or at least been fired at all. That they were never tested is astonishing; *Epervier* had recently sunk in a hurricane and been underwater in Halifax for days. As corrosive as salt water was known to be, any competent seaman should have had the inclination to test his equipment following such an episode, but not Commander Wales.

While this was not uncommon in Royal Navy ships, an earlier Admiralty directive had explicitly ordered captains in the North American squadron to pay greater attention to gunnery:

> Their Lordships trust that all of the Officers of His Majesty's Naval Service must be convinced that upon the good discipline and the proper training of their Ships Companies to the expert management of the Guns, the preservation of the high character of the British navy most essentially depends, and that other works on which it is not unusual to employ the Men are of very trifling importance, when Compared with a due Preparation (by instruction and practice) for the effectual Services on the day of Battle.[16]

12 TNA, ADM 1/5447, CM *Epervier*: Testimonies of Lt. John Hackett, David Genlan, Master, William Pearson, quartermaster.

13 TNA, ADM 1/5447, Testimony of Wales, CM *Epervier*.

14 TNA, ADM 1/5447, Testimony of Hackett, CM *Epervier*.

15 TNA, ADM 1/5447, CM *Epervier*: Testimonies of Wales, Hackett, Harvey, Genlan, Pearson.

16 Admiral Sir John Warren, RN, Standing Order on the North American station, Bermuda, 6 March 1813, *Naval War of 1812*, Vol.2, p.59.

Wales, it seems, thought pantomime drills were sufficient; the action with *Peacock* proved otherwise. Largely because of this, the *Peacock–Epervier* action is considered by many historians to be the most one-sided affair in the war, even though *Eperiver*'s broadside was only slightly lighter than her opponent.[17] In terms of fighting ability, *Epervier* did not stand a chance. In response to this loss, Vice Admiral Cochrane issued further orders regulating gunnery within the North American squadron, establishing a regular schedule and mandating proper live fire training.[18]

In their verdict, the court concluded that the defective carronade bolts were a decisive factor in the loss of the ship, and agreed with the officers that the 'inefficiency of her crew' meant that *Epervier* had gone into action against an enemy of 'very superior force.'[19] Yet the court did not blame Wales and his officers for either, instead praising them for taking '*Epervier* into action in a very skilled manner and … display[ing] themselves with gallantry and zeal.'[20] Despite Wales's responsibility for training his crew and ensuring that they and the ship were always ready for action, the court did not believe he was at fault. The primary reasons for the loss were all the fault of the commander in the months leading up to the action, but the court focused only on Wales's conduct in the action itself, and their examination often came down to a simple question posed to each officer: 'Was she [the ship] defended so long as she could be with any prospect of success?' Wales, Hackett, Harvey, and the master all definitively answered: 'no.'[21] In a letter written to the judges at the court, which was read into the minutes, Wales defended himself based upon his broader career and service: 'My conduct has been such at all times as to give a general satisfaction to the Commanders whom I have had the honour of serving under, and I sincerely hope, that for which I am brought before this honourable tribunal to answer for, will be found such as to merit their general approbation.'[22] The court was satisfied, and correctly concluded he had done everything in his power on the day of the action to fight and defend the sloop.

Why was the court martial so lenient to Wales? One suggestion is that the court did not wish actively to attack the conduct of the officer. Such a charge would be a serious offense, particularly as the verdicts from such trials were nearly always picked up in the press. Attacking Wales's conduct would have ruined his reputation, and damaged that of the Royal Navy by extension. The verdicts of courts martial where the individual was acquitted tended to follow a typical model that utilised very similar phrasing to describe the merits of officers. Unless the charge was serious, courts tended to use the same flowery and honourable language in any acquittal. In Wales's case, his failure in command of *Epervier* was not explicit. The court largely accepted his version of events and blamed the loss on the poor state of the crew rather than his

17 Roosevelt, *Naval War of 1812*, 313–315; Lambert, *The Challenge*, Chapter 6.

18 Thomas Malcolmson, *Order and Disorder in the British Navy, 1793–1815: Control, Resistance, Flogging and Hanging* (Woodbridge: Boydell Press, 2016) pp.74–76.

19 TNA, ADM 1/5447, Verdict, CM *Epervier*.

20 TNA, ADM 1/5447, Verdict, CM *Epervier*.

21 TNA, ADM 1/5447, CM *Epervier*: Testimonies of Wales, Hackett, Harvey, Genlan.

22 TNA, ADM 1/5447, Wales to the court, CM *Epervier*.

inability to train his men or prepare his ship for action. He certainly fared better than Captain Carden who had been criticized for losing *Macedonian*, which may have had something to do with the fact that, while Carden had no close ties to the Royal Navy, Wales's uncle was none other than Admiral John Warren himself.

This fact almost certainly influenced his post-war career, and he was quickly appointed to another sloop and received the step to post captain in the years following the war.[23] Hackett and Harvey were both promoted to commander in the following years. Harvey was the nephew of a flag officer in the Navy and continued in active service for some time while Hackett, who did not have any notable familial connections, died a vice admiral, managing to overtake both his commander and fellow lieutenant.[24]

Victories of USS *Wasp*, June to August 1814

Just a few days after *Peacock*'s rendezvous with *Epervier*, another heavily-built American sloop of war was putting to sea. USS *Wasp*, newly built and named for the *Wasp* which had defeated HMS *Frolic* in 1812, was armed with twenty 32-pound carronades and two chase guns and manned by a thoroughly trained crew of New Englanders under Master Commandment Johnston Blakely. Blakely intended to succeed where his colleague Allen had failed in *Argus* by conducting an extended cruise right under the nose of the British in the English Channel. He eluded the Royal Navy off the American coast and cruised alone into British waters, where he spent several weeks hunting for British merchants, taking five by the 28 June, when his lookouts spotted a British warship, HMS *Reindeer*.

At daybreak, lookouts from the British sloop reported an American man of war in the distance to Commander William Manners. His brig, *Reindeer*, was a sister of *Epervier*, an 18-gun brig-sloop of the *Cruizer* class. Unlike her sisters, though, *Reindeer* carried a main battery of sixteen 24-pound carronades rather than 32s, in part because (unlike her sisters) she was built of softer fir instead of oak, and a lighter armament reduced the strain on her timbers.[25] Like most British ships, *Reindeer* was under-manned, with 60 men fewer than the approaching American; but Manners was confident in the training and bravery of his men, and he himself was spoiling for a fight.[26] Here was an impetuous American warship in British waters, and it was his duty to teach them a lesson.

The two sloops slowly approached over the course of the morning, each endeavouring in the long hours to get to windward of the enemy. Manners managed to seize the advantage by deploying sweeps – long oars – and

23 Syrett and DiNardo, *Commissioned Sea Officers*, p.454; 'Richard Walter Wales, Esq.', *Royal Naval Biography*, Supplement, Part IV, pp.127–128.

24 Syrett and DiNardo, *Commissioned Sea Officers*, pp.193, 206; 'John Harvey (a), Esq.', *Royal Naval Biography*, Vol.4, Part II, pp.29–30; 'John Hackett, Esq.', *Royal Naval Biography*, Vol.4, Part II, p.308.

25 McCranie, *Utmost Gallantry*, p.231.

26 Roosevelt, *Naval War of 1812*, pp.321–322.

rowing the *Reindeer* upwind. *Reindeer* took a position astern of *Wasp*, and as the distance slowly closed Manners took command of the bow chasers. The guns were carefully loaded, aimed, and primed, and once set Manners grasped a lit matchstick and fired a shot into *Wasp*'s port quarter. The gun was reloaded and fired four more times and *Wasp*, on her current course, was unable to respond. After 10 minutes, Blakely veered his ship closer to the wind, coming around and taking a course parallel to that of the enemy. Both broadsides opened up at close range and for another 10 minutes continued to run yardarm to yardarm, firing shot after shot. In the light winds the smoke hung over the two ships and in the space between them, clouding the air. Gunners, unable to see much aside from the flash of the enemy's guns, loaded and fired relentlessly. Many were cut down by the carronades and musketry, including Manners himself, who was shot through both thighs by grape shot. The wounded commander, bleeding profusely, managed to struggle to his feet and realised he was badly outgunned.[27]

He ordered the quartermaster to steer for the enemy. With the short distance between the two vessels it was not difficult, even in the light winds, for *Reindeer* to drift through the water and crash against her side. Manners assembled his boarders, his men scurrying to the side with cutlasses, pikes, and small arms, and so too did the Americans. As the two ships crashed together, men along the sides began hacking at each other with their blades as topmen poured fire into the mass of boarders on either side. The lieutenant, Thomas Chambers, was shot in the hip, but remained on deck at his station as the commander made his way to the side. Cutlass in hand, Manners pushed through and led the boarders over the side, hacking their way onto the enemy's deck, when a musket ball fired by a marine in the maintop went clean through Manners's head. The British boarders who had followed Manners were appalled when their captain collapsed backwards, dead by the moment he fell onto his own deck. The remaining officers pushed on to rally the men as the Americans surged forwards. Chambers, after only a moment in acting command, fainted from blood loss. The master and every other officer were soon wounded as the British boarding effort collapsed under the weight of the advancing American pikes, relentless fire from the maintop, and carronades fired into the packed sides of the *Reindeer*. As the American boarders climbed over the side onto the British deck, resistance had disintegrated, and the wounded master had no choice but to surrender.[28]

With Manners dead and Chambers unconscious and badly wounded, the master took charge of the British as they were evacuated from *Reindeer*. Like *Wasp*, *Reindeer*'s hull had taken the brunt of the assault and was badly mauled, and before long she was set on fire and abandoned. *Wasp*'s damage was significant, but her rigging and masts were in good shape and she was able to make way for the nearest port not under British control, Lorient in Brittany. On route they encountered a Portuguese merchant, offloaded the

27 TNA, ADM 1/5444, Lieutenant Thomas Chambers to Vice Admiral William Domett, Plymouth, 4 July 1814, CM *Reindeer*.

28 TNA, ADM 1/5444, Chambers to Domett, 4 July 1814, CM *Reindeer*; McCranie, *Utmost Gallantry*, pp.231–232; Roosevelt, *Naval War of 1812*, pp.323–324.

prisoners, and took two more British merchants, bringing Blakely's total to seven. By now word had spread that there was a large American man of war operating in the Channel, and HM Sloop *Castilian* (another *Cruizer*-class vessel) was dispatched from Cork with a 10-gun schooner in tow, on the lookout for what they believed was an American privateer. Chambers, on board the Portuguese ship, made quick time to Plymouth, and there reported the loss to Vice Admiral Sir William Domett, commander of the forces at Plymouth.[29] Domett, much alarmed, dispatched HMS *Avon* and HMS *Scylla*, both *Cruizer*-class vessels, to join the hunt.

Upon reaching Lorient, *Wasp* was allowed to anchor and undergo repairs, remaining for six weeks before departing on 27 August to resume her cruise. Within days she had taken two more prizes, and on 1 September she was in chase of a small convoy. Not far away, HMS *Avon*, which had linked up with *Castilian*, was in pursuit of a privateer when her lookouts spotted the American warship. Her commander, James Arbuthnot, came about to investigate while signalling for *Castilian*, which was too far in the distance to see or hear him. As the sun set and night fell, *Avon* and *Wasp* approached each other. Neither could see the other very well; both had ensigns flying, but in the darkness they were invisible, and as they approached both ships prepared for action but held back. A voice from *Avon* demanded *Wasp*'s identity, but Blakely responded by demanding to know who *Avon* was. The voice from *Avon* replied with 'His Majesty's Brig *Avon*' but the howling night wind prevented anyone on board *Wasp* from hearing. Instead they asked again, irritating the British. This banter continued until the two ships were within short-range fire of each other, and a frustrated Blakely fired a shot across *Avon*'s bows. If the shot was meant to be one of warning, it did not work, and Arbuthnot responded by coming about and opening fire with his eight-gun broadside.[30]

Operating by the light of gun flashes, the action continued at close range. *Wasp* bore up and tried to get behind *Avon* to rake her, but Arbuthnot manoeuvred to counter, and the fighting continued in a serious of manoeuvres and broadsides in the dark, at such a close range that one Wasp was hit by a burning piece of wad that had been ejected from one of *Avon*'s carronade after the ball.[31] In the darkness neither could quite tell what was happening, but *Wasp*'s fire inflicted much more damage on *Avon* than she received. *Avon*'s rigging was cut up quickly, and shot after shot went into the hull, many impacting below the waterline. According to British accounts, the battle lasted two hours; the Americans assert it was over in 45 minutes. Either way, by the end *Avon* was completely dismasted and badly mauled, with water steadily gaining in the hold. *Wasp*, with the enemy disabled and unable to manoeuvre, secured a raking position off her stern and poured fire into the British sloop. Her fire began to slacken to a near halt, with enough time passing between shots for Blakely to notice and order his own guns to

---

29 TNA, ADM 1/5444, Chambers to Domett, 4 July 1814, CM *Reindeer*.

30 Roosevelt, *Naval War of 1812*, pp.329–330; McCranie, *Utmost Gallantry*, pp.235–236; TNA, ADM 1/5446, Testimony of Lt. John Harvey, CM *Avon*.

31 Roosevelt, *Naval War of 1812*, p.329.

cease. He called across to ask if *Avon* had struck, and the British replied by firing what few guns remained intact. Not long after the action resumed, Arbuthnot, with casualties mounting and the ship dismasted and nearly defenceless, ordered the ship to cease firing and surrender.[32] *Wasp* had won her second single-ship victory – the first American vessel since *Constitution* to claim two victories – and all in the span of two months. Blakely did not have long to savour his victory, however, nor even time to take possession of the prize.

The sound of gunfire in the distance had got *Castilian*'s attention. Under her acting commander, Lieutenant George Lloyd, she set off in pursuit, arriving within sight just a quarter of an hour after Arbuthnot had struck. Lloyd was distraught at the sight of the British ship, dismasted and rolling in the waves, next to the American sloop, and resolved to attack. Blakely had his men prepare to resume action, keeping back as he observed the nearby British sloop with one or two consorts somewhere in the darkness behind her. In actuality, *Castilian* was alone; there were no other ships. Nevertheless, Blakely saw something in the darkness, and his own anxiety over the approaching enemy's hurry and determination to bring him to action likely influenced how his tired eyes perceived shapes in the night.

At just 100 yards, *Castilian* opened fire with a ranging shot, but upon the gun's recoil her crew heard signal guns from the dismasted *Avon*. Signal guns and flares were fired off in a panic as hands rushed to the sides to wave frantically; they were sinking, and quickly. Reluctantly Lloyd abandoned the pursuit and turned to rescue to the Avons, managing to evacuate the entire crew before she slipped below the waves. In that time, Blakely, knowing his ship was already damaged and believing he was facing several ships of about the same force as his own, prudently fled into the night. *Castilian* sailed home with the exhausted crew of the *Avon*, and upon arrival there was a flurry of speculation about USS *Wasp*, the mysterious American ship which had now defeated two British warships. The Admiralty were frustrated that she had escaped, but assured Lloyd that he had done the right thing in rescuing the crew of the sinking *Avon*. The First Lord began speculating that, wounded as she was, *Wasp* must have later sunk in the night. Before long, further reports came in of *Wasp*'s raiding, putting a stopper on his hopes. However, reports of *Wasp*'s whereabouts trickled to a halt by autumn; she was last spotted by a Swedish brig on route to England, and likely foundered during a storm in the mid-Atlantic. Whatever the case, USS *Wasp* – one of the best cruisers of the United States Navy during the war – was never heard from again.

Impact of the actions in 1813 and 1814

Like the bulk of the letters written following losses to the Americans in this war, Chambers's and Arbuthnot's accounts did not rest their defence on the superiority of the enemy. Instead, they argued that they had fought as long as

32 Roosevelt, *Naval War of 1812*, pp.329–330; McCranie, *Utmost Gallantry*, pp.235–236; TNA, ADM 1/5446, Testimony of Harvey, CM *Avon*.

possible until the unmanageable state of their ship and the loss of life made further resistance impossible. Both did mention that *Wasp* was more heavily armed, especially against *Avon*, and in both cases this was done in reference to the 'steady and gallant conduct' of the officers and crew of the two lost brigs. Chambers stated that 'nothing could surpass the gallantry, and good conduct, displayed by every officer, seaman, and marine, onboard, during a contest with an enemy of such superior power; and I trust it will appear, that the honour of the British flag was nobly supported.'[33] Arbuthnot's account similarly praised the 'steady and gallant conduct of all the officers, seamen, and marines of His Majesty's Sloop under my command, engaged in this unequal contest.'[34] Both officers felt the bravery and determination shown by their men against such daunting odds had more than upheld the reputation of the Royal Navy, and were acquitted by courts martial held over the following months.[35]

Wasp's two cruises in the heart of British waters greatly distressed the British, as had the cruise of *Argus* in 1813. Anxieties about the cruise of several American warships in British waters resulted in the expansion of the Cork station (the ships responsible for protecting and patrolling the Irish sea and western English Channel). Even after the conclusion of the Napoleonic Wars, the Royal Navy did not reduce the overall size of the station.[36]

Some commentators in the *Naval Chronicle* had begun to show signs that the high following the *Shannon–Chesapeake* celebrations had peaked even before news of the losses of the four sloops reached England. Several reflected that, even with the glorious capture of *Chesapeake* and *Argus*, the American War was not going well at sea. 'We have surely little to console ourselves with,' one 'Albion' wrote.[37] Another, or perhaps the same, 'Albion' noted that 'the war with America has not yet been glorious to Britain; she has lost more than she has gained.'[38] 'Nestor' bemoaned that the American victories far outweighed the British ones, and called for a renewed effort: 'Smarting as our navy now does under the recollection of the successes of the Americans by sea, we cannot with honour, or self-gratification, lay down the sword, until her infant, but thriving navy, is swept away.'[39]

The *Chronicle* continued its calls for renewed action in North America. There were hopes that Cochrane, an officer with a reputation for bold action, would breathe new life into the naval campaigns.[40] The *Chronicle* followed news that additional warships were being sent to America, including coveted

33 TNA, ADM 1/5444, Lieutenant Thomas Chambers to Vice Admiral William Domett, CM *Reindeer*.

34 TNA, ADM 1/5446, Commander James Arbuthnot to Vice Admiral Herbert Sawyer, CM *Avon*.

35 TNA, ADM 1/5444, Verdict, CM *Reindeer*; TNA, ADM 1/5446, Verdict, CM *Avon*.

36 McCranie, *Utmost Gallantry*, pp.137–139.

37 'Albion' to the Editor, 6 February 1814, *The Naval Chronicle for 1814: Containing a General and Biographical History of The Royal Navy of the United Kingdom; With a Variety of Original Papers on Nautical Subjects*, Vol.31: January to June (London: Joyce Gold, 1814), pp.122–124.

38 'Albion' to the Editor, 16 December 1813, *Naval Chronicle*, Vol.31, pp.118–120.

39 'Nestor' to the Editor, 17 December 1814, *The Naval Chronicle for 1814: Containing a General and Biographical History of The Royal Navy of the United Kingdom; With a Variety of Original Papers on Nautical Subjects*, Vol.32: July to December (London: Joyce Gold, 1814), p.486.

40 'Albion' to the Editor, 6 February 1814, *Naval Chronicle*, Vol.31, pp.118–120.

heavy frigates like *Leander*, which were deemed to be a match for the American heavy frigates.[41] One commentator even wrote to the *Chronicle* searching for news of the construction and deployment of ships for the American conflict, hoping to learn if 'the A[dmiralty] B[oard] are going on preparing more heavy 50 gun frigates, and 20 gun sloops to enable us to cope with our American enemies on equal terms.'[42] Several commentators, as well as the editors, expressed hopes that Broke's victory, won on equal terms, would be replicated. There was a particular shift in the expectations and hopes from the *Chronicle*. In the wake of the shocking losses in 1812, many had begun calls for a strategy of overwhelming force and the destruction of the American Navy, and few were concerned about meeting the enemy on fair terms. That in itself was a shift from the general attitude of the Navy and public in the preceding decade, when victory against much greater forces had been common. Now, the *Chronicle* had settled into a new normal. Broke's victory had proved to the world that the Americans were not invincible and he had won his action in the purest of terms. Many commentators bemoaned that if only the Royal Navy could 'oftener meet the enemy as fairly, the same success would attend their efforts.'[43]

The remainder of 1813 yielded mixed results. HMS *Pelican* triumphed over USS *Argus*, but *Boxer* was defeated by *Enterprise* in a relatively even action. Little occurred early in 1814 aside from the victory of *Phoebe* over *Essex*, and even the editors of the *Chronicle* admitted 'owing to our superiority of force, we have nothing to boast, any farther than the smallness of our own loss.'[44] It was a victory, and one that reflected well on the honourable character of Captain Hillyar and the Royal Navy, but it was not another *Shannon–Chesapeake*. Still, there were high hopes that another such action would occur: 'from the last accounts we have from America, it would appear both sides were desirous to try their prowess again, as the *Shannon* and *Chesapeake* did.'[45]

In the 1814 June–July edition of the *Chronicle*, the editors anticipated that 'in our next we shall have to communicate events of greater interest', but had to admit in the following edition that 'contrary to our expectations, no news of importance has yet arrived from America.'[46] As before, the proceedings of the American War were not the only events of interest in the *Chronicle*. Through 1813 and 1814 the Napoleonic Wars were approaching what appeared to be a climatic finish, as the First French Empire collapsed under assault from the great powers of Europe. Commentators in the *Chronicle* wrote in on a variety of topics, including the contest with the Americans in the Atlantic and on the Great Lakes. Typically, those commenting on the Lakes campaigns focused on their strategic importance: the impact of victories and losses on the Lakes on the defence of Canada. However, the discussion of the battles in the

41 *Naval Chronicle*, Vol.31, p.244.
42 'Albion' to the Editor, 11 November 1814, *Naval Chronicle*, Vol.32, p.416.
43 'Albion' to the Editor, 16 December 1813, *Naval Chronicle*, Vol.31, pp.118–120.
44 *Naval Chronicle*, Vol.32, p.82.
45 'Albion' to the Editor, 8 April 1814, *Naval Chronicle*, Vol.31, pp.285–286.
46 *Naval Chronicle*, Vol.32, pp.134–153.

Atlantic remained linked to honour. The reputation of the Royal Navy was at stake here, rather than strategic considerations.

Throughout 1813 and 1814, the editors and readers of the *Chronicle* hoped that another of Britain's frigate captains would win a Broke-style victory. The events off New London proved to be the closest they came. As reports of the challenges in those waters reached London, some commentators began speculating about what had transpired. The idea of an action between *Endymion*, Britain's prize frigate, and the *United States* piqued the interest of one commentator in particular, who believed 'the American ships would have found them determined never to strike the British flag;' but that challenge never materialised, of course, and this commentator chose to pin the blame on 'the interference of the English admiral [Warren]' rather than on the 'gallant, enterprising, and judicious officer, Sir Thomas Hardy, the friend of Nelson.'[47] Of course Warren, who was widely scapegoated by the press for the apparent failures of the American war, had to have been to blame – how could blame attach to a protégé of Nelson himself? If anyone was willing to carry out the war in the brilliant manner the *Chronicle* hoped for, it was Hardy. Of course, copies of the correspondence between Hardy and Decatur eventually reached the *Chronicle*, and learning that Hardy had prohibited *Endymion* from meeting *United States* must have stung.

Still, with so many heavy frigates now on station, the *Chronicle* hoped that *Constitution* and her sisters would eventually be defeated. Still, the *Chronicle* had nothing to celebrate by the end of 1814, so the editors and commentators continued to analyse and make sense of the losses. As one commentator pointed out at the end of 1813, 'sufficient time has elapsed to allow full scope for the activity, zeal, and success of our squadrons, hitherto the never-failing characteristics of the British navy.'[48]

'C.H.' noted he had previously hoped Broke's victory 'would terminate their [America's] naval triumphs, and be the last of which we should have cause to lament. Events, however, have turned out far otherwise.'[49] The losses of *Boxer* and *Epervier* had demonstrated that British sloops appeared 'altogether as unfit to cope with the American sloops, as our frigates were with theirs of a like name; and the great difference in weight of metal, tonnage, and height, will, I fear, still secure to them the victory.'[50]

The commentators and editors continued to defend the valour of the men of the Royal Navy: upon news of the loss of *Reindeer*, it was reported that 'a braver crew than that of the *Reindeer* never sustained the lustre of the British flag.'[51] The defeats had still not tarnished the Royal Navy, in the view of the *Chronicle*, although it was distressing that the Americans continued to fall in with 'ships of inferior force.'[52]

47 'Albion' to the Editor, 8 April 1814, *Naval Chronicle*, Vol.31, pp.385–386.

48 'Albion' to the Editor, 16 December 1813, *Naval Chronicle*, Vol.31, pp.118–120.

49 'C.H.' to the Editor, Glasgow, 16 July 1814, *Naval Chronicle*, Vol.32, p.207.

50 'C.H.' to the Editor, Glasgow, 16 July 1814, *Naval Chronicle*, Vol.32, p.207.

51 *Naval Chronicle*, Vol.32, p.297.

52 'J.C.' to the Editor, Hitchin, Hertfordshire, 25 September 1814, *Naval Chronicle*, Vol.32, p.407.

The sense of dismay only grew, and upon news of the loss of HMS *Avon* the editors argued that the losses had without a doubt demonstrated

> The necessity of *immediately* building vessels capable of carrying MORE MEN, and HEAVIER METAL, as the present disparity is truly discouraging to both sailor and officer. The *Avon* was a very fine brig-sloop, and had a large complement of men. The *Wasp* is rated in the *American Navy List*, of the same force, though undoubtedly greatly superior in tonnage, and weight of metal, and number of hands.[53]

Four successive defeats had demoralised the editors, who believed that

> the truth is, that our navy contains scarcely a single sloop that is fairly a match for the weakest American built vessel of that class of ships of war. And most of them are so obviously deficient, that their commanders, whatever be their character for valour and skill, run the risk of compromising their reputation in the event of battle with an American, almost without a chance of victory.[54]

Even the news of the burning of the presidential mansion in Washington DC, reported in the same edition of the *Chronicle*, was not enough to dull the sting of the naval losses.

If the editors and commentators agreed that the recent losses were not a stain on British honour, they did not agree on whether to pursue peace with the United States. The editors contended that continuing the war would be long and costly, and that 'American cannot be conquered, but she may be half destroyed; whereby we should ultimately suffer.'[55] The Revolutionary War had proved impossible to win due to the titanic difficulties of waging war across the ocean and increasingly sour public sentiment towards the conflict. For some, this argument was not convincing; one commentator questioned why Britain was so weary of spending the necessary resources to see a fitting victory and end to the conflict, one which did justice to the Royal Navy and sufficiently punished the United States.[56] He was worried that making peace without achieving a sufficient victory would be disastrous:

> how often would our disasters be thrown in our teeth, and the loss of our ships be a subject for their triumph? – Besides – in order to keep up that character and consequence which it is so necessary for us to possess, we should make them feel the weight of our arm – *they have shewn to other nations that the British navy is not invincible* – these nations will not inquire the difference of force, but believe the Americans, and we cannot deny it, that THEIR FRIGATES *have* CAPTURED OURS?[57]

53 *Naval Chronicle*, Vol.32, p.243.
54 *Naval Chronicle*, Vol.32, p.244.
55 *Naval Chronicle*, Vol.31, pp.246–247.
56 'Arion' to the Editor, *Naval Chronicle*, Vol.33 (London: Joyce Gold, 1815), pp.127–128.
57 'C.H.' to the Editor, Glasgow, 16 July 1814, *Naval Chronicle*, Vol.32, pp.207–208.

The American victories had already, as some believed, emboldened the French; might not a quick peace with the United States threaten Britain's security in the coming decades? The editors responded to these views in the final edition of 1814:

> There are, however, those who think our hostility with the United States too soon terminated; and we confess it to be our wish that time had afforded us a few opportunities to redeem that portion of reputation supposed to be lost by the few nominal victories of our Trans-Atlantic antagonists; for surely the victories of strength opposed to comparative weakness, are entitled to no higher term.

That wish aside, the conflict had been ruinous and unnecessary. However unsatisfying, peace was 'at least a breathing time to both, however short, and the world so long distressed by war, requires it to renew her energies.'[58]

There was not the same clamour for or against peace in Halifax, however. While one letter submitted to the *Acadian Recorder* from 'A Briton' did argue that a dishonourable peace with the United States (as the war currently stood) would mean 'no end to the insolence of her citizens,'[59] the paper did not talk of peace much at all. It was only ever mentioned by the editors upon hearing news of the negotiations in Ghent, when they expressed their hope that the treaty would be favourable to the colonies.[60] Like the *Chronicle*, however, Halifax's *Acadian Recorder* made it clear that Haligonians were hoping that the reinforced North American squadron would bring the enemy to action.

In fact, the editors expressed a hope that HMS *Nymphe*, a 38-gun fifth-rate much like *Guerriere* or *Java*, would meet with *Constitution* single-handedly: 'That the *Nymphe* may single-handed meet the Constitution, is our most ardent wish, great as the odds are against her, we have no doubt of the result, our only *fear* is the loss of valuable British lives.'[61] Not all were so confident, and one letter submitted to the *Recorder* derided Captain Carden, who had 'before the war, seriously declared that 18-pounders were as good as 24's, and that he preferred his ship to the *United States*.'[62] He argued that the British ships were far outmatched and expressed his hope that more actions against 'numerically equal' opponents would follow: 'that *Brokes* will be found in every water ... I yet live in hopes of witnessing *another*, and *another*, and *another* fair demonstration.'[63] As the war had demonstrated, however, the Royal Navy had not had the fortune to fall in with any of the heavy frigates, and by contrast the Americans appeared

58 *Naval Chronicle*, Vol.33, pp.70–71.

59 NSA, *Acadian Recorder*, 9 April 1814, 2:15 (online), available at https://novascotia.ca/archives/newspapers/archives.asp?ID=819.

60 NSA, *Acadian Recorder*, 29 October 1814, 2:44 (online), available at https://novascotia.ca/archives/newspapers/archives.asp?ID=848; NSA, *Acadian Recorder*, 25 February 1815, 3:8 (online), available at https://novascotia.ca/archives/newspapers/archives.asp?ID=865.

61 NSA, *Acadian Recorder*, Monday 23 August 1813, 1:32 (online), available at https://novascotia.ca/archives/newspapers/archives.asp?ID=785.

62 NSA, *Acadian Recorder*, 1 January 1814, 2:1 (online), available at https://novascotia.ca/archives/newspapers/archives.asp?ID=804.

63 NSA, *Acadian Recorder*, 1 January 1814, 2:1.

> the luckiest people in the world. It seems almost impossible for any of our men-of-war to come athwart one of their's; without the former is of far inferior force. We have met *equal*, but in *two* instances: and then, we took their vessels, with much greater ease, than they did our's, where the odds were, at least, three to two in their favour.[64]

Speculation grew as the purpose-built heavy frigates, such as HMS *Leander*, arrived on station, and the *Recorder* pinned its hopes on her or her sisters finding *Constitution. Leander*, according to statements of force printed in British papers, appeared to be a match for *Constitution*, and to boot she was commanded by Sir George Collier, the distinguished son of another naval officer who had led a notable expedition in the last American war.[65]

The American heavy frigates were frequently mentioned in the *Recorder*, even in 1813 and 1814, when none of the three ships had much of an impact on the war. There was much speculation on the possibilities of action with these ships, particularly *Constitution*, which was mentioned in the paper twice as often as either of her sisters. After her stunning victories in 1812 and her continued avoidance of the Royal Navy's guns, 'Old Ironsides' and her sisters had become almost like bogeymen for the Haligonians. News of the escapes, movements, and whereabouts of American frigates were frequently printed in the *Recorder*, which relied on official reports, intelligence, and even rumours. Just as when its residents had followed news of Nelson's exploits a decade earlier, Halifax had little to go by. Their news chiefly came from British or American papers and from rumours brought in through the various ships that anchored in port; but the papers printed report and rumour all the same. The American frigates had a dual significance to Haligonians; they were the unpunished victors against their beloved Royal Navy, and the Haligonians hoped there would eventually be retribution for their defeated naval heroes. The frigates also mattered because of their potential impact on the war and on trade. This was particularly demonstrated following Capel and Broke's failed ploy off Boston in 1813, when 'the public mind is now wholly engrossed by the escape of Commodore RODGERS from Boston, a circumstance as unlooked for as unfortunate.'[66] Haligonians worried about the risk the American ships posed to trade and to the war effort in Canada, as merchant ships and military transports alike were easy prey to the daunting American frigates and it was acknowledged that such missions 'would more strengthen the American government than any other circumstance likely to occur.'[67]

As much of the news coverage in Halifax came from American newspapers, the *Recorder* included many accounts from the United States that differed considerably in view from their own. However, the nearest friendly ports

64 NSA, *Acadian Recorder*, 4 June 1814, 2:23 (online), available at https://novascotia.ca/archives/newspapers/archives.asp?ID=827.

65 NSA, *Acadian Recorder*, 17 September 1814, 2:38 (online), available at https://novascotia.ca/archives/newspapers/archives.asp?ID=842.

66 NSA, *Acadian Recorder*, 22 May 1813, Vol.1:19 (online), available at https://novascotia.ca/archives/newspapers/archives.asp?ID=771.

67 NSA, *Acadian Recorder*, 22 May 1813, Vol.1:19.

from which Halifax could reliably expect newspapers were Bermuda to the south and London to the east, so local papers had to turn to the American press for news on events at sea, whether the recent British losses or American views on the British victories. As the *Recorder*'s editor and other contributors were decidedly pro-British, they often engaged with the reports and views coming in from American sources as a means of disputing with them for the benefit of the readers. Following the *Shannon–Chesapeake* action, American papers came up with many means of explaining the loss (as British papers had done in similar circumstances), some accurate and others with no discernible basis in fact. The *Recorder* took umbrage with several rumours in particular: that *Shannon*'s complement had been massively enhanced before the action, that her crew had resorted to dishonourable tactics including the use of grenades, and that *Shannon* had won only narrowly, having been so mauled that she barely made it back to Halifax without being torn apart by wind and water. The *Recorder* broke those rumours down, among many others, and refuted them in detail.[68] As far as they were concerned, *Shannon* had won the action through the might, heroism, and training of her sailors, and they would not have American accounts throwing that into question. Even American rumours about minor actions, such as between a British packet *Morgiana* and an American privateer, were attacked in the *Recorder*.[69] It had been claimed that the privateer, *Saratoga*, had defeated a superior British ship, but the *Recorder* pointed out that *Morgiana* was not superior to *Saratoga*. The paper similarly refuted a rumour that USS *Argus* had defeated a 28-gun frigate.[70] There could be no questioning that the British were heroic, and that an inferior American ship could not defeat a larger British one.

The *Recorder* wished to avoid criticising the heroes of the Royal Navy in its reporting. When a report of the HMS *Macedonian* court martial reached Halifax, the editors included an extract from the court's verdict that highlighted Carden's bravery and conduct without the court's critique of his failure to bring the enemy to close action.[71] They went to great lengths to emphasise the bravery and honour of the men of the Royal Navy and to highlight the dishonourable conduct of the Americans. Similarly, the *Recorder* compared the fighting spirit of the two navies, unsurprisingly coming to the conclusion that the Royal Navy's was based on true heroism, while the Americans were deceitful and craven. The editor of the *Recorder* concluded that 'the Americans will not send any ships to sea, that are only a *little* superior to a very numerous class in our service, the 38-gun frigates', suggesting that United States ships only came out to fight when they had an advantage.[72] Even worse, he claimed, when faced with defeat, American ships would heave guns

68 NSA, *Acadian Recorder*, 3 July 1813, Vol.1:25 (online), available at https://novascotia.ca/archives/newspapers/archives.asp?ID=777.

69 NSA, *Acadian Recorder*, 2 April 1814, Vol.2:14 (online), available at https://novascotia.ca/archives/newspapers/archives.asp?ID=818.

70 NSA, *Acadian Recorder*, 9 April 1814, Vol.2:15.

71 NSA, *Acadian Recorder*, 3 July 1813, Vol.1:25 (online), available at https://novascotia.ca/archives/newspapers/archives.asp?ID=777.

72 NSA, *Acadian Recorder*, 2 July 1814, Vol.2:27 (online), available at https://novascotia.ca/archives/newspapers/archives.asp?ID=831.

overboard to exaggerate the superiority of force, which was what happened when USS *Frolic* surrendered to a superior force 'without firing a shot! – For this, a *British* Captain would deserve to be shot; – an *American* one will receive the plaudits of his countrymen!'[73] In actuality, the 22-gun *Frolic* threw overboard all her port guns in an attempt to escape from a 36-gun frigate and a 12-gun schooner – a force against which she stood no chance. The odds against her were greater even than the odds faced by Thomas, Lord Cochrane in *Speedy* in his famous action with *Gamo*, or by *Alert* against *Essex*. Flight was the only prudent response and heaving guns overboard was *Frolic*'s only hope of escaping and far from an act of cowardly deceit. The editor's perception of this episode was nevertheless influenced by the ethos of Royal Navy courage and bravery and by his frustration with the American Navy.

The movements of USS *Constitution* featured regularly in the *Recorder*'s arguments regarding the cowardly American fighting spirit, as demonstrated by her escape from HMS *Tenedos* and *Junon*, both fifth-rate frigates: 'The *Constitution*, in guns and men was not *near* so much inferior to the *Tenedos* and *Junon*, jointly, as she was *superior* to the *Guerriere*, or *Java*; yet each of the latter, with true British *rashness*, sought the unequal combat with their *Giant*-foe!'[74] Of course, this was not a fair comparison. *Constitution* certainly far outclassed a British fifth-rate, but not to the degree that she could easily defeat two 38-gun frigates with an advantage in broadside weight, an advantage in the number of guns and men, and an advantage in coordinating movements and fire from two ships. A contributor later claimed that both *President* and *Constitution* had even avoided action with single Royal Navy frigates such as the fifth-rates *La Pique*, *Alexandria* and *Nymphe*.[75] Whether these events actually happened is another matter; for the *Recorder*, they served as vital pieces of evidence that the American Navy was cowardly and devoid of honour. In contrast with this, the paper sought examples of British daring, including one notable action involving the 58-gun *razée* HMS *Majestic* and 22-gun *Cyane*:

> it cannot but be gratifying to the feelings of Britons, to compare the conduct of the captains of the *Cyane*, and *Majestic*, with that of the American naval commanders; notwithstanding the feats of valour performed by the latter, have been such as almost to turn the brains of their countrymen! … We are happy to announce to the public the Capture of the *Terpsichore*, French frigate, by H.M.S. *Majestic*. The gallantry displayed by Capt. Hayes, in a single ship (not larger than the *President*) chasing three ships and a brig; two of them 44-gun frigates, the other ship carrying 28 guns, and the brig armed, convince us, that the ST VINCENT and NELSON spirit still exists. – Had Capt. Hayes possessed Commodore Roger's *caution*, he would not have taken *Terpsichore*.[76]

73 NSA, *Acadian Recorder*, 2 July 1814, Vol.2:27.

74 NSA, *Acadian Recorder*, 16 April 1814, 2:16 (online), available at https://novascotia.ca/archives/newspapers/archives.asp?ID=820.

75 NSA, *Acadian Recorder*, 8 January 1814, 2:2 (online), available at https://novascotia.ca/archives/newspapers/archives.asp?ID=805; NSA, *Acadian Recorder*, 21 May 1814 2:21 (online), available at https://novascotia.ca/archives/newspapers/archives.asp?ID=825.

76 NSA, *Acadian Recorder*, 26 March 1814, 2:13 (online), available at https://novascotia.ca/archives/newspapers/archives.asp?ID=817.

Where the British are depicted as gallant and willing to engage into any action, even at long odds, the paper depicts the Americans timid and deceitful; their frigates and sloops were more heavily armed than their British counterparts, and yet even still they seemed shy about engaging the Royal Navy. One commentator even argued that the new *razéed* frigates, each armed more heavily than *Constitution* and her sisters, had inspired a deep sense of dread in the United States Navy.[77]

More generally, the *Recorder* sought to highlight the more chivalrous characteristics of Royal Navy officers in contrast with the Americans. Among other examples was a rumour that Captain Hillyar had issued a challenge of single combat to Captain Porter, when in fact the opposite had occurred.[78] When actual reports from the action arrived in Halifax, the editor candidly explained that

> With a disparity of force, certainly, far less than existed between our half a dozen unsuccessful ships and their American opponents, we should be ashamed to boast of any thing, beyond extreme good fortune in just nicking the time of Mr Porter's return to Valparaiso. We leave to the Americans to call such things '*brilliant Affairs – Splendid Achievements – Unrivalled Victories*'! – contented, as Britons, to have it always said of us, – that we never run from a ship of our own *rate*; although her great superiority in *actual force* and our temerity, may, now and then, obtain us a drubbing![79]

The editors then justifiably highlighted the contrast between Porter's account and Hillyar's. Porter was accused of downplaying the force under his command, principally by having,

> like his friend Rodgers, counted the hawse-hole, and quarter gallery window for two ports, mistaking, probably, a speaking trumpet, or a man's head, accidentally thrust out of the one, and a hand-spike, or some such thing, out of the other, for two long 18-pounders; or he has wilfully misstated the force of the *Phoebe*.[80]

His subsequent letters were also printed, in which the American captain expressed his frustration that Hillyar had not afforded him an event combat. The editor flatly rejected Porter's remarks as 'contemptible. … We could almost regret that the Captain of the *Phoebe* treated Capt. Porter and his officers, according to the rules of good breeding. Had Capt. Hillyar been cruising on this station, he would have learnt how to distinguish between an American officer, and a *gentleman*, and acted accordingly.'[81] By contrast,

---

77 NSA, *Acadian Recorder*, 20 August 1814, 2:34 (online), available at https://novascotia.ca/archives/newspapers/archives.asp?ID=838.

78 NSA, *Acadian Recorder*, 25 June 1814, 2:26 (online), available at https://novascotia.ca/archives/newspapers/archives.asp?ID=830.

79 NSA, *Acadian Recorder*, 17 September 1814, 2:38 (online), available at https://novascotia.ca/archives/newspapers/archives.asp?ID=842.

80 NSA, *Acadian Recorder*, 6 August 1814, 2:32 (online), available at https://novascotia.ca/archives/newspapers/archives.asp?ID=836.

81 NSA, *Acadian Recorder*, 6 August 1814, 2:32.

Hillyar's more gracious letter was praised for its gentlemanliness and for the gracious 'complement paid to his *unworthy* antagonist! – Who that reads the two letters, but would instantly pronounce one the production of a brave man, the other of a hectoring bully.'[82]

As always, the *Recorder* did not believe that *Constitution*'s captains were any less prone to deceit. Rumours reached Halifax that she had been ordered to sail to France to carry an ambassador, and the *Recorder* concluded that this was simply 'a Yankee trick,' as her neutral status would be used to get her safely to France where she could continue her voyage as 'a *belligerent*.'*83* Other passages from both the editors and commentators throughout 1814 accuse the American Navy and public of deceit, cowardice, cruelty, and general ungentlemanly behaviour in both victory and defeat.[84] The coverage in 1812 and 1813 in the *Recorder* had been much more measured and disciplined than the *Naval Chronicle*, but by 1814 that restraint seemed to have given way completely, and as the paper matured it took on a decisively more opinionated and patriotic tone.

The *Recorder* closely followed the exploits of Britain's frigate captains; letters, reports, and rumours alike found their way into its pages throughout the war, earning a place in Halifax public discourse alongside that of the Napoleonic Wars and the warfare in Canada. Reports and extracts from courts martial for the losses and victories of the Royal Navy frigates were all included in the *Recorder*, once the editor could get his hands on them, and generally any news of the frigate captains was welcome. Nelson had once taken on the aura of a public hero, and collectively the naval captains of the War of 1812 made a similar impression on the city and inspired a generation of young Nova Scotians who

> were eager to participate in the path that seemed to lead, by a few short steps, to honor, glory and fortune; and indeed when it is borne in mind that four or five Halifax lads rose to be admirals, we can hardly wonder at the school-boy's desire to wear the white stripe on his collar and the little ivory hilted dirk that indicated his authority to command men.[85]

One of those Halifax lads was Provo Wallis, who had brought the triumphant *Shannon* into port and eventually reached the rank of Admiral of the Fleet. Their naval heroes, whether born in Halifax or across the seas, embodied a lasting star power that during the War of 1812 captivated the town and its society, as one Nova Scotian historian remembered: 'Their courageous and adventurous life, – their unsophisticated manners, – their good-hearted,

82 NSA, *Acadian Recorder*, 6 August 1814, 2:32.

83 NSA, *Acadian Recorder*, 14 May 1814, 2:20 (online), available at https://novascotia.ca/archives/newspapers/archives.asp?ID=824.

84 NSA, *Acadian Recorder*, 21 May 1814, 2:21; NSA, *Acadian Recorder*, 4 June 1814, 2:23; NSA, *Acadian Recorder*, 31 December 1814, 3:1 (online), available at https://novascotia.ca/archives/newspapers/archives.asp?ID=857; NSA, *Acadian Recorder*, 2 July 1814, 2:27; NSA, *Acadian Recorder*, 3 July 1813, 1:25, https://novascotia.ca/archives/newspapers/archives.asp?ID=777; NSA, *Acadian Recorder*, 19 March 1814, 2:12.

85 Murdoch, *History of Nova Scotia*, p.351.

reckless generosity, and even their little faults and aberrations won them a place in the esteem and affection of our people. Their quaint phrases were re-echoed, and even their prejudices sometimes adopted.'[86] Such was the influence of the Royal Navy's exploits that Murdoch's 1867 *History of Nova Scotia* even included an account of the capture of USS *Essex*, an event that had taken place as far from Nova Scotia as was possible. This star power was even displayed in the case of Captain Hyde Parker, who was fined for illegally impressing a local trader. The *Acadian Recorder*, even while they attacked the offensive trampling of the local man's rights as a British subject, felt the need to remind their readers that Parker had served with distinction during the war.[87]

Of course, there was really little to discuss about the Royal Navy frigates following the *Shannon–Chesapeake* action. Like the *Chronicle*, commentators in the *Recorder* admitted that *Essex*'s defeat was not worthy of boasting. That then left the six sloop actions since *Shannon*'s victory. Following a British paper's account of *Reindeer*'s loss, the *Recorder* analysed the action and explained that *Reindeer* was significantly outgunned as a means of defending the honour of her captain and crew, adding that 'we cannot expect, we cannot wish, an action to be better fought than that between the *Reindeer* and *Wasp* … the loss … brings this consolation with it, that every man on board of her did his duty.'[88] A contributor offered a general analysis of the loss of *Frolic*, *Peacock*, and *Boxer*, arguing that, while the actions were between ships of equal broadside weight, the Americans had a considerable advantage in manpower and this was the primary factor in the defeat.[89]

A general analysis in June 1814 offered a slightly different view, arguing that the Americans had only triumphed due to their good fortune in only meeting British ships that were unprepared for action. Whereas 'in the *Shannon* and *Chesapeake*, our performance was a master-piece: in the *Pelican* and *Argus*, notwithstanding the equality of force, the difference of execution was as 5 to 1,' generally in the lost sloop actions the British gunnery had been pitifully inefficient, particularly in the case of *Epervier*. At the end of 1814, the paper again reflected on the poor state of gunnery in the lost ships: 'Nothing here said is intended, however to excuse the miserable gunnery exhibited, in nine cases out of ten, on board our national vessels. Yet, neither the crews, nor the commanders, of our ships can help this. The fault lies *higher-up*.'[90] The *Recorder* did not blindly defend the Royal Navy and provided a thoughtful and ongoing analysis which considered their deficiencies. However, the *Recorder* never blamed the officers for the poor state of their ship handling or crew's gunnery. It was instead blamed on other factors: a crew primarily made up on invalids, for instance, or the '*higher-ups*', most likely meaning the Admiralty, which had become the favourite scapegoat for the British papers

---

86 Murdoch, *History of Nova Scotia*, p.352.

87 Mercer, 'Sailors and citizens', p.107.

88 NSA, *Acadian Recorder*, 27 August 1814, 2:35 (online), available at https://novascotia.ca/archives/newspapers/archives.asp?ID=839.

89 NSA, *Acadian Recorder*, 21 May 1814, 2:21 (online), available at https://novascotia.ca/archives/newspapers/archives.asp?ID=825.

90 NSA, *Acadian Recorder*, 31 December 1814, 3:1.

early in 1812. Either way, the record thus far was poor; three victories, one against an inferior foe, to 10 losses, several of those in actions with relative parity in gunnery.

Still, by late 1814 the British had effectively won the war. The Americans were bankrupt, vastly outnumbered, and under a total economic blockade. The American economy was starved of commerce; over 700 prizes had been processed by Halifax's Vice Admiralty Court alone. Very few warships, privateers, or merchants were able to put to sea by the end of the conflict. The Royal Navy's maritime supremacy allowed for a prolonged series of amphibious raids and operations that saw thousands of African Americans freed from slavery, the destruction of several warships under construction, and the American capital sacked and set on fire. Madison's administration might have faced complete catastrophe had the British assaults on Plattsburg and Baltimore not stalled.[91]

Reading the *Chronicle* at the end of 1814, however, one would hardly know that the war was going so well. For the most part, the British public were not concerned about the War of 1812 insofar as it related to the strategic situation. Readers of the *Chronicle* and more informed observers did care about the protection of Canada and the war on the Great Lakes, but they did not think about the events in the Atlantic in the same context. The concern over the victories and losses in single-ship actions, and the urge for vengeance that sprang from it, was more emotional. *Shannon*'s victory on 1 June was not celebrated for its strategic impact, for it had none. It was celebrated because it was a vindication of Britain's honour and the public's perception of the Royal Navy. It was a victory for one of Britain's star frigate captains in as equal and brilliant a contest as the public could imagine. The actions of the sloops, on the other hand, would always be side-shows. The public paid attention to them insofar as they demonstrated the prowess (or lack thereof) of the Royal Navy, but with the titanic war in Europe, contemporaries and later historians focused more on the war against Napoleon. Reports of the sloop losses in 1814 did not make it into the *London Gazette* or any other paper in the way the losses of 1812 had done. The frigate losses and later victories were remembered as much due to the star power of Royal Navy frigate actions as they were for anything else, and the papers explored even the losses in detail. The sloop actions, lacking that same lustre, faded into history.

Things were a little different in Halifax. While the residents of Nova Scotia also followed and celebrated the news of the European war very closely and understood that it was of greater consequence than their own 'puny war,' the War of 1812 was more immediate to them. They were worried about the honour of the Royal Navy, but they were also worried about the threats posed to their trade and security. The papers reported on the sloop losses just as they had the frigate losses and victories, but it is clear they did not matter as much. There was not the same level of speculation about the actions of the sloops, nor were there the same reports on their movements and whereabouts. Halifax's fascination with the exploits of the American frigates

91 Lambert, *The Challenge*, Chapter 9; Gwyn, *Frigates and Foremasts*, pp.144–152.

was compelled by their fear of the *President* and *Constitution* and the power of stardom associated with frigate captains. By the end of 1814, Haligonians only had Broke's spectacular victory to console them. Neither *President* nor *Constitution* had been beaten in action; both were still at large; and among the many rumours that had reached Halifax was one that demonstrated the confidence of the United States Navy. It was reported that 'Commodore Decatur … has assured his friends, that, as he has now an opportunity of getting to sea in the *President*, he will have another British frigate before the war ends.'[92]

92 NSA, *Acadian Recorder*, 4 June 1813, 2:23 (online), available at https://novascotia.ca/archives/newspapers/archives.asp?ID=827.

8

'Gallantry and spirit on both sides': Triumph of the *Endymion* and *Constitution* in the war's final months, 1815

Through 1814, the United States Navy was increasingly crippled. The blockade only tightened as additional ships arrived and were better organised, first by Warren and then by Cochrane. Fewer American ships were getting to sea, further stifling trade and diminishing the impact of their warships and privateers on British commerce.[1] Secretary Jones's strategy of relying on single cruisers to cause as much a havoc as possible had limited success.[2] However, USS *Constitution* escaped from Boston yet again, taking advantage of the strange absence of the blockading ships – an absence that has not yet been explained – and put to sea on 18 December, heading south.[3] At sea, the war had effectively been won, even with *Constitution* having escaped. Both of her sisters remained in port and the Royal Navy controlled the Atlantic coastline. On land, the situation was more mixed.

By 1814, the Royal Navy had seized control of the Great Lakes, having launched the 112-gun first-rate HMS *St Lawrence* in Lake Ontario in September, and British forces were holding the Canadian border. Following success at Washington DC, however, Britain's assaults in the Chesapeake had stalled. In December, both countries, exhausted and eager for an end to hostilities, agreed to a peace settlement. The Treaty of Ghent restored the pre-war relations and borders, a *status quo ante bellum*. Neither side had won anything in the peace, but for Britain that was fine. They had not wanted the war anyway, and while the government entertained some possible concessions to extract from the United States, they recognised that to win a large enough victory and extract major concessions would require time

1 Gwyn, *Frigates and Foremasts*, pp.142–145.
2 McCranie, *Utmost Gallantry*, pp.238–241.
3 Gwyn, *Frigates and Foremasts*, p.148.

and money they did not want to invest.[4] It was more embarrassing for the United States, as they had launched an aggressive war with specific aims and had achieved none. The final peace treaty said nothing about maritime rights or impressment (impressment did come to an end with the end of the Napoleonic Wars, but this had only been a wartime policy anyway), nor did the United States gain any territorial concessions in Canada. The aggressor in a conflict can hardly claim victory when a war ends without any changes. The administration nevertheless successfully reframed the war as a sort of clash of honour, masking military failure and stalemate under a veneer of a few choice battles, which was enough to save the Madison government and influence memory of the conflict.[5]

Some in Canada lamented the war's conclusion upon the terms won, but overall peace was welcome and considered a success.[6] Canada, New Brunswick, Nova Scotia, and the other British North American colonies had survived as British territories, and their unique British Loyalist and anti-American culture continued to develop into an eventual Canadian identity, meaning that in the twenty-first century Canada remains a constitutional monarchy sharing a sovereign with the United Kingdom. This played an important role in world history, and in both 1914 and 1939, when the United Kingdom entered the next round of global conflicts, Canada stood by her side.[7]

The real losers of the war, though, were Britain's major allies – the various Native American tribes and nations that had allied with the British against the United States, in particular the Confederacy ruled by the Shawnee warrior Tecumseh. The British knew the Americans were terrified of the Natives, and this, along with their exceptional skills as warriors, made such an alliance particularly valuable. Their help had been instrumental to the campaigns along the border,[8] but upon Tecumseh's death at the Battle of the Thames the Confederacy and alliances slowly unravelled, and in the peace Britain abandoned their allies' demand for a recognised Native American state in the west and sought no concessions for their allies. The Natives had been abandoned, and within the next few decades the United States had wrested control of much of the western frontier from them.[9]

The Treaty of Ghent was signed in December, but the conflict did not immediately come to an end. Each side's government had to ratify the treaty, which would take time, as the United States Senate was unhelpfully on the other side of the Atlantic. The Prince Regent and His Majesty's Government in the United Kingdom ratified the treaty immediately, glad finally to be on the verge of peace and of putting an end to the costly conflict in America; but the American Senate did not ratify the treaty until 17 February 1815, and in the intervening two months operations continued as normal. *Constitution*,

4 Latimer, *1812*, pp.389–394.
5 Taylor, *Civil War of 1812*, p.407.
6 Latimer, *1812*, pp.398–399.
7 Latimer, *1812*, p.408.
8 Taylor, *Civil War of 1812*, pp.200–230.
9 Budiansky, *Perilous Fight*, p.360.

which had cemented herself as the most prominent of the American frigates, remained at sea, and on 14 January USS *President*, now under the command of Commodore Stephen Decatur, weighed anchor and proceeded to sea from New York, after a snowy gale had blown the blockading squadron off course. Once again, the notorious American frigate was at sea.

Capture of USS *President*, 15 January 1815

President had been in port for exactly 11 months, having dropped anchor in New York on 18 February 1814. By April, John Rodgers had had enough. He had commanded *President* since the beginning of the war, and conducted multiple cruises with her, taking a score of prizes unmatched by any other US commander aside from Porter. He had not, however, had the good fortune of a single-ship action with the enemy; the closest he came was in April 1813, when he suspected the British meant to lead him into a trap. A year after, in April 1814, he transferred to take command of the nearly complete USS *Guerriere* – a new heavy frigate under construction at Philadelphia, hoping she would bring him better luck.[10] As it turned out, however, she was not able to sail until the war ended.

Meanwhile, Decatur was happy for the opportunity of taking command of the Navy's crack frigate, one that Bainbridge had once offered $5,000 for the opportunity of commanding. He had been trapped in New London since June 1813, unable to get past the Royal Navy, and it was hoped *President* would have an easier time escaping from New York. It was certainly clear that he was never going to get out of New London anyway. He was joined by the officers and crew from *United States*, the same efficient complement which had taken *Macedonian* two years earlier. Throughout 1814 he prepared his ship to sail and waited for an opportunity, which came in January when a strong snowy gale blew the blockading squadron off station. Taking advantage of the storm, *President* weighed anchor and cruised out of the harbour, with a brig in company loaded with stores and provisions, intending to sail to the East Indies and prey on the valuable trade of the East India Company.

The blockade of New York was now commanded by Rear Admiral Henry Hotham, who was guarding the entrance to Long Island Sound. Captain John Hayes – a shipbuilder's son who had earned great distinction in the service, and who had served as a midshipman on board HMS *Boston* during her duel with *Embuscade* – commanded a detached squadron on the other side of the island at Sandy Hook, consisting of the slow and cumbersome *razée* HMS *Majestic*, the fifth-rates *Tenedos* and *Pomone*, and the impressive heavy frigate HMS *Endymion*.[11] Captain Henry Hope had with him a nearly full complement of well-trained seamen, among whom were 15 men recently pressed at Halifax.[12] The gale had blown all four ships 50 miles off station, and according to Hayes,

10 Budiansky, *Perilous Fight*, p.348; Lambert, *The Challenge*, Chapter 10.

11 McCranie, *Utmost Gallantry*, p.269.

12 James, *Naval Occurrences*, p.445.

> the very great attention paid to my orders and instructions by the respective Captains, in situations difficult to keep company, prevented separation; and whenever the wind did force us from the coast, I invariably on the gale moderating placed the squadron on that point of bearing from the Hook I judged it likely, from existing circumstances, would be the enemy's track.[13]

Hayes and his fellow captains expected Decatur to try and break out, and this gale had provided the perfect opportunity. They endeavoured to get back off Sandy Hook in time to intercept him. Hayes managed it superbly, coming up and spotting *President* on a path that cut her off from escaping into port. Unbeknownst to Hayes, *President* had been delayed after running aground on a sand bar – an impact that caused some damage, but more importantly slowed her escape enough for the British to intercept her. Decatur had been debating if he should return home; the damage was minor, but would become a problem in the coming voyage to the East Indies. Upon spotting the British squadron blocking his path home, he made up his mind. Prudently, he set sail and fled.[14]

Lookouts from the British ships spotted *President* and excitement spread through the squadron. Hayes, who had managed to bring his ships just in time to intercept the enemy, expressed his delight: 'We were made happy by the sight of a ship and brig standing to the southward and eastward, and not more than two miles on the *Majestic*'s weather bow; the night signal for a general chase was made, and promptly obeyed by all the ships.'[15] Just before daylight, a blue signal light was hoisted into *Majestic*'s rigging and three rockets were fired into the air, and the four frigates set off in pursuit of *President*. Decatur found his path to New York blocked by the squadron, and instead fled into the open water, setting as much sail as he could and running all morning. His ship was damaged, but even so she was fast and able to keep pace ahead of *Majestic* and the two fifth-rates. If he could maintain the distance until nightfall, he might escape. However, he soon found that *Endymion* was gaining on *President*, and early in the morning she had passed the rest of the squadron, quickly leaving them far behind. At noon the strong winds died down into a light breeze, and Hope and Decatur both called their topmen. Reefs in the sails were shaken out, and they set to work setting every remaining stretch of canvas: courses, royals, and studdingsails stretched out on the towering masts.[16]

The progress was slow for both frigates, but *Endymion*'s sailing qualities and Hope's skill proved decisive, and early in the afternoon Decatur could clearly observe that she had 'an evident advantage in sailing.'[17] His men set about attempting to lighten the ship; tons of water were pumped overboard, the massive bow anchors cut and dropped into the sea. Even with the

13 LAC, MG12 ADM1/508, Admiral's Dispatches, North America, C-12855, Captain John Hayes to Rear Admiral Henry Hotham, *Majestic*, at sea, 17 January 1815.

14 McCranie, *Utmost Gallantry*, p.269.

15 LAC, MG12 ADM1/508, Admiral's Dispatches, Hayes to Hotham, 17 January 1815.

16 Lambert, *The Challenge*, Chapter 10.

17 LAC, MG12 ADM1/508, Admiral's Dispatches, Hayes to Hotham, 17 January 1815.

anchors and tons of water gone, *Endymion* was still gaining. Just after 1:00 p.m., Captain Hope observed the Americans casting a host of spare cables, spars, casks of stores, and even several of the ship's boats overboard. The topmen wet the sails, Decatur hoping it would increase their draw and better catch the wind in the light breeze, but still *Endymion* gained, while the ship was cleared for action.[18]

At 2:00 p.m. she had closed within range of *President*'s 24-pounder chase guns, and the Americans opened fire. Half an hour later, *Endymion*'s smaller 18-pounder bow chasers were in range and opened fire in response. Both ships kept up a steady fire, repeatedly throwing shot at the enemy's rigging and cutting away spars and lines over the next two hours, by which time *Endymion* had closed the distance and taken a position off *President*'s starboard quarter. In this position, *President* could bring no guns to bear on the enemy, and over the next half-hour *Endymion* yawed three times, Hope bringing his ship around and firing a full broadside into the enemy's quarterdeck before coming back around and resuming the chase. The area around the ship's wheel was badly cut up, and among the casualties were Decatur and his First Lieutenant, the latter mortally wounded.

With night falling, the rest of the British squadron were not in sight, but they could follow the gun flashes easily enough, and Decatur knew he could not stay in this position forever. Eventually the British squadron would catch up. To this point, both captains had focused on firing into the enemy's rigging, and as such both ships' sails were tattered. Decatur had been relying on the tactics which had defeated *Macedonian*: firing to cripple the British ship, and so control the engagement. This time, though, Hope had the better of him; his ship was faster and seemingly answered the helm better, and every gain made by shooting away *Endymion*'s rigging was countered by damage done to *President*'s sails. At the moment, his ship was unable to return fire. Decatur, then, came up with a new strategy; he called his men aft and told them he was determined to come about and board the enemy. His crew was larger, and in a boarding action they would have an advantage. Even more boldly, he determined that, once secured, they would scuttle *President* and escape in the faster ship. *Endymion*, surely, could outrun the distant British squadron, and another conquest could be added to the United States Navy's record.[19]

At 5:30 p.m. *President* bore up closer to the wind. To Hope, it appeared that she was trying to cross *Endymion*'s bows and rake her, and he immediately ordered his ship turned in response. Again, the superior sailing qualities of *Endymion* were decisive; she answered her helm more quickly and managed to prevent Decatur from closing, and instead both frigates found themselves running parallel just a quarter of a mile apart. The 24-pounders and carronades of each broadside opened fire, beginning a fierce cannonade that would last for two hours. Decatur's men continued to fire at *Endymion*'s

18 Lambert, *The Challenge*, Chapter 10; James, *Naval Occurrences*, p.427; LAC, MG12 ADM1/508, Admiral's Dispatches, Hayes to Hotham, 17 January 1815.

19 Commodore Stephen Decatur to the American Secretary of the Navy, HBM Ship *Endymion*, 18 January 1815, in James, *Naval Occurrences*, pp.clxxiv–clxxxviii.

Captain Henry Hope of HMS *Endymion*, Britain's fastest frigate, Sir Henry Raeburn. (Eskenazi Museum of Art)

rigging, anything to slow her down and cripple her. Meanwhile, Hope ordered his men to concentrate on the enemy's hull. Decatur had trained his men well, and this had been demonstrated in their engagement with *Macedonian*; but Hope had trained his men thoroughly as well, and had even adopted some of Broke's gunnery drill techniques. Honed by this training, they fired devastatingly quickly and accurately, and over the next two hours smashed the enemy frigate. The ferocious firing lit up the dark January night sky around the two frigates, running yardarm to yardarm as the rest of the British squadron slowly gained.[20]

Over the next two and a half hours, *President*'s hull was continuously battered. Her bulwarks and lower masts and sails were badly cut up and her hull was perforated with shot. Her crew fared little better, and many were cut down in the cannonade, killed and wounded by lead balls and jagged splinters from their own ship's sides. Another lieutenant was struck and carried below, and Decatur was wounded again. Two jagged splinters – remnants of a bit of bulwark smashed by the enemy's 24-pound shot – struck him, leaving the commodore bleeding profusely from the forehead and with a broken rib. Still, Decatur remained on deck and directed the action. The *President*'s marines put up a heavy fight, firing between them over 5,000 musket cartridges at the British. Nevertheless, after 7:30 p.m. her fire slackened, just as *Endymion* began slowing, her rigging effectively shot to pieces. At 7:50 p.m. *President* bore away from the British frigate, and firing on both ships stopped. Eight minutes later, the British observed a signal light in what remained of *President*'s rigging – a common means of signalling a surrender at night when striking one's colours could not be observed.[21] In consequence, *Endymion* halted the action, even as *President* drifted and presented her stern to the British ship.[22] It is not quite clear what was happening, as the Americans denied surrendering at this moment and instead maintained they thought Hope had surrendered, having had enough. From the American's perspective this seemed likely; *Endymion* was effectively dismasted and had halted firing, believing that Decatur had given up.

The British maintained Hope had won the action. Some even accused Decatur of surrendering and then attempting to escape anyway, a serious accusation in a world where honour was so important. The Americans, on the other hand, insisted that Hope had been defeated and *Endymion* battered into submission. Kevin McCranie's analysis is the most balanced, and

20 Lambert, *The Challenge*, Chapter 10.

21 Lambert, *The Challenge*, Chapter 10; McCranie, *Utmost Gallantry*, p.271; James, *Naval Occurrences*, pp.430–433.

22 Lambert, *The Challenge*, Chapter 10; Budiansky, *Perilous Fight*, p.348.

probably the most correct: in the confusion of a night action, both captains mistook the other's actions as a surrender. Hope observed a signal light which appeared to be a sign that she had surrendered; Decatur, meanwhile, had drifted away from *Endymion* and also believed that Hope had been defeated, based on the lack of continued gunfire. In fact, *Endymion* was not in that bad a shape. Her rigging was badly cut up, but she had suffered little damage in the hull and had few casualties. *President*, meanwhile, was in horrible shape.[23] The sequence of events lined up perfectly for both captains to come to the wrong conclusion, and so the two frigates drifted apart, each believing they had won. There is also the question of signal light that the British observed, and so the question remains: what light did the British observe, and why was it flying? None of the surviving American sources explain why – or if – it was there, but the British accounts agree that it was. It is possible that *President* had surrendered, but Decatur changed his mind upon seeing *Endymion*'s state and thinking she was done in herself. It may not have been the most honourable course of action, but Decatur had a duty to preserve his ship and his men from capture.

Whatever actually happened, Decatur had no intention of waiting around for the approaching squadron to catch him. With his ship in a poor state, he needed to escape, and that meant abandoning what he thought was a defeated prize ship. Hope, meanwhile, did not try to take possession of *President*. The two ships had drifted apart – very slowly, in the light breeze – out of hailing distance, and Hope had no means of reaching her. Every one of the ship's boats had been smashed in the cannonade, and her rigging was in tatters. Instead, Hope and his men set about repairing the rigging. But at 8:30 p.m. *President* was again under weigh in an attempt to head back out to sea. She was in a pitiful state now, badly mauled, taking on water, and slowed by damaged rigging. *Pomone* and *Tenedos* were coming up quickly, heading for *President*; they were unencumbered by any rigging or battle damage, and 20 minutes later they passed *Endymion* making good progress in hoisting new masts. Decatur's ship was now in no fit state to fight. Her decks and bulwarks were badly cut up, many of her guns had been dislodged, their carriages and fastenings smashed, and over 100 men had been killed or wounded. As the two fifth-rates approached, Decatur consulted with his two remaining lieutenants and they decided to surrender.

Pomone came up into range just after 9:00 p.m., at which time *Endymion* was back under sail and slowly in pursuit. *Pomone* fired two distant and ineffectual broadsides at *President* before they heard Decatur hailing his surrender. It was not until 10:00 p.m. that boats from HMS *Tenedos* took possession of *President*. According to some accounts, Decatur indicated that he wished to surrender to the senior captain of the squadron; according to others, he indicated that he was surrendering to 'the black ship,' meaning the all-black *Endymion*, which finally came up with the three frigates at midnight. *Majestic*, carrying Hayes, took another two hours to come up with

23 Lambert, *The Challenge*, Chapter 10; McCranie, *Utmost Gallantry*, p.271.

the rest of the squadron, at which point the defeated American commodore went aboard and presented his sword to the British senior captain.[24]

The historiography is split on the question of which of the two frigates won the engagement. Like many contentious questions of the War of 1812, it had almost no real strategic significance, but because of its emotional and morale importance, the interpretations fell along national lines. British and Canadian accounts argued that Hope had won, while American accounts argue for Decatur. That the present work is published in the United Kingdom and authored by a Canadian, whose ancestors would have cheered the victories of Broke and his fellows, no doubt has some bearing on the perspective presented here; that aside, the evidence does suggest that *Endymion* won the action, albeit with some important caveats.

Without a doubt, when both ships broke off the action, *President* was in a near-ruinous state. Her rigging was badly cut up and her hull was even worse. Over 100 men, including most of her officers and the commodore, were wounded or dead. She was slowly taking on water, a situation that would only worsen as time went on. Decatur had failed in his aim to cripple and board *Endymion*, and instead *Endymion* had effectively crippled *his* ship, which proved fatal as the rest of the British squadron was approaching. *President* was left in a state unable either to run or to resist, and so she surrendered. She had entered the action slightly wounded from her grounding, but she was still a formidable warship, heavily built and with an armament slightly surpassing that of *Endymion*. *Endymion*'s hull was much weaker, and she was outclassed in terms of broadside weight by five to four.[25] Decatur's men were well-trained and had previously fought and captured *Macedonian*, but *Endymion* was no *Macedonian* and Hope was no Carden. The experienced crew of *President* was matched by the well-trained crew of *Endymion*, and so, even with the odds against her, *Endymion* triumphed in the long cannonade.

It was an impressive achievement, one that was rightly celebrated by the Royal Navy, but it should be remembered that the action was not a real single-ship action. From the beginning, the action was influenced by the distant squadron. This significantly limited Decatur's options in the fight. He had to keep moving, and his primary goal was to get away and avoid capture. He did not have the freedom of manoeuvre he had enjoyed in his action with *Macedonian*, and felt compelled to focus his fire on *Endymion*'s rigging. While some of *President*'s shot did hit *Endymion*'s hull, as demonstrated by the two dozen casualties and the smashed boats, overall this meant that *President* was subjected to two hours of brutal pounding from *Endymion* without being able to respond in the most destructive way.

Perhaps in recognition of the hazy nature of his achievement, Hope's official letter to Hayes, the senior officer, on the action was rather modest: 'Sir, I have great satisfaction in acquainting you that we closed with the United States frigate, *President* and brought her to close action at half-past

24 Commodore Stephen Decatur to the American Secretary of the Navy, HBM ship *Endymion*, 18 January 1815, quoted in James, *Naval Occurrences*, pp.clxxiv–clxxxviii; Lambert, *The Challenge*, Chapter 10; McCranie, *Utmost Gallantry*, 271–272.

25 Tucker, *Stephen Decatur*, p.144; Lambert, *The Challenge*, Chapter 10

five in the afternoon and continued in that position for two hours and a half, when we succeeded in crippling her very materially.'[26] He did little aside from praise the conduct of his crew, in particular Lieutenant William Morgan, and emphasise the damage that his ship inflicted on the enemy: 'But I trust the loss and damage sustained by the enemy's frigate, will show the steady and well directed fire kept up by His Majesty's Ship under my command. Altho' our loss has been severe, I am happy to state that it is trifling when compared to that of the enemy.'[27] Though modest, Hope's account rammed home the role his ship had played in the action by crippling *President* and effectively guaranteeing her capture. The letter does not mention her supposed surrender, but the ship's log does specify that Hope observed her signal light and assumed it to be a sign of surrender. The account was only a brief one, because Hayes, as the senior officer, was responsible for the official dispatch and account of the action. Therefore, Hope only needed to draft an account that was straight to the point and highlighted the role his ship and crew had played. He did not discuss the particulars of the action beyond stating that they 'brought her [the ship] to close action,' so there was no need to weigh in on Decatur's surrender and the conclusion of the fight. Hope had not taken possession of the prize, after all, and although he stated his losses were severe, he would later more accurately point out that in comparison to the *President*'s losses they were very light. In a letter to his distant cousin and prominent army officer Sir Alexander Hope, he stated that 'my brother officers all regret that we had not met single handed.'[28]

Hayes, by contrast, was far less modest and heaped praise upon Hope and his crew, particularly praising 'Captain Hope's exertions [which] enabled him to get his ship alongside of the enemy, and commence close action.'[29] Hayes makes it clear that he attributed *President*'s surrender to *Endymion* alone, as at the conclusion of the action:

> the *Endymion*'s sails being cut from the yards, the enemy got ahead; Captain Hope taking this opportunity to bend new sails, to enable him to get his ship alongside again, the action ceased, till the *Pomone* getting up at half past eleven at night and firing a few shots, the enemy hailed to say he had already surrendered.[30]

According to Hayes, then, *Endymion* was not out of action when *President* began sailing away at 8:30 p.m. Rather, he was conducting repairs necessary to pursue when the two fifth-rates came up and assisted him. *Constitution* and *United States* had both taken a moment in their victorious actions to repair damage and hoist new sails, and with her rigging so cut up *Endymion* needed to do the same. Crucially, Hayes stated that *President* hailed to say she had already struck when *Pomone* came up.

26 LAC, MG12 ADM1/508, Admiral's Dispatches, North America, C-12855, Captain Henry Hope to Captain John Hayes, His Majesty's Ship *Endymion*, at sea, 16 January 1815.
27 LAC, MG12 ADM1/508, Admiral's Dispatches, C-12855, Hope to Hayes, 16 January 1815.
28 National Archives of Scotland, GD 364/1/1267/23, Captain Henry Hope to Alexander Hope, 2 February 1815, quoted in McCranie, *Utmost Gallantry*, p.272.
29 LAC, MG12 ADM1/508, Admiral's Dispatches, Hayes to Hotham, 17 January 1815.
30 LAC, MG12 ADM1/508, Admiral's Dispatches, Hayes to Hotham, 17 January 1815.

As Hayes described it, the action was not a single-ship action. It was a collective effort, but one where *Endymion* contributed the lion's share of the fighting, and Hope was attributed with the credit for fighting *President* to the point where she could no longer retaliate. In fact, Hayes went a step further:

> And, now Sir, a very pleasing part of my duty, is the bearing testimony to the able and masterly manner in which the *Endymion* was conducted, and the gallantry with which she was fought, and when the effect produced by her well directed fire upon the *President* is witnessed, it cannot be doubted but that Captain Hope would have succeeded in either capturing or sinking her, had none of the squadron been in sight.[31]

President had been badly mauled by *Endymion*'s gunnery, and she was so damaged that 'had the present most severe gale commenced twelve hours sooner, the prize would undoubtedly have sunk.'[32] Given that *Endymion* was a lighter ship in terms of armament and the strength of her hull, it was a great achievement for Captain Hope – and Hayes had no interest in trying to take some of the credit. His letter points out that it was by 'very great attention paid to my orders' that they were able to find *President*, but he did not lay claim to her capture. That was Hope's triumph.

Hayes's letter was directed to Rear Admiral Hotham, who dispatched it directly to the Admiralty with his own preface. Nothing further was added, as Hayes's report spoke for itself. Secretary Croker, upon receipt of the letter, scribbled a minute for the Board of Admiralty that signified his approbation of 'the zeal and activity displayed by all the Capt. & ships company & the gallantly & seamanship with which Capt. Hope brought his ship into action & the distinguished bravery and good conduct with which it was maintained by him & all the other officers & ships company of the Endymion.'[33] It was a collective effort, but again Hotham and Croker singled out Hope and *Endymion* in the account. Hotham then directed a second letter to the commander-in-chief, Alexander Cochrane:

> United States Ship *President* ... sailed on the proceeding evening, under the command of Commodore Decatur, but the present season of the year, and the dark nights of which he availed himself, have not enabled him to elude ... Captain Hayes and the commanders of His Majesty's Ships under his orders, who have well discharged the important duty assigned to them, and I beg leave to offer you my congratulations on that *malignant design* of the American Government being defeated.[34]

31 LAC, MG12 ADM1/508, Admiral's Dispatches, Hayes to Hotham, 17 January 1815.

32 LAC, MG12 ADM1/508, Admiral's Dispatches, Hayes to Hotham, 17 January 1815.

33 LAC, MG12 ADM1/508, Admiral's Dispatches, North America, C-12855, Rear Admiral Henry Hotham to Secretary John Croker, *Superb* at anchor before New London, 23 January 1815.

34 LAC, MG12 ADM1/508, Admiral's Dispatches, North America, C-12855, Rear Admiral Henry Hotham to Vice Admiral Alexander Cochrane, *Superb* at anchor before New London, 23 January 1815.

Again, Hotham referred to the collective nature of the action but singled out Hope's efforts. Hotham made his own argument regarding Hope as the victor:

> the ardor displayed by Captain Hope in the pursuit, the intrepidity with which he brought the enemy's ship to close action, and the undaunted spirit with which the *Endymion*'s inferior force was singly employed, for the space of two hours and a half, ... and of the destructive precision of her fire, and the sinking state of her antagonist, the heavy loss sustained by the enemy, and his inability to make further resistance, when the *Pomone* arrived up with him; while the loss and damage sustained by the *Endymion* was comparatively small.[35]

Like Hayes, Hotham argued that the damage inflicted on *President* in the action signified a victory for *Endymion*. Cochrane too, upon hearing word of *President*'s capture wrote to the Admiralty to offer his congratulations, and characterised the action as Hope's victory with 'the *Majestic*, *Pomone*, and *Tenedos* in sight.'[36] Upon hearing the news, Rear Admiral Philip Durham, the commander of the Leeward Islands station, agreed; he wrote to Cochrane on 14 February: 'I wish you joy, the *President* being in your possession. The *Endymion* did her business in a grand style.'[37]

President was immediately commissioned into the service by Cochrane, and both Hotham and Cochrane sent dispatches to Britain to inform the Admiralty so they could 'receive the earliest information of that fortunate event' and the gallantry with 'which Captain Hope commenced and maintained his action with so superior an enemy and the bravery and discipline displayed by his Officers and Ships Company.'[38] Those same officers received the approbation they had earned. First Lieutenant William Thomas Morgan, who had only been a commissioned officer since 1809, was immediately promoted to commander,[39] and a midshipman of Hope's choosing was granted a lieutenant's commission. Before the end of the year, another of *Endymion*'s lieutenants, Arthur Fanshawe, was also promoted to commander after less than three years as a lieutenant. Fanshawe went on to reach the rank of admiral of the white – one of the highest ranks available in the Royal Navy. Morgan, too, remained in active service, and his career may have been as illustrious as that of Fanshawe or Provo Wallis, but tragically he drowned while still a commander in 1822.[40]

---

35 LAC, MG12 ADM1/508, Admiral's Dispatches, Hotham to Cochrane, 23 January 1815.

36 LAC, MG12 ADM1/508, Admiral's Dispatches, North America, C-12855, Vice Admiral Alexander Cochrane to Secretary John Croker, *Tonnant*, Havana, 28 February 1815.

37 Rear Admiral Philip Durham to Vice Admiral Alexander Cochrane, 14 February 1814 [sic: 1815], in Hilary Rubinstein (ed), *The Durham Papers: Selections from the Papers of Admiral Sir Philip Charles Henderson Calderwood Durham, G.C.B. (1763–1845)* (London and New York: Routledge/Navy Records Society, 2019), p.437

38 LAC, MG12 ADM1/509, Admiral's Dispatches, North America, C-12855, Vice Admiral Alexander Cochrane to Secretary John Croker, *Tonnant*, at sea off St Mary's Coast of Georgia, 13 March 1815.

39 Syrett and DiNardo, *Commissioned Sea Officers*, p.320.

40 Syrett and DiNardo, *Commissioned Sea Officers*, p.150.

Hope's senior officers, and the Navy overall, characterised the action in a way that danced the line between accuracy and falsity. Their accounts were true and their conclusions based in fact, but they ignored the crucial factor that the victory was complicated by the distant presence of the rest of the squadron. Hayes and Hotham could not be completely sure that, had *Endymion* and *President* met alone, the British would have prevailed. Regardless of that fact, the state of *President* and her opponent clearly demonstrated that *Endymion* had come out on top from the action, and the British were not going to let nuance get in the way of the story. Finally, one of the American heavy frigates had been defeated. It was a final, climatic ending to the War of 1812 at sea for the Royal Navy, the culmination of the narrative. Faced with the shocking losses in 1812, the Royal Navy had endeavoured to seek revenge – even by violating orders – for the sake of national honour. Philip Broke had won a spectacular victory in 1813, and was rightly celebrated as a national hero. However, *Chesapeake* was not a sister of *Constitution* or *United States*, which had inflicted the losses. The capture of *President* presented a final moment of victory – an American heavy frigate in British hands. *Endymion* had fought a long action with *President*, much of it running yardarm to yardarm, for several hours and had battered her into submission. For the British, that was enough: a fitting end to the story. Of course, history is not a novel that follows narrative rules of progression and climax. While *President* was carried to Bermuda, another shocking loss occurred far off in the Atlantic, inflicted by none other than 'Old Ironsides'.

Final victory of USS *Constitution*, 20 February 1815

In January, word reached the Admiralty that *Constitution* was at sea, cruising somewhere in the mid-Atlantic. Immediately ships were detached from the Channel Fleet to find her and provide some trade protection, while Sir George Collier (with the 58-gun frigates *Leander* and *Newcastle* and the 40-gun *Acasta*) left his station off North America to join the search. Collier mistakenly believed she was in company with *Congress* and would be linking up with *President* and *Hornet*, making the concentration of force on his part fully necessary.[41] With any luck, the two massive *razéed* frigates would come up with their intended matches, *Constitution* and *President*. In fact, neither squadron fell in with her before *Constitution* had scored yet another victory against the Royal Navy, after chancing upon two British sixth-rates near Gibraltar on 20 February 1815.

The ships in question were HMS *Levant*, a 20-gun post-ship armed primarily with 32-pounder carronades, and HMS *Cyane*, nominally a 22-gun ship but carrying 34 guns in all, primarily carronades. Lookouts from *Cyane* spotted a sail on the horizon early in the afternoon, and by 4:00 p.m. her captain, Gordon Falcon, concluded that she was an enemy and cruised within hailing distance to inform Captain George Douglas, *Levant*'s captain

41 LAC, MG12 ADM1/508, Admiral's Dispatches, Hotham to Cochrane, 23 January 1815; McCranie, *Utmost Gallantry*, p.259.

and the senior of the two. In his report, Douglas stated that he then intended to bring the enemy to action, understanding the risks but hoping to disable the enemy frigate and prevent her from finding and attacking two valuable and lightly defended convoys in the vicinity. *Constitution* was a faster ship and had a crew larger than *Cyane* and *Levant*'s combined, and while the total weight of metal between the two British ships was heavier than *Constitution*'s, that advantage only amounted to 50 pounds. Plus, the guns on *Constitution* had a much longer range and a greater hitting power, making the odds steep at best. As the defeat of *Essex* demonstrated, carronades were no match for long guns unless the action was exclusively at close range.[42] According to McCranie, the convoys in question were not really in any danger;[43] more likely, Douglas saw a chance at action with the enemy and seized it, even with his anxieties about facing 'a frigate of the largest class' with two sixth-rates.[44]

The two ships stood on towards *Constitution* over the next two hours, and *Constitution* fired ranging shots 5:00 p.m. but they fell short. The cannonade proper did not begin until 6:05 p.m., with the winter darkness falling quickly over the seas. *Levant* had taken position opposite *Constitution*'s bows, and *Cyane* was a bit aft her beam when they opened fire a few hundred yards apart. The British ships were not in a good situation; they mounted carronades, which meant they needed to fight a close action, but doing so exposed them to the murderous impact of *Constitution*'s full broadside. However, staying off meant they could barely hit the enemy at all, and Captain Charles Stewart of *Constitution* managed to keep his ship just beyond the effective range of the enemy for most of the action. Before long, *Cyane*, which had borne the brunt of the enemy's fire, was badly cut up and had drifted astern, freeing *Constitution* to pour a murderous broadside into *Levant*. *Levant* was devastated by the broadside and drifted before the wind. Captain Douglas managed to make repairs and move *Levant* back into play; Falcon endeavoured to follow, but with the damage to his ship's rigging her progress was slow.[45]

Captain Stewart of *Constitution* then assumed a raking position behind *Levant* and poured in two full broadsides. Damaged and helpless, *Levant* was ripped apart by the heavy shot of *Constitution* smashing through her stern gallery and passing through bulkheads; gun carriages and men turned the decks into a mess of broken bodies and splintered wood. With *Levant* mauled, Falcon finally managed to get *Cyane* before the wind and brought her guns to bear and opened fire. As shot flew into *Constitution*, Stewart brought his ship about and concentrated on *Cyane*, pouring shot after shot into the already disabled ship. *Levant*, badly damaged, had once again drifted away, and Falcon found himself alone fighting against the heavier ship in the

42 Roosevelt, *Naval War of 1812*, pp.420–421

43 McCranie, *Utmost Gallantry*, pp.265–266.

44 TNA, ADM 1/5449, Court Martial *Cyane*, Captain Gordon Falcon to Captain George Douglas, United States Ship of the War *Constitution*, 22 February 1815, at sea; TNA, ADM 1/5449, Court Martial *Levant*, Captain George Douglas to Secretary John Croker, United States Frigate *Constitution*, at sea, 22 February 1815 (quote).

45 TNA, ADM 1/5449, CM *Cyane*, Falcon to Douglas, 22 February 1815; McCranie, *Utmost Gallantry*, pp.265–266.

dark: 'not in a situation to afford support, without which I could not have any reasonable prospect of making any impression as to very superior a force as I was then singly opposed to.'[46]

Falcon consulted with the officers, who 'were of opinion that the situation and crippled state of the ship, prevented any prospect of success against a force considerably more than double even ours, or even of effecting our escape.'[47] Without *Levant*, which was somewhere in the darkness, *Cyane* stood no chance and had no real possibility of escaping. Nevertheless, Falcon hoped that he had distracted *Constitution* long enough for Douglas to hoist new sails and effect her escape. With no option left, Falcon and his officers judged that further resistance was futile and carried out his 'painful duty to direct the colours to be struck.'[48] At 7:00 p.m. *Cyane* was out of the fight and soon after taken possession of by boats from *Constitution*.

Meanwhile, on board *Levant*, Douglas was not quite sure what was going on. His ship had been disabled and had drifted away from the action, and in the darkness all he could see were distant flashes. He and his men did what they could to repair the damage and to re-rig the sails before standing in towards *Constitution* again in a suicidal attempt to renew the action. If *Cyane* was still in the fight, he was determined to come to her aid. As she approached, *Levant* came about and

> Passed close under his lee, and gave him our starboard broadside, as long as the guns would bear, receiving at the same time, a most heavy and destructive fire from the enemy, both in the rigging and hull, at 9:30pm finding that the *Cyane* had undoubtedly been obliged to striker her colours, the *Levant* was again put before the wind.[49]

She had passed broadside to broadside of the heavier frigate, and *Levant* paid dearly for it. Much to his dismay, Douglas's attempt to renew the action and come to Falcon's rescue had been for nothing. *Constitutions*' murderous fire had undone the repair work his men had laboured on in the dark. All that was left to do now was to run:

> Every effort was made to make ... sail, but owing to the crippled state ... the whole of the lower and running rigging, the wheel, main topgallant yard, mizzentopmast and the [studdingsail boom] being shot away, the lower masts much wounded and the sails shot and torn to pieces, caused an unavoidable delay – the enemy keeping up a constant fire upon us with his bow guns, during the chase, and coming fast up with us.[50]

---

46 TNA, ADM 1/5449, CM *Cyane*, Falcon to Douglas, 22 February 1815.
47 TNA, ADM 1/5449, CM *Cyane*, Falcon to Douglas, 22 February 1815.
48 TNA, ADM 1/5449, CM *Cyane*, Falcon to Douglas, 22 February 1815.
49 TNA, ADM 1/5449, CM *Levant*, Douglas to Croker, 22 February 1815; Roosevelt, *Naval War of 1812*, pp.418–422.
50 TNA, ADM 1/5449, CM *Levant*, Douglas to Croker, 22 February 1815.

Even without the extensive damage *Levant* had received, *Constitution* was still faster. Stewart directed a relentless fire from the 24-pounder bow chasers that further tore up *Levant*'s rigging, slowing the British ship to the point where *Constitution* could afford to yaw. Douglas observed that she 'was coming up on our larboard quarter with the intention of giving us his broadside, and having consulted the opinion of the officers, who agreed with me, that any further resistance would only be a useless sacrifice of more lives.'[51] Having done everything they could to fight and flee, *Levant*'s colours were struck.

Meanwhile, Sir George Collier was prowling the area in search of *Constitution*, still unsure if she was in company with any other frigates. On 11 March 1815, they stood in towards Porto Praya, a Portuguese port in the Verde islands off West Africa, where lookouts spotted *Constitution* slipping out of harbour with two sixth-rate prizes in tow. Captain Stewart had anchored in the neutral port to make repairs, but upon spotting the approaching British ships they weighed anchor and made a run for it. With Collier was *Leander* and *Newcastle*, each more than a match for *Constitution* alone. With *Acasta* in company as well, anything but flight would have been madness. *Newcastle* led the chase with the two others a few miles behind, and before long Stewart worryingly perceived that the British were gaining. He signalled for *Cyane* to tack and sail on a different course, hoping to draw away one of the British ships, but none did. Sometime later he tried the gambit again and signalled for *Levant* to tack out of the chase. This time, however, the entire British squadron veered after her, much to Stewart's amazement. Whereas Stewart had believed they were gaining on him, from Collier's perspective *Constitution* was slowly increasing the gap. As the chase went on, he began to worry that he would never actually catch *Constitution* at all, and so when *Levant* tacked away he resolved to capture at least one of the two lost sixth-rates. Stewart was able to escape, and later collected *Cyane* without any interference.[52]

Having collected *Cyane*, *Constitution* made her way home, yet another victorious action to her name. In America, the action was hailed as a great victory, as put forward by Captain Stewart himself:

> Considering the advantages derived by the enemy, from a divided and more active force, as also their superiority in the weight and number of guns, I deem the speedy and decisive result of this action the strongest assurance which can be given the government, that all under my command did their duty, and gallantly supported the reputation of American seamen.[53]

Without a doubt it was a considerable achievement. Stewart had engaged two separate warships on his own, managing to counter their freedom of movement, even managing to separate them so he could concentrate his fire on one at a time and batter both into submission. Still, as McCranie and

51 TNA, ADM 1/5449, CM *Levant*, Douglas to Croker, 22 February 1815.

52 McCranie, *Utmost Gallantry*, pp.268–269.

53 Captain Charles Stewart to Secretary Ben. W. Crowninshield, in James, *Naval Occurrences*, p.cxcv.

Roosevelt point out, the heavier broadside weight and number of guns on the British side were deceptive, as *Constitution*'s broadside was far more dangerous than her opponents, and the stronger and more durable hull of *Constitution* and her better sailing qualities were important factors.[54] Not dissimilar to *Endymion*'s victory, *Constitution*'s was not as clear cut as it initially seemed. Whereas *Endymion* had decisively won an engagement with a superior foe, it was complicated by the presence of the distant British squadron and the confusion at the end of the cannonade. *Constitution* had won an engagement against two different ships, displaying exceptional manoeuvring and tactics, but even with their forces combined *Cyane* and *Levant* faced nearly unsurmountable odds when facing *Constitution*'s superior sailing qualities, exceptionally strong hull, and devastating broadside.

Both Douglas and Falcon, in their subsequent courts martial held at Halifax, focused on those factors. They had faced a very superior force, which could outrange and out sail them to render the conclusion nearly inevitable. In the course of the action they had been outmanoeuvred and their ships badly mauled, losing important spars and rigging and having gun carriages smashed and dismounted. Douglas defended his decision to bring *Constitution* to action even when 'aware of the superiority of the enemy's force', starting that he had a duty to protect local convoys.[55] Of course, the convoys were not in as much danger as he implied.[56] Douglas's hope that together his ships could take on *Constitution* had been a long shot, but Douglas and Falcon had some notion that it was possible, stating that had their ships met 'a more equal force or … succeeded in bringing the enemy to close action the result would have been very different.'[57]

The courts martial concurred, stating that the losses were attributed to 'the very superior force of the enemy ship, aided by her superior sailing,' and that their carronades had little effect on the enemy, especially compared with the constant fire of the *Constitution*'s 24-pounders.[58] In contrast with the court martial for *Constitution*'s last two victories and the victory of *United States*, the verdicts of both courts martial highlighted the impact of the fire of *Constitution*'s 'seventeen long twenty-four pounders' which had made her such a 'superior force.' In the case of 18-pounder frigates in 1812, it was not thought necessary to mention the difference in gun calibre; the Royal Navy's experience over the last two decades had convinced them, as Carden had once explained to Decatur, that an 18-pounder frigate could defeat a 24-pounder frigate. Nevertheless, the case of *Cyane* and *Levant* was different from those of *Guerriere*, *Macedonian*, and *Java* two and a half years earlier.

Both *Cyane* and *Levant* were armed with carronades, so fighting at a longer distance placed them in a very unfavourable position, and the enemy's superior armament came into play in a more obvious way. Even at close range, the hitting power of the guns of a sixth-rate were nothing compared

54 McCranie, *Utmost Gallantry*, pp.265–266; Roosevelt, *Naval War of 1812*, pp.420–421.

55 TNA, ADM 1/5449, CM *Levant*, Douglas to Croker, 22 February 1815.

56 McCranie, *Utmost Gallantry*, p.266.

57 TNA, ADM 1/5449, CM *Cyane*, Falcon to Douglas, 22 February 1815.

58 TNA, ADM 1/5449, Verdict, CM *Cyane*; Verdict, CM *Levant*.

to that of a heavy frigate like *Constitution*. Actions had been won against similar great odds before, but even the Royal Navy considered exploits like Thomas Cochrane's capture of a Spanish frigate in a 14-gun brig-sloop to be rarities. After three years of discourse on the 1812 losses, the American heavy frigates had taken on an imposing reputation. Losing to such a force was no longer shocking. Still, Douglas and Falcon were praised for their conduct in the action, and for having carried it out against such a superior force for as long as they held 'the smallest prospect of success.'[59] However long the odds, the Royal Navy was always confident they had a chance. Douglas had been confident, despite the odds, and he and Falcon had fought until that prospect was extinguished.

George Douglas's naval career effectively ended following the action, and he remained on half-pay for the next decade.[60] Gordon Falcon, meanwhile, continued in active service for some time.[61] Of the possible candidates for their lieutenants, none advanced to the rank of command except in retirement.[62] The fate of Captain Sir George Collier, however, was much, much worse.

Sir George Collier finished the war with a long, distinguished record behind him. He had served throughout the French Revolutionary and Napoleonic Wars, having participated in many minor and major actions that won him quick promotions, and by the end of the conflict he had the prestigious command of HMS *Leander* and a baronetcy. After a brief period ashore, he was made commodore of the West African Squadron and led the slavery suppression efforts for several years. He had a strong following in the Navy and in the civilian presses, including the *Acadian Recorder*, which had run a piece on him and his new frigate HMS *Leander* during the war. However, during the peace, some began criticising him for his role in *Constitution*'s escape. William James brought that criticism to national attention in his *Naval History*, where he attacked Collier's honour and courage:

> the only ship [*Newcastle*], that could have pursued her with any chance of success, had been ordered by the *Leander* to tack from her. Most sincerely do we regret, on personal, as well as on public grounds, that this last and most triumphant escape of the *Constitution*, the first frigate of the United States that had humbled the proud flag of Britain, had not long ago, been brought under the scrutiny of a court-martial. The blame would then have fallen where it ought to have fallen; and, in the unpleasant task of detailing, what, the more it is investigated, the more it will show itself to be, the most blundering piece of business recorded in these six volumes, we should neither have had our statements called in question nor our motives misunderstood.[63]

59 TNA, ADM 1/5449, Verdict, CM *Levant*.

60 Syrett and DiNardo, *Commissioned Sea Officers*, p.129; 'Hon. George Douglas', in *Royal Naval Biography*, Supplement, Part III, pp.57–61.

61 Syrett and DiNardo, *Commissioned Sea Officers*, p.149; 'Gordon Thomas Falcon, Esq.', in *Royal Naval Biography*, Supplement, Part III, pp.161–162.

62 Syrett and DiNardo, *Commissioned Sea Officers*, pp.213, 243, 291.

63 James, *Naval History*, Vol.6, pp.383

James's accusation was remarkable: that Collier letting *Constitution* escape was the 'most blundering piece of business' of the last two decades of warfare was quite a claim. While not everyone ascribed to James's harsh interpretation of events, many did, and Collier was deeply hurt by the shaming of his public reputation. His honour and courage had been called into question, and the weight of the drama saw his mental state quickly deteriorate. In March 1824, just a year after the remarks were first published, Collier took his own life. In the *Royal Naval Biography*, Lieutenant John Marshall, one of Collier's sympathisers, suggests that the event was no secret, simply stating his 'melancholy and untimely death, the particulars of which are too well known to require repetition.'[64]

Understanding and remembering the naval war's final actions

By the end of the conflict, 'Old Ironsides' had won three major victories, and she became the symbol of the American government's celebrations of the war and of their particular spin on history. The same was happening in Britain with her sister, *President*. She was immediately taken into the service as HMS *President*, and set out for Portsmouth with *Endymion* as the symbol of the Royal Navy's triumph against the seemingly invincible American heavy frigates. Throughout February and March, reports of *President*'s capture made their way through newspapers across Britain, appearing in papers throughout the British Isles. The *London Courier* celebrated the 'CAPTURE OF THE AMERICAN LINE OF BATTLE SHIP, *PRESIDENT*, BY THE *ENDYMION* FRIGATE', describing the action as one won by an inferior frigate yardarm to yardarm after *Endymion* and *President* had left the rest of the squadron far behind. A line of battle ship *President* was not, but many circles in the Navy and the press had labelled her and her sisters as such, and she was compared in broadside weight to the old, obsolete fourth-rates from the mid-eighteenth century. The *Courier* argued that once *Pomone* had come up and fired 'a shot or two, Commodore Decatur hailed to say he had *already* surrendered ... the glory of the capture, therefore, is all the *Endymion*'s.'[65]

The *Hampshire Chronicle* described the action in great detail, concluding that once *President* ceased the fighting and hoisted her signal light: 'she then got a little a-head, the *Endymion* ..., bent new courses, repaired other damages, and was soon again in nearly her former position. ... *Pomone* and *Tenedos* came up, and their boats took possession, the whole of *Endymion*'s boats having been destroyed.' The greater casualties and damage on board *President* were highlighted, as was the fact that 'many of the *Endymion*'s shot went through both sides of the *President*, which was not the case in a single instance on board the *Endymion*.'[66] The *Hampshire Chronicle* were firmly of opinion that it was *Endymion*'s victory, as proved by the signal of surrender

64 'Sir George Ralph Collier, Bart.', in *Royal Naval Biography*, Vol.2, Part II, p.540.

65 *London Courier and Evening Gazette*, 18 February 1815.

66 *Hampshire Chronicle*, 6 March 1815.

made by Decatur and by the extensive damage inflicted on the American frigate.

In Halifax, the story was picked up and celebrated immediately, leading the front page of the *Acadian Recorder* more than once in the month of March. News first arrived from a copy of the *Bermuda Royal Gazette*, which printed an account of the action in its entirety. This account also hinged on the respective damage inflicted on the two frigates and the weight of force in favour of the heavier and better-manned *President*, arguing that suggestions of the outcome being anything other than a victory for *Endymion* were flatly false. The editors of the *Recorder* concurred, stating that based on 'the best information we can obtain, the *President* struck to the *Endymion*, but the *Pomone*, owing to its being a night action, was not aware of it, and fired some guns.' They noted the 'admirable' conduct of Hope's seamanship and gunnery, the quality of which gave them the assurance that 'the action would have terminated as it has, had the other frigates been at Spithead.'[67] Just a few weeks later, the *Recorder* responded to Decatur's American version of the event, accusing Decatur of libel and suggesting that 'We can partly conceive the feelings of the conqueror of the *Macedonian*, at finding himself so unexpectedly boarded by that very ship, to which, just twelve months before, he sent a flaming challenge.'[68] A bitter, perhaps jealous, Decatur had succumbed to the all-too-common (as the *Recorder* put it) tendency of American officers to spout lies and falsehoods to diminish the achievements of Britain's naval heroes.

From London to Halifax, newspapers were making a similar argument, which formed the basis of the British perception of the action. It was thought of by most of the popular press in both England and Halifax as an exceptional victory won by *Endymion*, and the presence of the rest of the squadron mattered little to its outcome. The editors of the *Naval Chronicle* opened the first edition of 1815 by declaring that

> Our hopes have been most honourably realized in the capture of the United States Ship *President*, Commodore Decatur commander, by the British frigate *Endymion*; and we most cordially congratulate Captain Hope, his officers and men, on the merited success of their gallantry and skill, in so bravely maintaining the reputation of their country – accustomed to capture and destroy, in a few hours, whole fleets of powerful and superior magnitude. We say, *maintaining* the reputation of this country; for, surely, it can never have been seriously considered as lost by *two* or *three* instances of advantage obtained by a morally-insuperable superiority of force.[69]

The account praised the 'vigilance and exertions' of the entire squadron, but most of all they recognised Hope and his crew who had actually caught and

67 NSA, *Acadian Recorder*, 4 March 1815, 3:9 (online), available at https://novascotia.ca/archives/newspapers/archives.asp?ID=866.

68 NSA, *Acadian Recorder*, 18 March 1815 (online), available at 3:11, https://novascotia.ca/archives/newspapers/archives.asp?ID=868.

69 *Naval Chronicle*, Vol.33, pp.156–157.

fought the enemy into submission. Like other publications, the account stated that *Endymion* had won the action, and that the arrival and intervention of *Pomone* only revealed that Decatur had already surrendered to Hope. The disparity in force was described in detail, as was the editor's hope that 'the remaining principals' of the American Navy would soon be captured.[70]

However, one story in *Cobbett*'s *Weekly Political Register*, a paper that espoused radicalism and staunchly anti-government views, agreed with the American account: Decatur believed he had won the action based on his misinterpretation of *Endymion* ceasing to fire as a mark of surrender, or at the very least of her having been disabled. The *Register* stated that *Endymion* was 'disabled in the action, and would, it is more than probable, have become a prize to the *President*, had not the rest of our squadron come to her relief,' and attacked the wider British press, particularly *The Times* and the aforementioned *London Courier*, for implying that *Endymion* had won single-handedly.[71] It was a minority view, however, and most of the paper's political views were staunchly in opposition to the governing order.

The action had come at the end of a war that offered little to console the British people. It was not a war they had wanted, and unlike the war against France, there seemed to be little of significance in the conflict. The losses in 1812 had shocked the nation, but finally the Americans had been punished by having one of their precious frigates snatched away. Civilians and naval men alike latched onto the event as a great victory. It was certainly a complicated one, and many accounts sought to make it *Endymion*'s victory rather than the victory of the entire squadron. Mostly the arguments hinged on the far greater damage inflicted on *President* than on *Endymion*. In part this can be attributed to the fact that Decatur, who was trying to disable his opponent to effect his escape, focused *President*'s fire on *Endymion*'s rigging, a detail lost on the average news reader or journalist. However, another factor was that Henry Hope had adopted the meticulous gunnery practice methods employed by Philip Broke. He had turned his ship's company into a crack team able to fire quickly and accurately, and that was demonstrated in the cannonade which battered *President*. The greater extent of that damage was key to Britain's perception of the action; it served as a crucial piece of evidence that supported their assertions that *Endymion* had won on her own and would have triumphed all the same had the rest of the squadron stayed home. Britain desperately wanted to accept this action as a one-on-one fight with one of the American heavy frigates.

Of course, *President*'s capture was only one of the two frigate actions from the final months of the war; not long after news of *Endymion's* victory flooded British newspapers the news of the capture of *Cyane* and *Levant* would have reached England. According to one twenty-first century historian, David Fitz-Enz, 'the newspapers in London were absolutely silent. It quickly passed into history, and, as we all know, "history is an unending argument."'[72] The

70 *Naval Chronicle*, Vol.33, pp.156–157.

71 *Cobbett's Weekly Political Register*, 6 May 1815, 27.

72 Fitz-Enz, *Old Ironsides*, p.190.

papers were not all that silent; some, like the *Norfolk Chronicle*, announced news of the action, but few papers picked up the story. At the conclusion of the War of 1812, it seemed that the United Kingdom cared little about it. One letter submitted to the *Naval Chronicle* expressed a distress at the conclusion of the American war generally, stating that he would be now 'Lamenting the fallen fortunes of my country, and the unavailing loss of so many brave men, I now take my leave of the American contest.'[73] The editors expressed their mortification at the triumph of *Constitution*, but little was said of the event.[74] The *Royal Gazette* of London, which regularly reported on victories and defeats of the Royal Navy, largely omitted the reports from *Cyane* and *Levant*, as they had several of the actions in 1814.

Halifax's *Acadian Recorder* offered a commentary on the action in June, over a month since they printed the first announcement of the action – from an American paper – largely in response to 'the hectoring of the Americans at the *Constitution* frigate capturing two British sloops-of-war.' The paper may have intended to let the action slide into history, but it appeared that the celebrations in the United States had struck a nerve. They defended the defeat, stating that *Cyane* and *Levant*, 'carrying carronades only,' attacked a ship that was comparable to a British 64-gun ship of the line.[75] Given the disparity in force, and particularly in the range and hitting power of the respective ships' guns, the battle was far from the glorious victory that the American press made it out to be. In fact, they went a step further and questioned whether two American sloops would 'venture to attack even a 36-gun frigate of ours, much more the *Leander*, *Newcastle*, the *Constitution*'s match? We are warranted in believing that, sooner than close with such a ship, they would throw overboard every gun, boat, and spar; and start their water and provisions.'[76] Continuing the trend in 1814, the *Recorder* praised the gallantry of the British sailors for engaging in such an outmatched fight, while insinuating that the Americans lacked that same spirit of gallantry. What they lacked in gallantry, though, they seemed to make up for in celebrating their achievements in a way that annoyed Haligonians. The *Recorder* was sick of the celebrations, and concluded the piece by sarcastically remarking: '"Brilliant affair" – Is there any act done by the Americans since the war began, that has not been so?'[77] Another month later, they included an account of the verdict of the courts martial for *Cyane* and *Levant* – a reassuring statement that both ships' brave naval heroes were honourably acquitted had faced a very superior force.

* * *

73 'Albion' to the Editor, 12 March 1815, *Naval Chronicle*, Vol.33, p.296.

74 *Naval Chronicle*, Vol.33, pp.431.

75 NSA, *Acadian Recorder*, 3 June 1815, 3:22 (online), available at https://novascotia.ca/archives/newspapers/archives.asp?ID=879.

76 NSA, *Acadian Recorder*, 3 June 1815, 3:22 (online), available at https://novascotia.ca/archives/newspapers/archives.asp?ID=879.

77 NSA, *Acadian Recorder*, 3 June 1815, 3:22 (online), available at https://novascotia.ca/archives/newspapers/archives.asp?ID=879.

While the vestiges of public discussion went on about the final actions and the last courts martial from the conflict were being held, peace in Europe was shattered. In March, Napoleon Bonaparte escaped from Elba back to France, and within days had gained control of the army and the government. The might of the Seventh Coalition, principally Britain, Prussia, Austria, and Russia, began mobilising their armies to confront the resurrected emperor. Together they could field well over a million soldiers, but assembling these forces and moving them to the French border would take time. Meanwhile, Napoleon launched a lightning offensive and invaded Flanders with his quickly assembled *Armée du Nord*. There, the border was defended by two coalition armies: the Anglo–Allied Army of Flanders under the Duke of Wellington, and the Prussian Army of the Lower Rhine under Gebhard von Blücher.

If the two armies could be destroyed in detail, then Napoleon could even the odds. He had smashed the Prussians before, and had decisively defeated the Austrians and Russians combined more than once. Europe's fate hinged on this campaign. In June, Napoleon attacked the Prussians at the Battle of Ligny, and while he drove the Prussians from the field, he did not destroy Blücher's army. The later retreated in good order, and on 18 June managed to come to the aid of Wellington's British, Dutch, Belgian, and German troops fighting the French at the Battle of Waterloo. With the Prussians assaulting his right flank, Napoleon opted to send his undefeated Imperial Guard to try and break the weary British; instead, the Guard shattered under the weight of British volley fire, and the two allied armies advanced and crushed the French army. It was as climatic a moment as one can find in history, and in the course of a few hours the reign of Napoleon Bonaparte was brought to an end, as were the over 20 years of warfare that had erupted during the French Revolution.

To the reader it might seem strange that the book has diverted to the Hundred Days campaign, which had absolutely no impact on the War of 1812 and simply distracts from the main narrative. Yet that is precisely why it is here, because the public in Britain were also distracted by the final campaign against Napoleon. The Hundred Days overshadowed everything from the end of the war – the peace with America, the final show-down and capture of *President*, and the victory of *Constitution*. The very last action of the war, fought in the Pacific in March between USS *Hornet* and HMS *Penguin*, occurred days after Napoleon escaped from Elba, and as such it barely registered in the public discourse once news of the action reached home. Even the defeat of *President* faded into history, along with much of the war.

President's capture had occurred after years of longing for such a victory, and the naval-interested public in Britain and Halifax were perfectly happy to accept the narrative that she had been fairly beaten by *Endymion*. Some outlets inaccurately inflated the British achievement by failing to mention that *Endymion* was not alone, while others argued that the particulars of the event were ample proof that *Endymion* would still have won if the rest of her squadron remained home. Eager to capitalise on the fanfare, *Endymion* and her prize were quickly sent home, and they arrived in late March to the cheers of 'the numerous spectators' that had assembled in Portsmouth.[78] However, *President* did not come home in a vacuum; she had arrived in the midst of the scare of Napoleon's return. The Royal Navy was remobilising for the coming war, and the events of the War of 1812 slowly faded from the headlines and from public memory.

78 *Naval Chronicle*, Vol.33, p.283.

Epilogue

Upon the Coalition partners declaring war against Napoleon Bonaparte in 1815, Henry Hotham was immediately transferred home and given command of a portion of the Channel Fleet as it mobilised to resume the blockade of France. With him was Hope in *Endymion*, having just left *President* in Portsmouth. The war did not last long; just a month after the Battle of Waterloo, Bonaparte surrendered to one of Hotham's ships, HMS *Bellerophon*, and the long two decades of conflict were finally over. To make sure of that, the Coalition members decided to exile Napoleon deep into the South Atlantic on St Helena, where he lived out his last days far from European society. The Royal Navy, meanwhile, was demobilised, and hundreds of officers went on half-pay. Hope returned home and paid off *Endymion* in August, and she remained there until 1833 when she underwent an extensive refit. Even then, she was still one of the fastest sailing frigates in the Navy and continued to see active service through the 1840s.[1] Upon being broken up she was followed by a steam frigate in 1865, one of the last wooden frigates built by the Royal Navy.

Broke's old 'wooden wife' was put in ordinary upon coming home, and later placed back in commission for a three year cruise in the Caribbean, hunting pirates and slave ships.[2] She was renamed in the 1840s, freeing up the now famous name for a state-of-the-art steam frigate launched in 1855, whose crew won distinction at the Siege of Lucknow during the Indian Rebellion. William Hall, an African Nova Scotian, earned a Victoria Cross in the battle while assisting his lieutenant in keeping a gun in operation while under heavy enemy fire; he was the first from that province and the first of African ancestry to earn that distinction. His parents had escaped slavery with the help of the North American squadron during the War of 1812. One of *Shannon*'s sisters survives today – HMS *Trincomalee*, completed just after the war. Alongside *Constitution*, she is the last of the sailing frigates that so captivated generations.

In America, the United States Navy took care to preserve their famous heavy frigate. USS *Constitution* remains in commission today – the oldest

1 Lambert, *The Challenge*, Chapter 13.

2 Martin Salmon, 'HMS *Shannon*'s later commissions', in Tim Voelcker (ed.), *Broke of the Shannon and the War of 1812* (Barnsley: Seaforth Publishing, 2013), p.179.

commissioned warship still afloat, surpassed in age only by the dry-docked HMS *Victory*. USS *United States* may have survived too, but during the Civil War she was seized by the fledgling Confederate Navy and later sunk when Norfolk was abandoned to the United States Navy. Waterlogged and old, the Union Navy raised the ship but sold her for scrap at the end of the war.[3] Her name was thrice resurrected for capital ships ordered in the twentieth century; a *Lexington*-class battlecruiser, cancelled following the Washington Naval Treaty, a *United States*-class aircraft carrier cancelled due to budget restraints, and an aircraft carrier laid down in 1993, which was later renamed by the Secretary of the Navy. The name *President*, however, was never reused in the United States Navy.

In Britain, *President* was immediately taken into the service. The existing HMS *President*, a former French frigate, was renamed to free up her name for the captured American frigate. After a few years, however, HMS *President* proved to be in too poor a shape to return to active service, and she was scrapped just after the war. An entirely new *President*, built to the exact same design as her namesake, was ordered in 1818, and later served as the flagship of the North America and West Indies Station under Admiral Sir George Cockburn, the naval officer who had landed the force that sacked Washington. She served not only as one of Britain's heavy frigates but also as a visual reminder to the United States of the Royal Navy's final triumph of the war. *Chesapeake*, on the other hand, served until just after the end of the war, when it was concluded she was also in poor condition and sold for breaking. She went to the yards alongside *Cherub*, the sloop that accompanied *Phoebe*'s attack on *Essex*, and timbers from the once-American ship contributed to the construction of Chesapeake Mill, another standing reminder to the United States.[4]

On both sides of the Atlantic, and on both sides of the then-fortified Canada–United States border, the frigate actions of the war retained some of their lustre. They had fascinated, frightened, and emboldened a generation of naval officers and civilians, but long afterwards they had mostly faded into memory. In Britain and Nova Scotia, of course, Napoleon Bonaparte had always been the biggest threat, and therefore the victories of Nelson and Wellington took precedence. Yet to contemporaries on both sides of the Atlantic the war still mattered. Canadians, even while recognising that theirs was a 'puny war,' had lived through a border war that engrossed their lives. Nova Scotians were deeply impacted by the commercial and maritime conflict in the Atlantic and followed the news of the single-ship actions of the two navies closely. In Britain, too, the contests of naval chivalry resonated disproportionately to their importance in the overall war. Literature analysing the actions soon flooded the market. William James, while in Halifax, published his first analysis of the conflict with the aim of defending Britain's reputation and honour, and he stated that 'The colonial public … gave the work a most flattering reception: in the short space of two months,

3 Toll, *Six Frigates*, pp.476–477.

4 John Wain, 'Chesapeake Mill', in Tim Voelcker (ed.), *Broke of the Shannon and the War of 1812* (Barnsley: Seaforth Publishing, 2013), pp.182–186.

nearly 2,000 copies went off; and the remainder, about 500 in number, the author brought with him to England.'[5] It was a considerable feat – if true, that is – as Halifax's population was only about 5,000 in 1815. In England, too, James's expanded and revised edition was a bestseller, and he followed it up with a more expansive *Naval History* of the entire war. Even decades later, some were still talking about the actions. In 1830, the Duke of Wellington told Philip Broke in a letter that 'there is no event of the late war to which I have looked with more interest than' *Shannon–Chesapeake*.[6] The new HMS *President* remained at the head of the North American squadron, ready to show the flag and remind the United States of their loss.

However, as several American historians have argued, the impact of the 1812 losses on the Royal Navy and on Britain had been profoundly shocking. As a result of that shock, the British developed a new-found respect for the United States as a naval power. According to Daughan, that respect shaped the post-war relationship between the two powers throughout the nineteenth and twentieth centuries. Several crises nearly led to war between the two powers, but both sides were weary of such a conflict and in every case better sense prevailed. As strange as it is to imagine now, the Americans were developing war plans aimed at Canada and the United Kingdom as late as the 1930s, and in Canada similar plans were also under consideration, but such a conflict never occurred: from the start, the post-war relationship was defined by a mutual respect, primarily built on the contests of naval chivalry during the War of 1812.[7]

Beyond that, the Royal Navy took some specific lessons from their experience in action against the Americans. One *Naval Chronicle* commentator helpfully suggested that, in the future, 'to cope effectually with America, we must have many large frigates (50 gun class) and sloops (20 guns), and we must have a large fleet on their coasts, as well as strong squadrons elsewhere.'[8] For the most part, the Admiralty was of a similar mind. They continued to build 18-pounder fifth-rates up until 1840, when the last *Seringapatam*-class was constructed, but for nearly every fifth-rate built in that time, a heavy fourth-rate frigate with 24-pounder main batteries was also constructed.[9] The Navy that had once rejected heavy frigates as an unnecessary expense, even in wartime, now focused on constructing large frigates during the peace.

This coincided with a revolution of scientific ship-building, and in the post-war years the size of naval vessels exploded. Ships of the line climbed in tonnage, and new construction methods enabled larger ships, able to carry heavier guns, to be launched. Around the 1840s, this trend allowed

5 James, *Naval Occurrences*, pp.vi–vii.

6 SRO, HA 9/9/330, Duke of Wellington to Admiral Philip Broke, 17 July 1830.

7 Daughan, *1812*, 416

8 'Albion' to the Editor, 2 December 1815, *The Naval Chronicle for 1815: Containing a General and Biographical History of The Royal Navy of the United Kingdom; With a Variety of Original Papers on Nautical Subjects*, Vol.34: July to December (London: Joyce Gold, 1815), pp.483–484.

9 Rif Winfield, *British Warships in the Age of Sail, 1817–1863: Design, Construction, Careers and Fates* (eBook edition) (York: Seaforth Publishing, 2014), Chapters 4–5.

new wooden sail and steam frigates to be launched with main batteries of 32-pounders, starting an evolution in ship design that led to HMS *Warrior*, an iron-hulled armoured frigate that forever changed the face of naval warfare.[10] *Warrior* is often regarded as an early battleship, but in fact she was a frigate – a warship whose primary armament was arranged on a single gun deck. From *Warrior* would emerge the modern capital ships of the Victorian and World War era that would fill the niche left empty by the gradually declining species of ships of the line.

Gunnery, too, took a more scientific route in the following decades. Philip Broke's meticulous devotion to gunnery science and training had been very unique during the wars, but following *Shannon*'s victory many in the Navy began to take a serious look at his methods and ideas.[11] Works and treatises on naval gunnery were published in the following decades as a result of this interest, and in 1829 a dedicated school was founded to train officers and gunners in scientific methods of gunnery, headed in 1845 by Henry Chads, who had become a renowned gunnery expert in his own right. During the War of 1812, Broke's success had inspired others to follow his lead; Hyde Parker, Broke's erstwhile companion off Boston, adopted many of his techniques. So too did Henry Hope, who had whipped his crew into an efficiently trained team of gunners in time for his show-down with *President*.

British historiography since the end of the War of 1812 has hinged on the general advantage in broadside weight held by the Americans in their victories in the War of 1812. In the case of the frigate actions, this was particularly astute – *Constitution* and *United States* had a 50 percent advantage over their opponents. Contemporaries in the public and in government clung to this excuse as well, using it to reconcile their conception of British naval mastery with the losses. In doing so they redefined what the British world expected of their Royal Navy; exceptional victories against superior forces were still welcome, but no longer expected. The celebrations of *Shannon–Chesapeake* signified this, as no single-ship action between even forces had ever been quite so celebrated. The British people began clamouring for such even combats for the rest of the war. Fighting and defeating a foe of equal force, one-on-one, came to be the measure of British greatness at sea.

Yet relying on this explanation, as many have, belies the fact that, for the Royal Navy, it was not an acceptable one. The barometer had not shifted in the Navy as much as it had with the public and in government. Naval officers did not let go of their belief that an 18-pounder frigate could take on a 24-pounder one. However, if serving officers of the Royal Navy did not want to blame the losses on the disparity in force between their fifth-rate frigates and the American heavy frigates, that leaves one other poignant explanation: the inadequate, and at times utterly incompetent, gunnery exhibited in the actions. In many cases, the British crews were not prepared for action. The crews of *Peacock*, *Boxer*, and *Epervier* in particular were woefully unprepared to meet an enemy as well-trained as the commanders

---

10 D.R. Brown, *Before the Ironclad: Development of Ship Design, Propulsion and Armament in the Royal Navy, 1815–60* (London: Conway Maritime Press, 1990), pp.25, 36, 173–174.

11 Bibbins, 'Gunnery zealot', p.103.

and crews of *Hornet*, *Enterprise*, and *Peacock*. As one Halifax paper had argued, the Americans had the good fortune to come across several Royal Navy warships embarrassingly unprepared for combat. When the Americans met a Royal Navy ship in a proper state of preparedness – indeed when her captain employed a meticulous, scientific methodology to hone his crew into fighting shape – the Royal Navy had triumphed. Broke's meticulous training regime gave the British a victory on 1 June 1813 and allowed *Endymion* to thoroughly batter *President* into submission – the crucial factor that allowed the British world to say definitively that it was a victory for *Endymion*.

Several courts martial examined the poor state of gunnery and training closely, though they were reluctant to comment publicly on it. Even in the case of *Epervier*, where the court agreed that the crew's inadequate performance in action was a cause of the loss, Commander Wales was not indicted for failing to train his men properly. In part, this may have been because of his uncle's influence. By contrast, John Carden was criticised in the verdict of his court martial, but he was not actually punished for the loss. Both officers had done everything in their power to fight on the day of the action, which was enough for acquittal. In fact, in every of one of the court martial verdicts, the judges considered only the conduct during the action itself in their decision to acquit the officers. So long as the officer had demonstrated brave and acceptable conduct and done everything in their power to effect victory, they were acquitted, even if the evidence showed they had doomed their chances by failing in preparation and leadership. Only Andrew Duncan, who by joining the throng of seamen on HMS *Alert* in pleading for the captain to surrender, was dismissed from the Royal Navy in disgrace. As the statements of courts martial verdicts of prominent cases like the loss of a ship in action were often made public, the judges of the court carefully considered their statements. The Navy had no interest in declaring that their officers and men had failed in their duty lest it worry the public even more and tarnish the reputation the Royal Navy had worked so hard to build over the last two centuries. Behind the scenes, though, an officer acquitted by court martial had no guarantee of a future career. One might be acquitted in public but effectively removed from active service for failure, or by simple fact of being unable to compete in the post-war slump.

With the decommissioning of much of the fleet, the already oversized officer corps was now far too big, and hundreds of officers went on half-pay. Understandably, those officers who commanded or participated in one of the victorious actions fared relatively well. Some, like Lieutenants Provo Wallis or Arthur Fanshawe, enjoyed fruitful post-war careers, each reaching flag rank in active service, and in the case of Wallis reaching the most senior rank of the Navy. Some lieutenants faded into obscurity even after having participated in victorious actions, though. Falkiner was promoted to commander after the *Shannon–Chesapeake* action, but never received a command. Charles Pearson fared better, enjoying active service into the 1830s and finishing his career as a captain. Victory alone was not enough to make a naval career; professional and personal connections still mattered. Over all, though, the officers who had participated in the victorious single-ship actions fared much better than their peers who had participated in the defeats. Of the defeated captains and commanders, only Dacres and Wales enjoyed a successful post-war career, and both had close ties to senior officers in the Navy. Even with his connections, however, Wales never reached the rank of admiral. Even George Douglas, a Scotsman of noble birth, could not escape half-pay following his loss to USS *Constitution*.

Societal and professional connections could save a defeated officer from obscurity and retirement, but they were not guarantees. Most of the Navy's officers depended only on their reputation and friendships within the Navy. In consequence, most of the defeated captains, commanders, and lieutenants during the War of 1812 ended their careers in obscurity and half-pay. Some lucky individuals did enjoy fruitful careers after the war, though; Chads, having distinguished himself in the eyes of the Navy for his conduct following the death of his captain in action with *Constitution* was promoted, and went on to serve with distinction for decades. David Hope enjoyed an active career into the 1820s, perhaps in part because he had impressed the naval service by criticising John Carden's decision not to close in his engagement with *United States*, which the Navy collectively decided may have given him a fighting chance. While Carden's career was over, Hope enjoyed a brief tenure as a commander. Reputation, in a crowded promotion and employment field, remained key to success.

Philip Broke remained on half-pay for the rest of his life; unlike his defeated peers, however, Broke did so voluntarily. By 1813 he was badly homesick, and the wounds he had received probably would have kept him from returning to service even if he had wanted to. Instead he retired to a life as a country gentleman with his beloved Louisa, having become a national hero. Hope, the conqueror of *President*, never served at sea again after paying off his ship in 1815. Like Broke, this may have been his preference, as he was showered with honours for the rest of his life. He was awarded a naval gold medal and made a Companion of the Bath, and was later appointed as a Naval Aide-de-Camp to King William IV, himself a former naval officer, and continued in the post under Queen Victoria.[12] Officially he remained in the active service, drawing full pay through his appointment as an Aide-de-Camp, and reached the rank of admiral of the red just before his death.[13] Of all of the officers who had fought in the glamourous actions of the War of 1812, he was surpassed in final rank only by Wallis, who reached admiral of the fleet some time before his death.

Broke and Hope were ready to return to a quiet life; they had won their honours and made their reputation and felt they had done their duty. However, many of the other officers involved in the chivalric contests of the War of 1812 did not have that closure. They had the chance denied to most of their comrades – the chance to fight a single-ship action. Victory could mean making one's career; it did for Wallis and Pearson, among others. Instead, though, they had lost. Societal connections and professional reputation could carry an officer through to the next stage of their career, but in that pivotal moment with the coming of peace and the memory of the losses of

12 Lambert, *The Challenge*, Chapter 13.

13 Syrett and DeNiro, *Commissioned Sea Officers*, p.228.

1812 still fresh, many officers prematurely finished their careers on half-pay and never returned to sea.

The losses also redefined how the public in Britain saw and appreciated naval victories and defeats. The defeats in 1812 were unprecedented, and after 20 years of non-stop victory the public had to find ways of coping with the thought that their beloved Navy might not be invincible after all. For many, this was done by redefining expectations. Before 1812, the ships of the Royal Navy had been expected to triumph against all odds, even when vastly outmatched – so much so that a captain who captured an enemy frigate of similar tonnage and broadside weight in 1805 could hardly have expected the treatment that awaited Philip Broke after his capture of USS *Chesapeake*.[14] Yet following the losses, many eventually concluded that the matches had been unfair, and the press throughout Britain and Nova Scotia called for retribution through even combat. In *Shannon–Chesapeake* Britain got that even combat – two ships as closely matched as could be hoped for. It was pure vindication for the British public.

The Admiralty, too, shifted their expectations. Their response to the losses was to implement policy to prevent them from ever happening again. Captains of fifth-rates were forbidden from engaging the American heavy frigates, and late in the war, captains of 74-gun ships of the line were similarly forbidden from engaging a new class of American ships of the line alone, as they appeared to carry something close to 90 guns in all. Many British captains rejected this, however. Some even defied orders to challenge the enemy, hoping for a chance to bring them to battle, superiority of force notwithstanding. Strategically, however, this was nonsensical. Britain had little to gain and everything to lose by risking their frigates in action with the tiny American Navy, just as the United States had nothing to gain by risking theirs with the Royal Navy. However, their importance lay in honour, not strategy. The honour of the Royal Navy had been stained, and its reputation of invincibility seemingly shattered. For officers like Broke and Hope, this was intolerable. '*Honor* is a jewel of more value than whole fleets & armies & public prejudice waits not to enquire into the particulars of a defeat where the result is so mortifying,' Broke had once wrote to his wife.[15] Many in the Navy agreed with him, and this impacted their actions during the War of 1812. Personal and professional honour demanded vindication. For the officers of the British Royal Navy, vindication lay in revenge – revenge in the name of honour.

14 McCranie, *Utmost Gallantry*, p.154

15 SRO, HA 93/9/128, Philip Broke to Louisa Broke, 14 December 1812.

Appendix I

Careers and fates of the British naval officers

Dramatis personae: summary of the careers and fates of every identified British Royal Navy officer who participated in the single-ship actions of the War of 1812.

Glossary

PIR	Promoted into retirement: some officers were rewarded upon retirement with a promotion, which increased their half-pay as a form of pension. Others were promoted much earlier in their lives but never received another appointment and were effectively shunted out of active service by being promoted
KIA	Killed in action: killed in battle or due to wounds received in action.
DIS	Died/drowned in service: died while remaining in active service.
RAS	Remained officially in active service without retiring, until passing away of natural causes
Unknown	Details could not be found in available sources. Individuals without an exact date of retirement are also individuals whose service was relatively obscure, and therefore hard to track. It is unlikely that any remained employed for very long after 1815.

1812

Ship and rank	Date of lieutenant's commission	Date of promotion to commander	Date of promotion to post captain	Active service until
Thomas Lamb Polden Laugharne Commander, *Alert*	8 Aug 1806	12 Feb 1811	4 Apr 1832	Nov 1815, PIR, 1832
Andrew Duncan 1st Lieutenant, *Alert*	5 Nov 1806	–	–	1812, Dismissed
Philip Pitt Nind 2nd Lieutenant, *Alert*	17 Mar 1810	–	5 Jan 1844	Unknown
James Richard Dacres Captain, *Guerriere*	15 Nov 1804	5 Jul 1805	14 Jan 1806	1848: PIR Vice Admiral
Bartholomew Kent 1st Lieutenant, *Guerriere*	2 May 1804	29 Mar 1815	–	Unknown
Henry Ready 2nd Lieutenant, *Guerriere*	8 Jul 1807	13 Aug 1812	–	KIA, 1812
John Pullman 3rd Lieutenant, *Guerriere*	18 Sep 1810	–	–	Unknown
John Surman Carden Captain, *Macedonian*	24 Jul 1794	25 Oct 1798	22 Jan 1806	1813
David Hope 1st Lieutenant, *Macedonian*	30 Aug 1806	15 Jun 1814	4 Feb 1830	1820s
Samuel Mottley 2nd Lieutenant, *Macedonian*	20 May 1808	30 Apr 1845	–	1845, PIR
John Bulford 3rd Lieutenant, *Macedonian*	27 Jan 1809	16 Aug 1854	–	1854, PIR
Thomas Whinyates Commander, *Frolic*	7 Sep 1799	16 May 1805	12 Aug 1812	1816, later PIR, Rear Admiral
Charles McKay 1st Lieutenant, *Frolic*	Unknown	–	–	KIA, 1812
Fred Broughton Wintle 2nd Lieutenant, *Frolic*	5 Sep 1810	–	–	KIA, 1817
Henry Lambert Captain, *Java*	15 Apr 1801	5 Apr 1803	10 Apr 1805	KIA, 1813
Henry Ducie Chads 1st Lieutenant, *Java*	5 Nov 1806	28 May 1813	25 Jul 1815	RAS, 1868
William A. Herrington 2nd Lieutenant, *Java*	2 Nov 1810	16 Jan 1818	10 Jan 1837	1832, later PIR, Rear Admiral, in 1851
George Buchanan 3rd Lieutenant, *Java*	21 May 1812	–	–	Unknown

1813

Ship and rank	Date of lieutenant's commission	Date of promotion to commander	Date of promotion to post captain	Active service until
William Peake				
Commander, *Peacock*	21 Jul 1797	22 Jan 1806	–	KIA, 1813
Frederick A. Wright				
1st Lieutenant, *Peacock*	13 Jun 1807	–	–	Unknown
Philip Bowes Vere Broke				
Captain, *Shannon*	19 Aug 1797	2 Jan 1799	14 Feb 1801	Voluntarily retired in 1813
George T.L. Watt				
1st Lieutenant, *Shannon*	20 Jan 1806	–	–	KIA, 1813
Provo William Parry Wallis				
2nd Lieutenant, *Shannon*	30 Nov 1808	9 Jul 1813	12 Aug 1819	RAS, 1892, Admiral of the Fleet
Charles L. Falkiner				
3rd Lieutenant, *Shannon*	4 Jan 1810	9 Jul 1813	5 Apr 1848	1813, PIR, 1848
John Fordyce Maples				
Commander, *Pelican*	16 May 1795	21 Oct 1810	23 Aug 1813	Unknown, PIR, 1846
Thomas Welsh				
1st Lieutenant, *Pelican*	2 Feb 1809	–	–	Unknown
Samuel Blyth				
Commander, *Boxer*	7 Feb 1806	5 Sep 1811	–	1813
David McCrery				
1st Lieutenant, *Boxer*	31 Aug 1810	–	–	Unknown

1814

Ship and rank	Date of lieutenant's commission	Date of promotion to commander	Date of promotion to post captain	Active service until
James Hillyar				
Captain, *Phoebe*	8 Mar 1794	16 Apr 1800	29 Feb 1804	Retired following promotion to Vice Admiral
William Ingram				
1st Lieutenant, *Phoebe*	22 Jan 1806	–	–	KIA, 1814
Charles Pearson				
2nd Lieutenant, *Phoebe*	8 Nov 1808	29 Jul 1814	3 Apr 1837	1830s
Thomas Tudor Tucker				
Commander, *Cherub*	20 May 1800	15 Feb 1808	1 Aug 1811	1816
Remaining officers from Battle of Valparaiso unidentified				
Richard Walter Wales				
Commander, *Epervier*	13 Jul 1799	16 Jun 1808	1 Jan 1817	Unknown, never reached Rear Admiral
John Harvey (a)				
1st Lieutenant, *Epervier*	13 Nov 1813	2 Apr 1819	1 Apr 1856	Unknown, PIR, 1856

Ship and rank	Date of lieutenant's commission	Date of promotion to commander	Date of promotion to post captain	Active service until
John Hackett				
2nd Lieutenant, *Epervier*	11 May 1811	2 Sep 1828	28 Jun 1838	Retired following promotion to Vice Admiral
William Manners				
Commander, *Reindeer*	14 Aug 1806	7 Feb 1812	–	KIA, 1814
Thomas Chambers				
1st Lieutenant, *Reindeer*	22 May 1810	–	–	DIS 1818
James Arbuthnot				
Commander, *Avon*	28 Apr 1810	27 Oct 1813	–	DIS 1817
John Harvey (b)				
1st Lieutenant, *Avon*	24 Jul 1812	–	–	DIS 1814

1815

Ship and rank	Date of lieutenant's commission	Date of promotion to commander	Date of promotion to post captain	Active service until
Henry Hope				
Captain, *Endymion*	3 May 1804	22 Jan 1806	24 May 1808	Last sea service 1815, remained employed ashore, retired as Admiral of the Red
William Thomas Morgan				
1st Lieutenant, *Endymion*	30 Nov 1809	18 Feb 1815	–	DIS, 1822
Arthur Fanshawe				
2nd Lieutenant, *Endymion*	22 Apr 1813	2 Oct 1815	17 Oct 1816	Retired following promotion to Admiral of the White
George Douglas				
Captain, *Levant*	8 Aug 1807	8 Aug 1809	28 Feb 1812	1815
Gordon Falcon				
Captain, *Cyane*	15 May 1800	8 Mar 1811	29 Oct 1813	1820s
Remaining lieutenants from 1815 actions unidentified				

Appendix II

Dispositions of Frigates in North American waters, July 1813

Glossary

LoB	Line of battle ships (64–120 guns)
24pdr	Frigates armed with main batteries of 24-pounder guns, including *razées*
18pdr	Frigates armed with main batteries of 18-pounder guns
12pdr	Frigates armed with main batteries of 12-pounder guns

North America: Admiral Sir John Borlase Warren – 50 ships

LoB:	Ten 74s, including *San Domingo* (flagship)
24pdr:	58: *Majestic*
18pdr:	38: *Nymphe, Junon, Tenedos, Spartan, Shannon, Armide, Lacedaemonian*
	36: *Maidstone, Belvidera, Barrosa*
	32: *Narcissus, Aeolus*
12pdr:	32: *Cleopatra, Minerva*
Other:	Two 6th rates, 25 sloops, three schooners, two receiving ships, one prison ship

South America: Rear Admiral Manly Dixon – 14 ships

LoB:	One 74, *Montagu* (flagship)
24pdr:	44: *Indefatigable*
18pdr:	38: *Nisus*
	36: *Inconstant*
	32: *Nereus*
12pdr:	32: *Aquilon*
Other:	Three 6th rates, three sloops, two cutters

Jamaica: Rear Admiral Brown

LoB: Two 74s, including *Vengeance* (flagship, and one 44)
Other: Five 6th rates, six sloops, two gun-brigs, one receiving ship

Leeward Islands: Rear Admiral Sir Francis Laforey – 40 ships

LoB: Two 74s, including *Cressy* (flagship), one 50
18pdr: 38: *Statira, Surprise, Phin*
36: *Orpheus, Pique, Venus*
12pdr: 32: *Circe, Castor*
Other: Three 6th rates, 20 sloops, three gun-brigs, two schooners, one cutter

Newfoundland: Vice Admiral Sir Richard Goodwin Keats

LoB: One 74, Bellerophon (flagship)
18pdr: 38: *Sybille, Crescent*
36: *Dryad*
32: *Hyperion*
12pdr: 32: *Quebec*
Other: Two 6th rates, four sloops, one cutter, one prison ship

Unappropriated vessels which would soon be sent to North America

24pdr: 50: *Akbar* – under construction to be converted to a frigate, would join squadron shortly
40: *Endymion* – completing refit, would join squadron shortly
18pdr: 38: *Cydnus* – would join squadron shortly

Frigates assigned to convoys and particular services

18pdr: 36: *Theban* and *Doris* were sent to hunt down USS *Essex* in Pacific
36: *Phoebe* was *en route* to the Pacific escorting convoys[1]

1 Gardiner, *Frigates of the Napoleonic Wars*, pp.185–190.

Bibliography

Archival sources

Library and Archives, Ottawa, Canada (LAC)

Admiralty Records (Microform Copies) (MG12 ADM 1):
Admirals Dispatches (Extracts) – Copies of ADM 1/502–509, The National Archives:
ADM 1/502, C-12863: Admiral's Dispatches, North America, 1812
ADM 1/503, C-12854: Admiral's Dispatches, North America, 1812–1813
ADM 1/504, C-12854: Admiral's Dispatches, North America, 1813
ADM 1/505, C-12855: Admiral's Dispatches, North America, 1814
ADM 1/506, C-12855: Admiral's Dispatches, North America, 1814
ADM 1/508, C-12855: Admiral's Dispatches, North America, 1815
ADM 1/509, C-12855: Admiral's Dispatches, North America, 1815
Captain's Letters (Extracts) – Copies of ADM 1/1454–2800, The National Archives:
MG12 ADM 1/1454–1455, B-2605: Captain's Letters A
MG12 ADM 1/1553–1557, B-2608: Captain's Letters B
MG12 ADM 1/1663–1664, B-2612: Captain's Letters C
MG12 ADM 1/1734–1736, B-2614: Captain's Letters D
MG12 ADM 1/1946–1948, B-2623: Captain's Letters H
MG12 ADM 1/2536, B-2800: Captain's Letters S

The National Archives, London (TNA)

Admiralty Papers (ADM 1):
Admiral's Dispatches: Newfoundland (ADM 1/477)
Courts Martial:
ADM 1/5431, Court Martial *Alert*
ADM 1/5431, Court Martial *Guerriere*
ADM 1/5434, Court Martial *Frolic*
ADM 1/5435, Court Martial *Java*
ADM 1/5436, Court Martial *Macedonian*
ADM 1/5436, Court Martial *Peacock*
ADM 1/5444, Court Martial *Reindeer*
ADM 1/5446, Court Martial *Avon*
ADM 1/5447, Court Martial *Epervier*
ADM 1/5449, Court Martial *Cyane*
ADM 1/5449, Court Martial *Levant*
Admiralty Papers Officer Service Records (ADM 196):
John Carden, ADM 196/3/363
James Dacres, ADM 196/3/582
Gordon Falcon, ADM 196/4/177
Charles Falkiner, ADM 196/4/180
William Herringham, ADM 196/4/517
David Hope, ADM 196/4/583

Thomas Laugharne, ADM 196/5/61
Samuel Mottley, ADM 196/5/347
Thomas Whinyates, ADM 196/6/559
Samuel Whiteway, ADM 196/6/584
James Hillyar, ADM 196/68/355

Suffolk Record Office, Ipswich, UK (SRO)

HA93/6: Broke, Sir Philip. Broke Papers, De Saumarez Collection, 1813
HA93/9: Broke, Sir Philip. Broke Papers, De Saumarez Collection, 1811–1813

Newspapers

Acadia Recorder (Halifax, NS), 1813–1815, Nova Scotia Archives (online), available at: https://novascotia.ca/archives/newspapers/results.asp?nTitle=Acadian+Recorder

The Royal Gazette (Halifax, NS), 1812–1813, Nova Scotia Archives, Microfilm Reel 8172

The London Gazette, 1812–1815 (online), available at: https://www.thegazette.co.uk/

London Courier and Evening Gazette, 1815 (online), available at: https://www.britishnewspaperarchive.co.uk/

Hampshire Chronicle, 1815 (online), available at: https://www.britishnewspaperarchive.co.uk/

Cobbett's Weekly Political Register, 1815 (online), available at: https://www.britishnewspaperarchive.co.uk/

Unpublished Sources

Drolet, Marc, 'The North American squadron of the Royal Navy, 1807–1815' (PhD dissertation, McGill University, 2008)

Kaizer, Nicholas James, 'Professionalism and the Fighting Spirit of the Royal Navy: Rules, Regulations, and Traditions that made the British Royal Navy an Effective Fighting Force during the French Revolutionary and Napoleonic Wars, 1793–1815' (Honours thesis, Acadia University, 2015)

Kaizer, Nicholas James, 'Regret, determination, and honour: the impact of the single ship losses in North American waters on the British Royal Navy, 1812–1813' (MA thesis, Dalhousie University, 2018)

Knight, Timothy, 'Navigating Networks in the Napoleonic Era: A Close Study of three British Naval Officers and their Deliberate use of Networking' (Masters thesis, California State University, 2016)

Published Sources

Allen, Douglas W., 'The British Navy rules: monitoring and incompatible incentives in the age of fighting sail', *Explorations in Economic History*, 39 (2002).

Anon (ed.). *The Naval Chronicle: Containing a General and Biographical History of The Royal Navy of the United Kingdom; with a Variety of Original Papers on Nautical Subjects*, Vols. 28–34 (London: Joyce Gold, 1812–1815).

Arthur, Brian, *How Britain Won the War of 1812: The Royal Navy's Blockade of the United States, 1812–1815* (Woodbridge: Boydell Press, 2011).

Bauer, K. Jack (ed.), *The New American State Papers: Naval Affairs*, Vol.4 (Wilmington, DE: Scholarly Resources, 1981).

Berton, Pierre, *The Invasion of Canada: 1812–1813* (Toronto: McClelland and Steward, 1980).

Brighton, J.G., *Admiral Sir P.B.V. Broke: Chiefly from Journals and Letters in the possession of Rear-Admiral Sir George Broke-Middleton* (London: Sampson, Low, Son, and Marson, 1867).

Brown, D.R., *Before the Ironclad: Development of Ship Design, Propulsion and Armament in the Royal Navy, 1815–60* (London: Conway Maritime Press, 1990).

Budiansky, Stephen, *Perilous Fight: America's Intrepid War with Britain on the High Seas, 1812–1815* (New York: Alfred A. Knopf, 2010).

Carden, James Surman, *A Curtail'd Memoir of Incidents and Occurrences in the Life of John Surman Carden, Vice Admiral in the British Navy* (Oxford: Clarendon Press, 1850).

Crawford, Michael J., Christine F. Hughes, Charles E. Brodine, and Carolyn M. Stallings (eds.), *The Naval War of 1812: A Documentary History*, Vol.3: 1814–1815 (Washington DC: Naval Historical Center, Department of the Navy, 2002).

Daughan, George C., *1812: The Navy's War* (New York: Basic Books, 2011).

Daughan, George C., *The Shining Sea: David Porter and the Epic Voyage of the USS* Essex *during the War of 1812* (New York: Basic Books, 2013).

Davey, James, *In Nelson's Wake: How the Royal Navy Ruled the Waves after Trafalgar* (New Haven, CT and London: Yale University Press, 2015).

Dietz, Anthony G., *For Their Safekeeping and Accommodation: British Prisoners of War in the United States During the War of 1812* (Harriett G. Dietz [Standard Copyright License], 2011).

Dillon, William Henry (ed. Michael A. Lewis), *A Narrative of My Professional Adventures* (London: Navy Records Society, 1953).

Douglas, Howard, *A Treatise on Naval Gunnery* (London: John Murray, 1860).

Dudley, Wade, *Splintering the Wooden Wall: The British Blockade of the United States, 1812–1815* (Annapolis, MD: Naval Institute Press, 2003).

Dudley, William S., Christine F. Hughes, and Tamara Moser Melia (eds), *The Naval War of 1812: A Documentary History, Vol.1: 1812* (Washington: Naval Historical Center, Dept. of Navy, 1985).

Dudley, William S., Christine F. Hughes, and Tamara Moser Melia (eds), *The Naval War of 1812: A Documentary History, Vol.2: 1813* (Washington DC: Naval Historical Center, Department of the Navy, 1992).

Duffy, Michael, 'The Gunnery at Trafalgar: Training, Tactics, or Temperament?', *Journal for Maritime Research*, 7:1 (2005), pp. 140–169.

Eustace, Nicole, *1812: War of the Passions of Patriotism* (Philadelphia, PA: University of Pennsylvania Press, 2012).

Farragut, Loyall, *The Life of David Glasgow Farragut: First Admiral of the United States Navy* (New York: D. Appleton and Company, 1879).

Fitz-Enz, Colonel David, *Old Ironsides: Eagle of the Sea – The Story of the USS* Constitution (Lanham, MD: Taylor Tree Publishing, 2004).

Gardiner, Robert, *Frigates of the Napoleonic Wars* (Annapolis, MD: Naval Institute Press, 2000)

Gwyn, Julian, *Frigates and Foremasts: The North American squadron in Nova Scotia Waters, 1745–1815* (Toronto and Vancouver: UBC Press, 2003).

Harris, Gardner W., *The Life and Services of Commodore William Bainbridge, United States Navy* (Philadelphia, PA: Carey Lea & Blanchard, 1837).

Herman, Arthur, *To Rule the Wales: How the British Navy Shaped the Modern World* (New York: Harper Collins, 2004).

Hannay, David, *Naval Courts Martial* (Cambridge: CUP, 1914).

Heathcote, T.A., *Nelson's Trafalgar: Captains & Their Battles* (Barnsley: Pen and Sword Books, 2005).

Hickey, Donald E., and Donald E. Graves, *Don't Give Up the Ship!: Myths of the War of 1812* (Montréal: R. Brass Studio, 2008).

Hickey, Donald E., *The War of 1812: A Forgotten Conflict* (Urbana and Chicago, IL: University of Illinois Press, 1990).

Hughes, Ben, *In Pursuit of the Essex: Heroism and Hubris on the High Seas in the War of 1812* (Annapolis, MD: Naval Institute Press, 2016).

James, William, *A Full and Correct Account of the Chief Naval Occurrences of the Late War Between Great Britain and the United States of America* (London: Joyce Gold, 1817).

James, William, *Naval History of Great Britain: From the Declaration of War by France in 1793 to the Accession of George IV* (London: Macmillan and Co., 1902).

Kelly, Morgan and Cormac Ó Gráda, 'Speed under sail during the early Industrial Revolution', *VOX: CEPR Policy Portal* (online), available at: https://voxeu.org/article/speed-under-sail-during-early-industrial-revolution (accessed 29 January 2019).

Lambert, Andrew, *The Challenge: Britain Against America in the Naval War of 1812* (eBook edition) (London: Faber and Faber, 2013).

Lardas, Mark, *American Heavy Frigates, 1794–1826* (Oxford: Osprey, 2003).

Lardas, Mark, *British Frigate vs. French Frigate: 1973–1814* (London: Osprey, 2013).

Latimer, Jon, *1812: War With America* (Cambridge, MA: Harvard University Press, 2007).

Lincoln, Margaret, *Representing the Royal Navy: British Sea Power, 1750–1815* (Aldershot: Ashgate and the National Maritime Museum, 2002).

Long, David F., Nothing *too Daring: A Life of Commodore David Porter, 1780–1843* (Annapolis, MD: Naval Institute Press, 1970).

Lossing, Benson *The Pictorial Field-Book of the War of 1812* (New York: Harper and Brothers, 1868).

Marshall, John, *Royal Naval Biography: Or, Memoirs of the Services of all the Flag-Officers, Superannuated Rear-Admirals, Retired-Captains, Post-Captains, and Commanders*, 12 Vols. (London: Longman, Hurst, Rees, Orme, and Brown, 1823–1835).

McCranie, Kevin D., 'Dueling with warships to satisfy honour: the use of naval challenges in the War of 1812', *International Journal of Maritime History*, 25:2 (2013).

McCranie, Kevin D., *Utmost Gallantry: The US and Royal Navies at Sea in the War of 1812* (Annapolis, MD: Naval Institute Press, 2011).

Morriss, Roger, *Cockburn and the British Navy in Transition: Admiral Sir George Cockburn, 1772–1853* (Columbia, SC: University of South Carolina Press, 1997).

Mercer, Keith, 'Colonial patriotism to "Mystical Chords of Memory": the Halifax celebrations and commemorations of the *Shannon–Chesapeake* battle', *Acadiensis* 44:1 (2015), pp. 36–63.

Mercer, Keith, 'Lord Nelson on the mind: naval victories and cultural memory in Nova Scotia', *Trafalgar Chronicle* 22 (2012), pp. 171–191.

Mercer, Keith, 'Sailors and citizens: press gangs and naval–civilian relations in Nova Scotia, 1756–1815', *Journal of the Royal Nova Scotia Historical Society*, 10 (2007), pp. 87–113.

Murdoch, Beamish, *A History of Nova Scotia, or Acadie*, Vol.3 (Halifax: J. Barnes, 1867).

Napier, Henry Edward, *New England Blockaded in 1814: The Journal of Henry Edward Napier, Lieutenant in HMS Nymphe*, ed. Walter Muir Whitehill (Salem, MA: Peabody Museum, 1939).

Neeser, Robert W., 'American naval gunnery: past and present', *The North American Review*, 196:685 (1912), pp. 770–791.

Nicolson, Adam, *Men of Honour: Trafalgar and the Making of the English Hero* (London, New York, Toronto, and Sydney: Harper Perennial, 2005).

Raddall, Thomas H., *Halifax: Warden of the North* (Halifax, NS: Nimbus Publishing, 2010).

Robson, Martin, *A History of the Royal Navy: The Napoleonic Wars* (London and New York: I.B. Tauris & Co., 2014).

Rodger, N.A.M., 'Honour and duty at sea', *Historical Research*, 75:190 (2002), pp. 425–447.

Rodger, N.A.M., *The Command of the Ocean: A Naval History of Britain, 1649–1815* (New York: W.W. Norton, 2005).

Ronald, D.A.B., *Young Nelsons: Boy Sailors During the Napoleonic Wars* (Oxford: Osprey, 2012).

Roosevelt, Theodore, *The Naval War of 1812 or the History of the United States Navy During the Last War with Great Britain* (New York: G.P. Putnam's Sons, 1882).

Rubinstein, Hilary (ed.), *The Durham Papers: Selections from the Papers of Admiral Sir Philip Charles Henderson Calderwood Durham, GCB (1763–1845)* (London and New York: Routledge/Navy Records Society, 2019).

Syrett, David and R.L. DiNardo, *The Commissioned Sea Officers of the Royal Navy, 1660–1815* (Aldershot: Scholar Press for the Navy Records Society, 1994).

Taylor, Alan, *The Civil War of 1812: American Citizens, British Subjects, Irish Rebels, and Indian Allies* (New York: Alfred A. Knopf, 2010).

Taylor, Stephen, *Storm and Conquest: The Battle for the Indian Ocean, 1808–1810* (London: Faber and Faber, 2007).

Toll, Ian W., *Six Frigates: The Epic History of the Founding of the US Navy* (New York and London: W.W. Norton and Company, 2006).

Tracy, Nicholas, *The Naval Chronicle: The Contemporary Record of the Royal Navy at War*, (London: Chatham Publishing, 1998-99).

Tucker, Spencer, *Stephen Decatur: A Life Most Bold and Daring* (Annapolis, MD: Naval Institute Press, 2005).

Vale, Brian (ed.), *The Naval Miscellany, Volume VIII* (London: Navy Records Society, 2017).

Voelcker, Tim (ed.) *Broke of the Shannon and the War of 1812* (Barnsley: Seaforth Publishing, 2013).

Wareham, Tom, 'The duration of frigate command during the Revolutionary and Napoleonic Wars', *The Mariner's Mirror*, 86:4 (2000).

Wareham, Tom, *The Star Captains: Frigate Command in the Napoleonic Wars* (London: Chatham Publishing, 2001).

Wilcox, Martin, '"These peaceable times are the devil:" Royal Navy officers in the post-war slump, 1815–1825', *The International Journal of Maritime History*, 26:3 (2014), pp. 471–488.
Willis, Sam, 'Capabilities of sailing warships', *The Northern Mariner*, 13:4 (2003), pp. 57–68.
Willis, Sam, *Fighting at Sea in the Eighteenth Century: The Art of Sailing Warfare* (Woodbridge: The Boydell Press, 2008).
Wilson, Evan, 'Social background and promotion prospects in the Royal Navy, 1775–1815', *English Historical Review*, 131:550 (2016).
Winfield, Rif, *British Warships in the Age of Sail, 1793–1817: Design, Construction, Careers and Fates* (London: Chatham Publishing, 2005).
Winfield, Rif, *British Warships in the Age of Sail, 1817–1863: Design, Construction, Careers and Fates* (eBook edition) (York: Seaforth Publishing, 2014).

Online Sources

Founders Online, National Archives (online), available at: https://founders.archives.gov/
Historic *Hansard Index, UK Parliament*, available at: https://api.parliament.uk/historic-hansard/index.html